Guide Library

Hillwood Museum
Washington, D.C.

ALSO BY RONALD HINGLEY

Russian Writers and Soviet Society: 1917–1978

A New Life of Anton Chekhov

Chekhov: A Biographical and Critical Study

The Undiscovered Dostoyevsky

Russian Writers and Society: 1825–1904

Nihilists

The Tsars: Russian Autocrats 1533–1917

A People in Turmoil: Revolutions in Russia

The Russian Secret Police

A Concise History of Russia

Joseph Stalin: Man and Legend

EDITOR AND TRANSLATOR OF:

The Oxford Chekhov:
Volumes 1–3 *(plays)*; Volumes 4–9 *(stories)*

TRANSLATOR OF:

Alexander Solzhenitsyn:
One Day in the Life of Ivan Denisovich
(with Max Hayward)

Nightingale Fever

Boris Pasternak

Marina Tsvetaeva

Anna Akhmatova

Osip Mandelstam

Ronald Hingley

Nightingale Fever

Russian Poets in Revolution

Alfred A. Knopf New York 1981

THIS IS A BORZOI BOOK
PUBLISHED BY ALFRED A. KNOPF, INC.

COPYRIGHT © 1981 BY RONALD HINGLEY
ALL RIGHTS RESERVED UNDER INTERNATIONAL AND PAN-AMERICAN COPYRIGHT
CONVENTIONS. PUBLISHED IN THE UNITED STATES BY ALFRED A. KNOPF, INC., NEW
YORK. DISTRIBUTED BY RANDOM HOUSE, INC., NEW YORK.

LIBRARY OF CONGRESS CATALOGING IN PUBLICATION DATA

Hingley, Ronald.
Nightingale fever.

Bibliography: p.
Includes index.
1. Russian poetry—20th century—History and
criticism. 2. Mandelstam, Osip Yemilyevich, 1891–1938—
Criticism and interpretation. 3. Akhmatova,
Anna Andreevna, 1889–1966—Criticism and interpretation.
4. Pasternak, Boris Leonidovich, 1890–1960—
Criticism and interpretation. 5. TŜvetaeva, Marina
Ivanovna Éfron, 1892–1941—Criticism and interpretation.
I. Title.
PG305G.H5   891.71'42'09   81-47498
ISBN 0-394-50451-8   AACR2

MANUFACTURED IN THE UNITED STATES OF AMERICA
FIRST EDITION

И ничем нельзя помочь,
Что в горячке соловьиной
Сердце теплое еще.

Osip Mandelstam, 1918

CONTENTS

Acknowledgements ix
Introduction xi

PART ONE: PEACE AND WAR (1889–1921)

1. *Motive for Murder* 5
2. *Torture by Happiness* 18
3. *Cloudburst of Light* 45
4. *My Craft Adrift* 72
5. *Black Velvet* 84

PART TWO: BETWEEN CONVULSIONS (1921–1930)

6. *Herbs for Alien Tribe* 105
7. *Rebel in Head and Womb* 116
8. *Time's Great Dislocation* 132
9. *Loving and Lopping* 147

PART THREE: TERROR AND BEYOND (1930–1966)

10. *Frolics and Pitfalls* 157
11. *Harder to Breathe* 174
12. *Doom's Black Whisper* 189
13. *All Change for Freedom Camp* 207
14. *Old Style, New Style* 221
15. *Two Voices Calling* 236

Appendix: *Translation Policy, Texts and Sources,*
Titles, Omissions, Transliteration, Dates 249
Reference Notes 254
Bibliography 260
Index 263

ACKNOWLEDGEMENTS

FOR his wise counsels over the last three decades I sadly record my thanks to my old friend Max Hayward, with whom I was privileged to discuss my labours in early 1979 during the few weeks before his death robbed modern Russian literature of one of its subtlest interpreters. To Sir Isaiah Berlin and to the Oxford University Press I am deeply grateful for their kindness in affording me prepublication access to his memoir "Meetings with Russian Poets in 1945 and 1956," to which a brief tribute is paid under "Texts and Sources" in the Appendix, and which is now available in his *Personal Impressions* (London, 1980; New York, 1981). Thanks are also due for their kind help and skilled advice to Dr. Jennifer Baines, Dr. Christopher Barnes, Mr. Michael Makin, Professor Guy de Mallac, Professor John Fennell, Dr. Virginia Llewellyn Smith, Dr. David Luke, Mr. Willem Meeuws, Dr. Jeremy Newton, Miss Isia Tlusty, and Mr. and Mrs. Harry Willetts. Finally, I most particularly thank my wife, whose editorial insights have been especially valuable.

Frilford, 1981   RONALD HINGLEY

INTRODUCTION

A FEW months after the Bolshevik Revolution of 1917 the Russian poet Osip Mandelstam wrote the lyric from which the title of this book is taken. It was the first occasion on which he expressed in verse the concept, which was to overshadow his later life, of "death as the penalty for poetic creation."[1] He himself would perish, according to his own diagnosis, from the occupational disease of poets that he calls "Nightingale Fever." The ailment will not be found in any medical dictionary, but its main symptom is easily described: an inability to stop singing regardless of the consequences.

That this complaint may be incurable Mandelstam indicates in the lines quoted in the epigraph to this book. They are, in translation:

> And there is no hope
> For heart still flushed
> With Nightingale Fever.[2]

Here is a reminder that the creative process poses a serious threat to poets everywhere in the world, and that the disease of being a poet has probably proved fatal more often in Russia than anywhere else.

In this book the evolution of Russian poetry is traced from the years immediately preceding the First World War to just beyond the outbreak of the Second, the investigation being based on the case histories of four particular fever patients. They are Mandelstam himself and the three comparably gifted contemporaries with whom he is most closely linked: Anna Akhmatova, Boris Pasternak, and Marina Tsvetayeva. They were all major writers who viewed the world from a poet's shifting and unpredictable angle of vision, reflecting an age of recurrent crises with a flair for the startling, piercingly phrased insight. And so their works (including prose) offer a valuable commentary on the cataclysms through which they lived, of which the Stalin Terror of the late 1930s was the climax. The study of their lives and writings, and of the memoirs about them, gives an impression of their times more vivid than any mere historical account can convey. The historical setting will not be ignored in this book, since it is crucial to the understanding of the poets and their work; but it is not their epoch, it is they themselves — as reflected in their lives and verses — who are the theme.

This is a study of poets against a background of revolution, not a study of revolution against a background of poets.

All four poets will be observed in violent collision with a state system which caused the physical destruction of two of them, and which kept the other two in fear for their lives and liberty over several decades. Yet this is no simple saga of talented rebels heroically challenging a tyrannical government and perishing in the cause of freedom, for the poets' revolt against their society was a quiet and protracted affair. Theirs was less a deliberate resolve to mutiny than a temperamental inability to yield to the pressures of their epoch — even when they would perhaps have wished to do so. Apart from Pasternak's action in releasing *Doctor Zhivago* for publication in the West in the late 1950s, none of the four poets ever took the deliberate decision to embrace martyrdom through mortal combat with the State. Rather did they blunder involuntarily into self-sacrifice because it was their nature to act in that way.

Though the four poets were all to be persecuted by Soviet authority, eventually becoming identified with opposition to the system, this important aspect of their lives always remained secondary to their creative evolution. They did not represent a political opposition, for art was overwhelmingly their chief concern, but they were manipulated into political postures by an officially imposed ideology so militant that the mere failure to simulate enthusiasm for it became a form of heresy. All four poets tended to be a-Soviet rather than anti-Soviet, while fluctuating in the degree of hostility to the system that they expressed at different times. Tsvetayeva left the country when the new dispensation was barely established — partly because she disliked it, but partly so that she could join her husband in emigration. At the other end of the scale Pasternak was for nearly twenty years a supporter, however wary and idiosyncratic, of the Leninist-Stalinist system — which may surprise those who know him chiefly for his steadfast opposition to authority in the Khrushchev era. At that and all earlier periods of his life Pasternak was, like the other three poets, a creative artist first and foremost. He was only secondarily a political figure or symbol.

Would the four have written less remarkable work if they had had an easier time? According to one view, poetry is so intimately concerned with the ultimate human realities of suffering and death that the more severely the poet is exposed to them, the better. Perhaps any artist is "extremely lucky who is presented with the worst possible ordeal which will not actually kill him."[3] If so, Russian poets have been particularly fortunate — except of course for those presented with ordeals that actually *have* killed them, in some instances after they have enjoyed for many years the full benefits that misery, privation, and terror can bestow. These blessings were showered on them so freely that Akhmatova sometimes spoke of Russian émigrés as "envying the sufferings" (how Russian a formulation!) of those who had stayed at home. Reporting this comment, Mandelstam's widow has dismissed it as grossly imperceptive. There was, says she, nothing in the least elevating about her own and her husband's sufferings: there was only terror and pain. "I don't envy a dog run over by a truck, or a cat thrown out of a ninth-floor window by a hooligan."[4]

Akhmatova herself has demonstrated that precisely the same point of view can be phrased in very different terms. "Shakespeare's plays — the sensational atrocities, passions, duels — are child's play compared to the life of each one of us. Of the sufferings of those executed and sent to concentration camps I dare not speak. . . . But even our disaster-free biographies are Shakespearian tragedy multiplied by a thousand."[5]

Nightingale Fever

Part One

Ah, had I known the way of it
When launching my career —
That verse is deadly, murderous
Haemorrhage gushing from throat!

All frolics with such pitfalls
I would have turned down flat.

BORIS PASTERNAK, 1932

1

MOTIVE FOR MURDER

FROM the great constellation of poets born in the Russian Empire of the late nineteenth century one closely grouped cluster of four stars shines with especial brightness. Anna Akhmatova, Boris Pasternak, Osip Mandelstam, and Marina Tsvetayeva entered the world in the order listed and in the successive years 1889 to 1892. This means that all were a year or two younger than Ezra Pound and T. S. Eliot, the two leading poets of their generation writing in English. As for contemporary nonpoets still more widely renowned or notorious, Akhmatova has pointed out that her own birth year, 1889, also gave Charles Chaplin and Adolf Hitler to humanity.[1]

The four poets were all in their middle to late twenties when they were overtaken by their country's two 1917 revolutions, being unceremoniously precipitated — together with other members of Russia's middle classes — from comfort into poverty, from safety into peril, from the known into the unknown. The chain of upheavals made its first impact at a time when they all had volumes of published verse behind them, and were beginning to become securely established in the literary firmament.

None of them was ever to regain the tranquillity of the pre-Revolutionary era, but all summoned enough courage and resourcefulness to face conditions so drastically transformed. Perhaps it was to their advantage that the convulsions of the period struck them in youth, and at so early a stage in what for each of them was to prove a complex evolution. Only after 1917 did they attain full artistic maturity. Each did so in an atmosphere of recurrent personal crisis, but also in constant awareness of the others' achievements, for they were closely united by admiration, rivalry, friendship, love, and occasional resentment.

The years of the poets' infancy were those of the last Russian Tsar-Emperor but one, Alexander III, who died in 1894. As the funeral

5

cortège passed through central Moscow, the four-year-old Pasternak was held up to watch it by his mother on the balcony of the city's Institute of Painting, Sculpture, and Architecture, where his father, Leonid Pasternak — a distinguished painter and teacher — was a professor. But the infant poet was less impressed by the Tsar's passing than by another experience of the same year. Awoken one evening by the strains of chamber music, he peeped into his parents' drawing-room and saw among the assembled guests a venerable figure. It was the great Lyov Tolstoy, a friend of the family whose novel *Resurrection* was to be illustrated by Pasternak's father. This sight affected the boy so powerfully that he wept, and was later to recall the episode as his first conscious memory. Another early recollection took him back to the age of six, when he was able to watch the coronation procession of Russia's new Tsar, Nicholas II, whose abdication was to bring both the Romanov dynasty and the Russian monarchy to an end in February 1917.[2]

This interweaving of historical, musical, artistic, and literary motifs was prophetic of the poet's whole career, since he was not only to play a significant role in the cultural life of his generation, but was also to become reluctantly prominent in its historical and political evolution. So too, in their very different ways, were the other three poets.

Anna Akhmatova was born near the Black Sea port of Odessa; but her childhood was chiefly spent near the Imperial Russian capital, St. Petersburg. Osip Mandelstam spent his early years in the same city after being born in Warsaw, then belonging to the Russian Empire's western marches. In the poet's birth year (1891), and at the far-flung Empire's eastern limits, an event of economic and symbolic significance occurred as the future Nicholas II ceremonially turned the first sod of the future Trans-Siberian Railway at Vladivostok. Forty-seven years later Mandelstam's fatal last journey was to take place along this intercontinental artery, as if destiny had conspired in the very year of his birth to institute preparations for his eventual elimination.

The youngest of the four poets, Marina Tsvetayeva, was no less patriotic a Muscovite than Pasternak, but she became the only member of the group to choose emigration from Russia. She too was to end her life in her native country, and as no less tragic a victim of her age than Mandelstam. How they both perished while the two other poets survived, living or partly living through disasters fatal to their colleagues, will be described in due course.

The first major period (or "Golden Age") of Russian verse had been that of Pushkin and his contemporaries — poets who also included Lermontov, Baratynsky, and Tyutchev, and who were chiefly active from the early 1820s to the early 1840s. Then the movement subsided, giving way to the great age of Russian prose fiction, which blossomed most impressively in the reign of Alexander II (1855–81) and was sustained through the next two decades by Anton Chekhov. Russian verse had not been wholly eclipsed, but only with the advent of Symbolism in the mid-1890s did it again acquire potent impetus, and begin to push prose into the background. This "Silver Age," as it is sometimes termed, was to survive both the decline of Symbolism and the revolutions of 1917.

The first phase of the Silver Age, the decade and a half ending in 1910, was dominated by the Symbolists. They were "modern" in caring little whether their verses "made sense" or not. They also liked to tantalize readers with glimpses into ultimate reality. But though some Symbolists saw themselves as high priests of a cult, they also pioneered the refinement of poetic craftsmanship, and so came to inspire later poets who considered themselves anything but Symbolists. When Symbolism collapsed as a coherent movement in about 1910 — partly because its members could not agree about which of them was in what degree of contact with the Ultimate — individual Symbolist poets nevertheless continued writing. Russian poetry was not enfeebled by Symbolism's decline, but branched out, with renewed vitality, into Futurism, Acmeism, and numerous other channels.

The four poets all belong to the Silver Age's second stage — that which embraced both the late, disunited Symbolists and the post-Symbolists, both prerevolutionary and early postrevolutionary Russia, and poetry written both on Russian soil and in emigration. Nor were the echoes of the Silver Age wholly silent so long as Pasternak and Akhmatova were still alive and writing, as they were into the early 1960s.

Russian verse of the Silver Age is phenomenally rich and varied. It is qualitatively impressive and quantitatively daunting, exhibiting a wider range, greater originality, and a larger gallery of significant poets than the earlier Golden Age. Their product can be avant-garde, decadent, esoteric, ingenious, and perverse. They may seek to shock with distorted grammar, as with jagged, jazzy, syncopated juxtapositions and paradoxes. Some invented new words, new sounds, a new Russian syntax, or even a new Russian language. And yet, sacerdotal, mystical, and solemn though Russian poetry of this period often is, it does not limit itself to insights into the transcendental. Much of it is anything but earnest, shocking readers with its stark simplicity and with those bald, spare statements to which the language lends itself as readily as to the writhings of anguished contrivance. Love, death, despair, the nature of

God, but also irony, humour, puns, whimsy — all these elements are prominent in poetry written by Russians from the late 1890s until well into the Soviet era. It may be questioned whether any other twentieth-century literature has produced a more impressive sequence of poetic explosions, or given so large a group of talented poets to humanity. They took their place in the modernist movement within the arts throughout the world — a movement that was not confined to poetry but included prose writing, ballet, theatre, painting, music, and other arts or crafts, in Russia as elsewhere.

The leading Russian Symbolist poet was Aleksandr Blok, other important representatives being Annensky, Balmont, Bely, Bryusov, Zinaida Gippius, Vyacheslav Ivanov, Kuzmin, and Sologub. Most of these influenced the four poets, but without converting them to Symbolism. Tsvetayeva was never closely affiliated to any literary group, and Pasternak was so only briefly — during the few years when he clung to the skirts of Futurism, of which Khlebnikov and Mayakovsky were the main representatives. Akhmatova and Mandelstam were less emancipated from the world of "ists" and "isms," forming — with Akhmatova's first husband, Nikolay Gumilyov — the core of the Acmeist group. Significant poets of the post-Symbolist period also include the two peasant bards Klyuyev and Yesenin.

Eighteen names have been mentioned. These, with a few added or subtracted to suit individual taste, form an élite — a score or so of outstandingly gifted twentieth-century Russian poets. As for the tally of minor versifiers, it defies computation. In emigration alone nearly four hundred volumes of Russian poetry, by over two hundred and fifty poets, are said to have been published in the forty years following the Revolution.[3] Still more poetry was published in Russia itself, under increasingly frustrating conditions. Yet the very oppressions inflicted on poets by the Soviet State were not the result of indifference to poetry, such as may be observed in some other countries. Rather did they proceed from overanxiety. Perhaps poetry was too important to be left to poets, always an unreliable breed? Or perhaps poetry was too important to be permitted at all?

The Russian public is no less sensitive to poetry than the Russian government, as is vividly illustrated by the warning once given to an American translator who had rashly described Blok as "highly over-rated"; he was told by a compatriot of Blok's that if he said such a thing in Russia he would be lynched on the spot.[4] Blok himself has commented: "Literature is a more vital force in Russia than anywhere else. Nowhere else does Word become Life, nowhere does it turn into bread or stone, as it does with us." Blok says that this is "perhaps why Russian writers die, come to grief, or simply fade away so early."[5]

One reason for the highly charged relationship between the Russian and his poets is the nonliterary role traditionally played by poetry in Russia. Along with other branches of imaginative literature, verse has long been a vehicle for opposition such as is expressed, in countries less authoritarian, by political groups and parties. In Russia, however — whether pre-Revolutionary or post-Revolutionary — such initiatives have been so severely restricted that imaginative writers have become accepted as political spokesmen. And poets have tended to be even more prominent mouthpieces of opposition than authors of prose fiction, if only because verse statements — tending to be shorter and more pointed than prose statements — can the more easily be got by heart or clandestinely circulated in manuscript, for which reason they are less vulnerable to censorship controls.

A special role has been played in modern Russia by public poetry recitals. They have occasionally developed — even during phases of particularly severe oppression — into spectacular scandals, and in effect into political demonstrations that luridly highlight the special relationship between the poet, the public, and political authority. At these functions audiences are sometimes less eager to hear the poetry than to monitor the poet. Will he blunder — or can he be steered — into some indiscretion that may (with luck) lead to his arrest and disgrace? Among many such public recitals or gladiatorial displays four particularly revealing episodes stand out: Mandelstam's triumphant performance in Leningrad in 1933, and the no less dramatic appearances made in Moscow's Polytechnic Museum in 1921, 1944, and 1948 by Tsvetayeva, Akhmatova, and Pasternak, respectively. These will be described in detail in due course.

The conflict between the Russian poet and the Russian State goes back to the early nineteenth century, when one minor poet (Ryleyev) was hanged and others were imprisoned or exiled for involvement in the abortive Decembrist coup which followed the death of the Emperor Alexander I in 1825. The country's poet of poets, Aleksandr Pushkin, was also implicated in this affair, as a friend of the conspirators and as author of certain notorious clandestinely circulated youthful revolutionary verses. Pushkin narrowly escaped arrest after the Decembrist rising, and was induced to abandon subversive topics by Alexander I's successor, Nicholas I. But the great poet was never tamed, and he remained an emblem of opposition until his death in a duel at the age of thirty-seven. The tyrannical Nicholas has been blamed for his responsibility in permitting or provoking this tragedy by several generations of Russian poetry-lovers — none of them more eloquent than Marina Tsvetayeva — but the accusation has often been overstated.

If Pushkin's premature death is solidly in the Russian tradition, so too is the zest with which antiauthoritarian or anti-Tsarist Russian commentators have pounced on the great poet's fate in order to pillory a disliked political system. The tragedy was followed only four years later by the death of Pushkin's most gifted immediate successor, Mikhail Lermontov — another author of subversive lyrics — at the even earlier age of twenty-six, also in a duel that might have been prevented had authority been more vigilant in protecting the country's most gifted artists. A convention was accordingly established whereby it has almost been expected of any Russian poet worthy of the name, at least in certain historical periods, that he should challenge the power of the State, that his clandestinely circulated verses should hearten and inspire his government's victims and opponents, that he himself should perish by violence at an early age, and that his funeral should provoke political demonstrations. "Only in Russia is poetry respected," Mandelstam once remarked. "It gets people killed. Where else is poetry so common a motive for murder?"[6]

Where indeed? Still, no Russian poet of significance came to grief through head-on conflict with society between Lermontov's death and the fall of the autocracy. Only in the Soviet period did Russia resume, and much extend, the practice of honouring its bards by exterminating them. Mandelstam himself and Nikolay Klyuyev were the two most celebrated poets among the many twentieth-century writers who vanished into Stalin's prison camps; but just how, when, and where these and most other victimized individuals died will, presumably, never be known with certainty. More information is available on the doom of another leading poet, Akhmatova's divorced husband Nikolay Gumilyov, since he chanced to fall foul of authority before the tradition of enshrouding poets' and others' deaths in mystery had been established. When he was executed in August 1921 for alleged participation in a counter-revolutionary conspiracy, an official announcement to that effect was published in the press.[7] To these, the three most important twentieth-century poets directly exterminated by the State, may be added three others, whose response to the pressures of their era, and of their personal lives, was to die by their own hands: Yesenin, Mayakovsky, and Tsvetayeva.

Modern Russian writers have by no means all perished through State-inflicted or self-inflicted violence. But every important poet who survived the 1917 revolutions was quelled, frustrated, traumatized, or terrorized in some degree by the conditions of his age. Bryusov is perhaps an exception, though some might regard his fate — becoming a literary official empowered to determine his fellow authors' place on the food-rationing scale — as the most distasteful of all. Among others victimized or degraded in more conventional fashion, Blok died in 1921 at the age of forty, broken and disillusioned by the revolutionary society that he had openly welcomed in its earliest phase. The thirty-six-year-old Khlebnikov perished a year later of neglect and exposure to the hardships of the Civil War period. Others chose emigration, living in poverty and isolation: Balmont, Gippius, Khodasevich, the Ivanovs — Georgy and Vyacheslav. Hence the claim that "Soviet cultural policies brought total tragedy to every single one of the eighteen major poets who were active at the time of the Revolution."[8] The tragedy might be suffered vicariously, as it was by Akhmatova and Pasternak: they were victimized less in their own persons than by the persecution of those closest to them, and by officially sponsored public vilification.

These and similar facts have been rehearsed so often that one almost feels obliged to apologize for mentioning them. "Perhaps we have been sufficiently informed as to the martyrdom of Russian writers?" Such is the comment of a leading American authority on Mandelstam, Clarence Brown.[9] Another helpful interpreter of Russian poetry, Roman Jakobson, suggested in 1931 that a concern with these matters was typical of journalists rather than scholars — in particular of those who "bear Russia a grudge" and who express it by demonstrating with chapter and verse, and with historical precedent, "that it is dangerous to practice the trade of poet in Russia." Jakobson further claims: "What distinguishes Russia is not so much the fact that her great poets have ceased to be, but rather that not long ago she had so many of them."[10] That is admirably put. And yet, how can these men and women be understood if they are considered in isolation from the sufferings and anxieties that overwhelmingly dominated their lives? Russian poets themselves have repeatedly alluded, both in their verse and in more casual comments, to the hazardous, the almost melodramatic role imposed on the Russian poet by Russian conditions. Some of their finest verses — many of the disturbing lyrics from the doomed Mandelstam's last years, for example — hardly make sense at all if the historical context is ignored.

All the four poets were exposed, for prolonged periods and in fluctuating degree, to the danger of sudden or lingering death, either for writing certain kinds of verse or for not writing certain other kinds, for continuing to write when required not to do so, or for failing to write when required to do so. They were not endangered solely in their capacity as authors, for they naturally shared the general vulnerability of their fellow citizens during the forty-year period of intense agony that afflicted their country, with only minor remissions, between the outbreak of the First World War in 1914 and the death of Stalin in 1953.

The first phase in this sequence of tribulations included five major crises: the First World War of 1914–18; the February and October revolutions of 1917 — both of which occurred while Russia and Germany were still fighting; the Russian Civil War of 1918–21; and the major famine that followed the Civil War. A brief period of relative calm ensued in the middle and late 1920s, but even in those years Russians were actively preparing to inflict on each other the massive ordeals by mutual destruction that were to begin with the onset of Stalin's fully developed dictatorship in 1930. The Stalin period embraced the enforced collectivization of agriculture in the early 1930s, the generalized political terror of the late 1930s, the Second World War, and the oppressions of the dictator's last years. In each of these phases millions perished prematurely — whether in battle, by famine, through epidemic disease, or in concentration camps, the Stalin epoch being considerably longer and more severe than that of the First World War, the revolutions, and the Civil War combined.

The four poets had lived relatively carefree lives before 1917, and had been little affected by the political restrictions of that era. Imperial Russia too had its authoritarian pretensions. But they have been grossly exaggerated by the successor administration, and the fact is that Russian poets and Russian citizens in general were relatively secure during the last decades of the Empire. They risked serious consequences only if they chose to seek them through the open advocacy of revolutionary views or persistence in political conspiracy. The late Tsarist state might censor its poets' work. But it did not kill, harm, or threaten them, sportingly permitting them, as they are permitted in most non-authoritarian countries, to destroy themselves. Such is the way of poets all over the world.

Little inconvenienced by the political conditions of their youth, the four poets all reached adulthood without having to worry unduly about their material circumstances. All committed, by the mere process of being born, what was to be retrospectively deemed in their country of origin a crime punishable (in some cases) with death: that of springing from the respectable middle class. Tsvetayeva's father was — like Pasternak's — a professor of art, while Akhmatova's father was a naval engineer, and Mandelstam's a moderately successful leather merchant.

All four poets were brought up in or near one of Russia's two great metropolitan centres, St. Petersburg and Moscow. St. Petersburg was the country's administrative capital, the centre of the Imperial court, a thriving port, and one of Europe's most cosmopolitan cities, whereas Moscow — the country's capital until the early eighteenth century, to be reinstated as such in early 1918 — was notoriously old-fashioned, sprawling like a gigantic village. The poets were equally divided between these two metropolises. Pasternak and Tsvetayeva were born and bred in Moscow, while St. Petersburg (to be called Petrograd in 1914–24, and after that Leningrad) became the home of the infant Osip Mandelstam not long after his birth in Warsaw. Akhmatova's childhood was spent only a few miles from St. Petersburg, at Tsarskoye Selo (since renamed Pushkin). She later lived for many years in Petrograd/Leningrad. Each poet was to develop a powerful emotional relationship towards his or her native metropolis, and a whole anthology of magnificent eulogies and denunciations of the two cities could be culled from their works.

Though the poets did not meet in their earliest years, their evolution proceeded on roughly parallel lines. All four received the kind of rigorous education that was available to members of their class. They were taught from an early age by foreign governesses or tutors — hence their command of the French and German tongues. The Russian language was all around them in infancy, of course, Tsvetayeva being its most precocious champion. She not only read Pushkin for herself from the age of six, but she also reversed the old Russian poetic tradition whereby an infant poet is told endless fairy stories at the knee of his peasant nurse: in this case it was child who entertained nurse with nursery tales and recitations of poetry. In adolescence all four poets attended schools with exacting curricula, emphasis being laid both on native Russian traditions and on those of Western European culture as a whole. Mandelstam went to a well-known private school in St. Petersburg — Tenishev's, which he was later to describe in his autobiographical sketch *Buzz of Time*, and where Vladimir Nabokov was to be a pupil. The other three all attended *gimnazii* — State grammar schools with syllabuses that included some training in Latin and ancient Greek. Insight into classical civilization was imparted, and was to leave its imprint on some enchanting lyrics. But no member of the quartet can be called a classical scholar — unlike their older contemporaries Vyacheslav Ivanov and Innokenty Annensky, who were both teachers and translators of ancient Greek as well as major authors of original Russian verse. It should also be noted that Tsvetayeva was expelled from her Moscow *gimnaziya* for being cheeky to the staff.

The poets' education benefited from repeated visits, sometimes lasting months or years, to Western Europe. Armed with their fluent French and (except for Akhmatova) German, besides being young and eager for experience, they immersed themselves in European life and culture. They did not confine themselves to France and Germany, but also visited Italy and absorbed its enchantment through the language of art, architecture, and landscape; later in life Akhmatova and Mandelstam were to become ardent students of Dante. England was never part of their European tours, but it does not follow that English culture passed them by. Though only Akhmatova and Pasternak learnt to read the language of Shakespeare, they were all familiar with his work, and allusions to it abound in their verse. Pasternak was to become one of Russia's most distinguished Shakespearian translators.

As these details emphasize, the poets were all citizens of the world, or at least citizens of Europe, which is one of the many important factors uniting them. It also contrasts them with two Russian poets of comparable renown belonging to their generation — Yesenin and Mayakovsky, whose knowledge of European culture and whose interest in it were slight. Those two might tour the world giving flamboyant recitals of their work in the original Russian; but they knew little of, and they cared less for, the native traditions of the countries that they visited.

Unlike some of their contemporaries, the four poets could admire the new without disparaging, abusing, or ignoring the old, just as they could embrace Western European culture without being disloyal to their native traditions, and without feeling that the Russian and the non-Russian cultural heritage must necessarily be hostile to each other. Their devotion to the European tradition as a whole, their knowledge of Western and (to some extent) classical languages and literatures, are of particular importance, since all four poets can be seen without undue distortion as champions of the West against the post-Revolutionary forces in their native country that have violently rejected the West. The four had the same natural instinct as any ancient Greek — to oppose the barbarian in this "insane epoch when all the principles of social life, all the foundations of European — and consequently of Russian — culture were being eradicated."[11]

Though all the four poets sprang from the privileged strata of pre-Revolutionary Russian society, it also happens that all belonged to categories subject to adverse discrimination. The two poetesses did so by virtue of being women, while the poets had the disadvantage of being Jewish — by descent, not by language or religion.

For many years before the poets' birth the revolutionary and reformist opponents of the Tsar's government had been campaigning for sexual and racial equality — with limited success, since conditions throughout the country at large remained unfavourable both to the female sex and to the Empire's numerous minority nationalities. Yet there is little trace of any handicap being imposed on the four poets by their origins. Higher education was a prime area of discrimination, for example; but none of them seems to have suffered educationally through being a Jew or a woman.

The two girls each married shortly after leaving school, and neither seems to have hankered after higher education in any formal sense, though Akhmatova somewhat casually pursued a course in law at Kiev. In any case, both came to know Russian and world literature more thoroughly than many an honours graduate in those subjects. As for the young men, the quotas imposed on Jewish university applicants did not prevent Pasternak and Mandelstam from attending the universities of Moscow and St. Petersburg, respectively. The point is not so much that the regulations restricting Jewish university entry were laxly administered, like so many Russian regulations, as that they applied only to those who professed the Jewish religion. A Jew could escape the restrictions by embracing Orthodox Christianity, and it seems likely that Mandelstam adopted this course so that he could attend St. Petersburg University. Pasternak, whose Jewish parents practised no religion, happened to have been christened in the Orthodox Church at the insistence of his nurse, and so he experienced no difficulty in gaining entry to Moscow University. Neither Pasternak nor Mandelstam knew Yiddish or Hebrew, and both were to all intents and purposes educated Russians. But it does not follow that they were exempt from occasional anti-Semitic sneers — a feature of their society — either at school or later.

Victims of discrimination or not, the four poets were pioneers in that they included the first outstanding authors of Jewish origin to arise in Russian literature, while also furnishing (if the earlier poet Zinaida Gippius may be forgotten) the country's first major woman writers.

Not only were these four young people little affected by the racially, sexually, and politically repressive practices of the late Russian Empire, not only were they tolerably provided for, reasonably well-versed in European languages and literatures, and strikingly well-versed in their own, but they also enjoyed the boon of high spirits, vigour, and handsome or impressive appearance as they embarked on their literary careers in the relatively untroubled epoch between the unsuccessful Russian Revolution of 1905 and the period of upheavals that began with the First World War. Born within a year or two of each other; sharing comparably high reputations together with similar cultural, educational, and social backgrounds; maturing as artists before the 1917 revolutions, but producing their major work after it; propelled into hostility towards a political system of which all became victims — the four poets have more than enough in common to justify the decision to treat them as a group, especially as they were all aware of each other's work, keenly reacting to it, and praising or abusing it throughout their lives, besides being united by friendship and mutual respect. Their group unity is emphasized even more eloquently if it is asked what fifth Russian poet could conceivably be attached in order to convert them into a quintet. There is none, except that Gumilyov might have qualified, had he survived into the period following the Civil War. The four were, however, disunited to the extent that they never belonged to a single poetic school, though it is true that neither Akhmatova nor Mandelstam was ever to renounce the Acmeist movement which they helped Gumilyov to form in the early 1910s.

The four poets by no means presented a common front towards the avant-garde movement in the arts. They varied, to put it crudely, in the degree to which their poems "made sense" by yielding up their surface meaning without placing excessive demands on the reader's close and sympathetic attention. Diverging in this respect at the outset of their careers, each went on to pursue his or her individual pattern of intelligibility. The result is that all four have written with limpid precision at some periods, but have also gone through phases in which they have cultivated a considerable degree of obscurity.

Both in their simple and their complex veins, all have composed superb poetry. At their more obscure they indulge in sudden swoops, changes of subject, tortured syntax, arcane allusions, and elusive ambiguities. And yet, even at their most inventive, ingenious, and obscure, they remain superficially conventional in their prosody. There is little *vers libre* such as is common in the work of contemporaries writing in other languages. There is, on the contrary, a strong tendency for them to deploy their verses in regular stanzas, often quatrains, each of which repeats the same metric pattern — and to do this even when they are cultivating a high degree of semantic obliquity. Simple metres — iambics, trochees, anapaests, dactyls — tend to predominate, and there is a reluctance to abandon rhyme, although unrhymed iambic pentameters are by no means unknown. A poem such as Mandelstam's "Horseshoe Finder," his longest and one of his most impressive, is therefore exceptional since it follows a superficially free and nonrepetitive rhythmic pattern, like parts of Eliot's *The Waste Land* and Pound's *Cantos;* so successful was this pilot model that one may wonder in passing why Mandelstam did not put *vers libre* into regular production.

To the sensitive eye and ear the poets' seemingly tame or conventional approach is nothing of the sort. Both at its most simple-seeming and at its most opaque, their verse conceals much artfully contrived rhyme, internal rhyme, near-rhyme, ellipsis, metrical syncopation, enjambment, and dislocated syntax, together with prosodic pyrotechnics of many other kinds. They shock, they hypnotize, they leap adroitly from one stylistic level to another. They also exhibit that paradoxical element — call it serious playfulness or playful seriousness — which is a fundamental element in poetry all over the world.

Though innovation is crucial to poetry, so too is tradition, and the four poets were all profoundly aware of the poetic heritage of their own country. It need hardly be said that they were saturated in Pushkin. But Pushkin faced them, as he has faced all Russian poets of the last hundred and fifty years, with an acute problem: how could they operate within the orbit of so potent a predecessor without either parodying or self-consciously diverging from him? The poets all overcame that difficulty, and also absorbed other nineteenth-century influences, especially from Lermontov, Baratynsky, and Tyutchev. Among their older contemporaries Blok was pre-eminent as an admired figure whose poetic personality was so powerful that he too could easily betray his juniors into parody or imitation. Innokenty Annensky — very much a poet's poet, and one whose name deserves to be more widely known outside Russia than it is — was also highly influential.

Despite the wealth of cultural influences, both Russian and foreign, that may be traced in the work of all four poets, the more closely one investigates this and other aspects of their writings, the more one is impressed by their profound originality.

2

TORTURE BY HAPPINESS

ANNA AKHMATOVA was the first of the four poets to have a poem published. She was still a schoolgirl when it appeared in 1907, in an obscure, short-lived Russian magazine — *Sirius* — brought out in Paris by Nikolay Gumilyov. He was three years her senior, he had already published a volume of his own verses — *Path of the Conquistadors*, and he himself was to become one of the foremost Russian poets of his age. He was also to become famous as a traveller to Egypt, Abyssinia, and Somaliland who exploited tropical themes in his verse. Sometimes described as grotesquely ugly — his head seemed to come to a point, as if it had been maltreated at origin by a midwife's forceps — Gumilyov was a dashing, reckless young man with a commanding presence. He was adored by women.

If this twentieth-century conquistador was ever to feel passions comparable to those that he ignited, their object would obviously have to be a woman who did not take him and his advances too seriously. Such, it happens, was the teen-aged Akhmatova's instinctive reaction. But Gumilyov countered repeated rebuffs with typical panache and is said to have attempted suicide no fewer than four times in five years for love of Akhmatova. At last his bizarre approach proved successful, and in April 1910 poet duly married poet.

They were no sooner united than — as might have been expected in so highly charged an atmosphere — they began to draw apart. Each was, perhaps, too fiercely independent a spirit to make concessions to the other, besides which, as may be true of many a happier wife and husband, "neither seemed really to understand what being married was all about."[1] It also seems likely, from Akhmatova's later evolution, that she possessed only a limited talent for intimate personal relations, whether as spouse, mistress, or mother. Her gift was, rather, for transmuting unsatisfactory emotional experiences into poetry. And so she had a permanent vested interest in cultivating disharmony.

The wedding ceremony was followed by no sudden rupture, but by the progressive discovery that bride and groom lacked the aptitude for living together, particularly as Gumilyov too was the kind of poet whose art thrived on emotional drama more torrid than is easily reconciled with established domesticity. Artists of this type perhaps require only as much domesticated love as is necessary to reveal some new dimension of conflict, and then they are off. Akhmatova and Gumilyov were to remain on friendly terms; and they were always to regard each other as literary allies, even though there is not much in common between the two bodies of verse. But they drifted further and further apart in their personal relations.

A few months after the capture of Akhmatova, Gumilyov went off on one of his African expeditions, leaving his bride behind at their home in Tsarskoye Selo. She was lonely, she felt abandoned, and she infused her first book of poems — *Evening,* published in 1912 — with these sensations. A second collection, *Rosary,* followed two years later, by which time the attractive young poetess was already the object of an extravagant literary and personal cult in St. Petersburg. She was also the mother of a baby son, Lyov; but, proving no better fitted for the maternal than for the conjugal role, she had the child brought up in the countryside of Tver Province by her mother-in-law. The "bad mother" whom she mentions in a lyric of 1915 is, in effect, herself.[2]

Was Akhmatova truly beautiful or not? There was some dispute on this among her contemporaries, the general view being overwhelmingly favourable. And no one questioned the devastating impact that her appearance and personality made on all who saw her. She was tall, with long, dark hair, shapely white hands, and a perpetual look of sadness even when she smiled; she bore herself like an empress nursing some secret sorrow. Her appearance became famous for certain features: her fringe of hair, her shawl, her muff. She herself has drawn a poetical self-portrait incorporating these details.

A rosary of small beads on the neck,
I hide my hands in broad muff. . . .

And mauve silk
Makes my face look paler.
My uncurled fringe
Nearly touches my brows.[3]

Others were not slow to commemorate her beauty and talent until, it has been claimed, over a hundred other poets had dedicated verse to her. Among the most illustrious was Blok, whose poem to her of 1913 and its various drafts refer to her demoniac beauty, her pensive, nonchalant

air, and her famous shawl. Mandelstam described her as a "black angel
in the snow," and as the personification of statuesque grief.

> Drooping from your shoulders,
> Pseudo-classical shawl became stone.

He went on to compare her to Phèdre as played by the French tragic
actress Rachel.[4]

Akhmatova had other advantages besides her striking looks. What
conquered the lovesick conquistador and her many other admirers, male
and female, was the combination of beauty, talent, and personality with
a congenital indifference to the effect that they might have on anyone
else. Here was no effortless consciousness of superiority, but superiority
so innate that there was no need for her to be conscious of it at all. This
indifference is expressed at the very outset of her literary career, in the
letter that she wrote commenting on the publication of her poem in
Sirius. She alludes to her own first appearance in print and to her
publisher Gumilyov as if both were self-evidently absurd.[5] Her vocation
as a poet seems to have been so strong — and she had been writing
verses from about the age of eleven — that the reception of her work
barely concerned her, and she was equally unimpressed by her social
success. Nothing could have been better calculated to inflame the atmo-
sphere of adulation surrounding her than this air of nonchalance.

Akhmatova seems to have derived little satisfaction from her vogue
as a poet and a woman. That it caused her acute suffering is the burden
of verses written in 1955, when she was in her middle sixties and was
attempting to sum up the experiences of her youth.

> The more they praised me,
> And the more I was admired —
> The more I dreaded life on earth,
> The more I longed to come awake.
> And I knew I would pay a hundredfold
> In prison, tomb, madhouse:
> Wherever such as I should wake.
> But torture by happiness continued.[6]

Though the world saw the young poet as the spoilt darling of
fortune, she had early conceived a tragic outlook on the scheme of
things. She was quick to sense that the cosmopolitan, glittering city of
St. Petersburg, which so eagerly acclaimed her, was but a Waste Land,
the capital of the world's most accident-prone large country in what was

to become its most accident-prone century. Nor was she spared family misfortunes. Her parents separated when she was in her teens, and she remained with her mother. Her father had strongly objected to his daughter writing poetry, and so she abandoned her family name, Gorenko, in favour of Akhmatova; the pseudonym purportedly revives the surname of a Tatar great-grandmother.[7] The decision was a lucky one, perhaps, since the Gorenkos seemed marked out by fate for extinction before their time. One of the poet's sisters had died at the age of four; she herself came close to death from a mysterious illness contracted at the age of ten; her other sister was to perish from tuberculosis (from which Akhmatova also suffered) in her twenties; a brother was to commit suicide.

The fatalities, tragedies, and misunderstandings surrounding the young poet help to explain the obsession with mortality that led to the word *smert* ("death") and its derivatives occurring no fewer than twenty-five times in *Rosary*.[8] This concern with death was shared by Marina Tsvetayeva; but Tsvetayeva could contemplate the skull beneath the skin with a youthful vitality and gusto that Akhmatova was never to express. Despite her tragic aspects, the young Akhmatova could be a vivacious companion, even though the liveliness of her recorded conversation finds little expression in her poetry. Its dominant tone is serious without being ponderous or earnest.

Akhmatova's verse of the period 1907–14 includes more than a hundred and forty lyrics, of which over a hundred appeared in collected form in the two books *Evening* and *Rosary*, while others were published only in magazines, or have been rescued from oblivion posthumously. There is also a single long poem, *By the Sea Shore*, dated 1914.

Her dominant theme is love. In the lyric that flies "Love" as its title she sees that emotion in protean guises: as a curled snake, as a cooing dove, as hoar frost, as flowers; she "senses it in the drowsiness of stocks." But her main point is that love, however conceived,

> Surely, secretly leads
> Away from joy and calm.[9]

The couplet might be taken as the motto for Akhmatova's many love poems as a whole. Hers is the poetry of partings envisaged before meetings have even taken place. Her lovers fall into the two classes of those whom she rejects and those, more numerous, who have rejected her, are engaged in rejecting her, or are about to reject her.

While usually shunning the evocation of love in the abstract, the poet more commonly provides information about what — at some moment of tense emotional involvement — she was doing with her muff, her hands, her glove. The vegetational background is lightly sketched in with some information on the trees and flowers that embellished the scene. These details are hard and sharp, but the emotional involvements are managed very differently. The reader is given only vague indications of their nature, being treated as an intimate confidant who already knows all the background details. It is a sort of coyness. Many of the lyrics suggest the dimly discerned phantom of a background plot. "Elements of the novella or novel have found refuge in her verse after remaining neglected in the heyday of the Symbolist lyric."[10] There is the unidentified heroine and speaker, "I," who may be equated with Akhmatova herself; and there is usually some unidentified "thou" or "he": her lover, who has been, is, or soon will be suffering or inflicting suffering in some manner no more than vaguely specified. A celebrated instance is "Song of the Last Meeting," in which the heroine's confusion of spirit is reflected in a detail about her glove.

> My breast was so cold, so helpless;
> But light was my tread.
> I put left glove
> On right hand.
>
> There were many steps, it seemed;
> Yet I knew there were but three.
> Autumnal whisper among maples
> Urged: "Die with me.
>
> I'm betrayed by my woeful,
> Fickle, dire fate."
> I answered: "Dearest,
> So am I. I'll die with you."
>
> This is our last meeting's song.
> I glanced at dark house.
> Just candles burning in bedroom —
> Uncaring, yellow-flamed.[11]

Concrete details about candles and gloves, an intense emotional crisis that is merely glimpsed — the combination is typical of many another lyric of the period, including the following.

> I clasped my hands beneath dark veil.
> "Why so pale today?"
> "Because I gave him bitter grief
> To drink till he was drunk."

Can I forget? He left, stumbling;
Mouth twisted, anguished.
I ran down, not touching baluster;
Ran after him to gate.

Gasping, I cried: "I was just
Joking. I'll die if you go."
He smiled calmly, eerily;
Said: "Don't stand out in the cold."[12]

Among the unidentified lovers or would-be lovers who people these poems is a "boy," sometimes called a "poor boy" or a "grey-eyed boy," who seeks the poet's favours in vain. Another is a potent, demoniac figure to whom she submits, but who is cold, lustful, and no true soul mate. It was, as already indicated, a staple feature of Akhmatova's technique to people her verses with these unidentified "he's," "thou's," and "you's," whom contemporary readers other than close friends could not possibly identify, whose identity may still elude the biographer, and who were not all necessarily equated in the poet's mind with specific individuals. In the earliest verses the "he's" and "thou's" — together with the second partner in the occasional "both of us" — may often be plausibly equated with Nikolay Gumilyov. But other men were involved too, and increasingly so over the years: Akhmatova was to become famous for the number and variety of her lovers. On the identity of her individual "he's" the reader is usually left to speculate in vain — part flattered, part exasperated by being treated as if he were already initiated into these intimacies and needed only to be instructed on such externals as the smell of oysters or a wasp sting.

Her lyric about the wasp is striking in once again combining precise factual detail with a vaguely indicated violent crisis in personal relations.

I went mad, strange boy,
At three on Wednesday.
A droning wasp stung
My ring finger. . . .

Shall I weep for you, strange one,
Will your face smile at me?[13]

In the poem referring to oysters, "In the Evening," the fusion of emotion and attendant detail is especially subtle.

Band in park.
Unutterable grief's jangling.
Fresh, sharp marine tang
Of oysters in dish of ice.

He said: "I am your true love."
He touched my dress.
How uncaressing
Those hands' contact.

Thus one strokes cat or bird,
Watches lithe horsewomen.
There is laughter, though, in calm eyes
Under lashes' light gold.

And grieved fiddles' voices
Chant beyond settling smoke:
"Give thanks to heaven, then,
Alone with your love for the first time."[14]

As these passages indicate, the young Akhmatova shuns the obscurity so characteristic of avant-garde verse. When she published her first poems, Russian readers had long been accustomed to expect new poetry not to yield its secrets as easily as hers does. True, her lyrics normally convey no more than an elusive and vague impression of emotions that are themselves elusive and vague. But they are otherwise largely free from obscurity, their originality being that of startling simplicity. The language is straightforward, conversational — at times even prosaic. The mystery lies more in the poet's personality than in her way of expressing herself.

She writes without obtrusive stylistic devices, most lyrics consisting of three or four four-line stanzas, with regular metre, often iambic, and with alternate rhyming lines. But this seeming lack of adventurousness conceals much elegant workmanship, and owes some of its success to surprise; it was not what readers had come to expect in an age when art often consisted less of concealing art than of flaunting artifice.

Despite her obsession with love Akhmatova is no erotic writer. The point is stressed because of the rumours surrounding her private life, imputing to her an extreme degree of sexual promiscuity, and embodied in the notorious formula "half nun, half whore." This description of the poet was to be offered, during the official witch-hunt mounted against her in 1946, by the Stalinist cultural satrap Andrey Zhdanov, who had borrowed it from the literary critic Boris Eykhenbaum. Writing in the early 1920s, Eykhenbaum had put the point more circuitously, as befitted his calling, while relating his comment to the "I" of Akhmatova's poems rather than to herself directly. "One begins to sense the image, paradoxical in its duality — or rather oxymoronic quality — of a heroine who is partly a fallen woman with tumultuous passions, and partly a poor nun capable of praying successfully for God's forgiveness."[15]

The image of a nun finds some support in the religious motifs that occur in Akhmatova's work from the beginning, but without being as obtrusive as in the later Pasternak. Though the reader can indeed sense the "tumultuous passions," he is also conscious of the discipline and control with which the poet deploys them. The general tone is cool, and so the comparison with Sappho sometimes made — and gracefully repeated by Oxford University's public orator during the poet's visit to England in 1965 — can be misleading. If Akhmatova is seized by convulsive trembling, if she is paler than grass, nigh unto death with frozen tongue and fire flickering under her skin (to quote a few Sapphic images), she manages to convey those experiences in a more clinical, less vibrant spirit than does the bard of Lesbos. Russia's answer to Sappho was not to be Anna Akhmatova, but her more volcanic contemporary Marina Tsvetayeva.

The early Akhmatova did not offer, as was claimed by Aleksandra Kollontay (a leading early Bolshevik and famous apostle of free love) "an entire volume of the female soul." Still less was she — at least in her earlier years — "concerned with the necessity of giving voice to the woman's point of view," as has been suggested by a recent biographer.[16] It is hard to see Akhmatova as a typical woman or a typical anything. She did not regard herself as the mouthpiece of collective womanhood, natural though this impression may be in view of her status as the first Russian woman writer to attain such prominence. She expressed *a* woman's point of view, but for *the* woman's point of view her readers had to wait for *Requiem,* written many years later. She was not an apostle of feminism, however justifiably that cause had been preached in Russia since the mid-nineteenth century, being perhaps too self-possessed to feel that she needed to assert herself, either "as a woman" or in any other capacity. Nor was she the kind of mean spirit that chiefly sees itself as the representative of a social or sexual category. But her self-possession was combined with great vulnerability: here is a leading paradox among the many that lend her fascination.

Vulnerable or not, Akhmatova displays control and inner strength in her writing from the beginning. This claim is not contradicted by the tragic, pessimistic, gloomy sentiments that she often voices. They are not the wailings of self-pity. They are rather a dispassionate adverse diagnosis of the human condition offered by one free from illusions who believes in her need and capacity for a great love that (she knows, even as she craves for it) can never be anything but transitory and disappointing. Hers is an unruffled appraisal of a complex situation, not a cry of pain.

Every young poet has the right and perhaps the duty to be self-centered, and the young Akhmatova certainly was so. She herself, her emotions, her experiences, her needs, her disappointments, dominate her work without monopolizing it. Her early lyrics include evocations of her homeland: of the Crimea and southern Russia, where she was born and was a frequent visitor. They also commemorate the north: St. Petersburg, where much of her adult life was to be spent, and nearby Tsarskoye Selo, her childhood home. While attending the *lycée* at Tsarskoye Selo, Pushkin had incidentally read and imitated Evariste Parny and other French poets. He figures in Akhmatova's delightful eight-line lyric of 1911 recalling his activities of the 1810s.

> The swarthy youth strolled these paths,
> Grieved by lake's shores.
> For a century we've cherished
> That tread's faint rustle.
>
> Pine needles — dense, spiny —
> Cover low stumps.
> Here lay his cocked hat,
> His dog-eared Parny.[17]

Advancing nearly a century in time, Akhmatova commemorated, in verses of January 1914, a visit that she had made in St. Petersburg to the poet Aleksandr Blok.

> I visited the poet.
> Noon. Sunday.
> Calm of ample room,
> Frost beyond windows,
>
> And sun — crimson
> Over ragged, dove-grey smoke.
> How bright my silent
> Host's gaze at me.
>
> Such eyes —
> Unforgettable.
> Better, though, for me discreetly
> Not to look at them at all.

But I shall remember our talk
And Sunday's hazy noontide
In tall grey house
By Neva's sea gates.[18]

There were, inevitably, rumours of a romance between the two
poets, both so illustrious — and in neither case for the practice of celi-
bacy. In later life Akhmatova went out of her way to deny what was
commonly assumed, that she and Blok had been lovers.[19]

The St. Petersburg poets of the prewar period were accustomed to
recite their verses and to hobnob with painters, actresses, and other
members of the capital's artistic bohemia at the Stray Dog, a famous
basement night club. Gumilyov and Akhmatova were habitués, and she
has described the scene in a disapproving lyric. She contradicts more
conventional memoirists, to whom the Dog was the liveliest cultural
night spot in town, by portraying the customers as drunkards or whores
united in common misery. The poet has done her best to raise morale
by donning a tight skirt "to seem even more graceful." But she finds
herself brooding agonizingly on the hour of her own death.[20]

The Stray Dog was also a favourite haunt of Osip Mandelstam,
who is closely linked with Akhmatova as a fellow resident of St. Peters-
burg and as a co-founder of the Acmeist movement. A third St. Peters-
burger, Akhmatova's husband Gumilyov, was Acmeism's leading spirit
and principal philosopher.

Among these three leading Acmeists Mandelstam least resembled
a conquistador, being smallish, shortish, and slightish, with receding
curly ginger hair. His large head was set on a thin neck, and was usually
canted backwards at a characteristic angle that made people think of a
young chicken. That he resembled a goldfinch, alert to danger and
ready for flight, he himself implied in one of his late lyrics.[21] His gait
was bouncy; his ears stuck out, and he tried to disguise the fact by
growing side-whiskers; his brilliant eyes were like a camel's; his eyelids
looked inflamed; he was forever smoking cigarettes and using his shoul-
der as an ashtray. He was "extremely ugly, with a hint of the absurd,
which makes a man more than merely ugly," according to a celebrated
beauty of the period, Princess Salomeya Andronikova. In this descrip-
tion of the poet, dated 1961, she ill repays the two exquisite lyrics that
he had addressed to her back in 1916.[22]

This is one view of Mandelstam. But the many photographs of the
young poet do not bear out such testimony; there is an authoritative air

about him, suggesting that the emphasis on his small, comic, bird-like appearance may have proceeded from the grudge that minor talents often bear towards a major talent. An American professor has shown that Mandelstam was taller than Ilya Ehrenburg, one of the chief propagators of the "tiny bird" image, and has even adduced evidence, using language of awesome delicacy, to suggest that the poet's penis was of impressive dimensions.[23] Mandelstam spoke with complete confidence whenever the subject of poetry came up, and on such occasions he could seem more like a supreme arbiter than a homeless flutterer. Just as Akhmatova combined self-confidence and vulnerability, so too Mandelstam could seem outstandingly timid and courageous by turns. A fellow poet, Mikhail Lozinsky, nicknamed him "Rabbit-Leopard." But perhaps it would be better to forget the many zoological images that the young Mandelstam evoked and remember him as the high-spirited, light-hearted, talented youth which he was.

His early history resembles Pasternak's, and contrasts him with the two women poets, in revealing a vague interest in politics combined with the left-wing sympathies that were almost de rigueur among Russian intellectuals in the last decades of the Imperial régime. At one time the young Mandelstam had been "a thoroughly mature and finished Marxist," according to his own memoir, *Buzz of Time*, written in his thirties.[24] But the phrase is ironical. He also flirted with the Socialist Revolutionaries, Russia's main revolutionary rivals to Marxism, and he is even reported as seeking to join their Fighting Organization, which was heavily engaged in assassinating high Russian officials. In Paris in 1908 he insisted on attending a memorial service for the famous Socialist Revolutionary assassin Grigory Gershuni, who had died in emigration; an address was given by the even more famous political terrorist Boris Savinkov. Yet it is clear that Mandelstam's flirtation with politics was superficial, as was the no less transitory sympathy that he also expressed for Roman Catholicism. He was far more interested in reciting the poetry of Bryusov and Verlaine. He was also known, during his Paris sojourn, to profess his appreciation of bourgeois comfort, a sentiment profoundly alien to any true revolutionary.[25]

Mandelstam was to become neither a revolutionary nor a counter-revolutionary, being incapable of adopting or simulating a political stance even to save his life. The most eloquent pointer to his future is his remarkable reaction, as a five-year-old boy, to the unfamiliar word "progress" when he chanced to hear it used in adult conversation. He had not the faintest idea what the word meant, but it conveyed so potent a whiff of evil that he immediately burst into tears.[26] The episode must establish a record for a poet's prophetic precociousness. Here was an infant who indeed felt the future in his bones.

What of the literary movement that Mandelstam and Akhmatova joined in the early 1910s as colleagues of its main sponsor and spokesman, Gumilyov? The essence of Acmeism was, at least in theory, the pursuit of clarity, precision, order, and balance, with which may be contrasted the vagueness often generated by Symbolism. Acmeists also claimed to be down-to-earth, once again diverging from the Symbolists, who were so often obsessed with a dimly defined other world perceived through a transcendentalist or occultist haze. To the Acmeists a rose was, they insisted, significant as a rose — significant for its petals and its scent, and not as an emblem of beauty. The Acmeists were also cultural traditionalists devoted to the heritage of Western Europe, with its classical and Mediterranean roots. They disagreed on this issue with the Futurists, who formed the chief among the rival movements disputing the succession to Symbolism, and who were apt to reject the consolidated artistic achievements of humanity's regrettable pre-Futurist phase as fit only for the rubbish dump. To the Acmeists, by contrast, "nostalgia for world culture" was all-important, as Mandelstam himself once claimed.[27]

There are some affinities, largely coincidental, with a vigorous contemporary movement in English poetry, Imagism. But though there was little traffic between the two movements, the leading Imagist Ezra Pound shared with the Acmeists, especially Mandelstam, an enthusiasm for the unity of European culture going back through the Middle Ages, while laying particular emphasis on its classical and Mediterranean origins. Both authors, the American and the Russian, also showed a flair for converting their cultural enthusiasms into magnificent poetry.

Mandelstam's first published verses — five lyrics — appeared in 1910 in an issue of the elegant, recently founded St. Petersburg journal *Apollon*. A collection of twenty-three lyrics, *Stone*, appeared in 1913; and there are, in all, up to a hundred lyrics written before the First World War. Among them the following most aptly illustrates the Acmeist cult of the precise.

On pale blue
April-hued enamel
Birches lifted boughs
Unobtrusively crepuscular.

Sharp, delicate pattern,
Fragile network frozen.
Precisely drawn design
On porcelain plate,

When gracious artist limns it
On glassy base,

Aware of his brief power,
Forgetful of sad death.[28]

Mandelstam had a formidable ability to conjure up silence and emptiness, as in this four-line poem.

Dull, discreet plop
Of fruit dropped by tree
Amid lively hum
Of forest's dead silence.[29]

Still more silent, still emptier, is the following.

Acute hearing tautens sail.
Void are dilated eyes.
Floats through silence
Midnight birds' unsinging chorus.

I am poor as Nature,
Simple as sky.
Chimerical my freedom
As birds' midnight voices.

I see the unbreathing moon,
Sky deader than canvas.
Your weird, ailing world
I welcome, Nothingness.[30]

The idea of the artist overcoming death underlies what may well be the most famous of all Mandelstam's poems; it is also one of his earliest, having been written in 1909. Though it has been much anthologized and translated, it is here rendered anew.

I have a body. Tell me what to do
With it — so integral, so wholly me?

For the calm joy of breathing and of life
To whom, I wonder, do I owe my thanks?

I am the gardener, I the blossom too;
In the world's dungeon I am not alone.

Already on eternity's glass pane
My exhalation and my warmth are fixed.

On it shall be imprinted a design
Unknowable till recently.

But though the evanescent blur may fade
The graceful pattern cannot be erased.[31]

The lines about eternity's windows are by no means the only
passage in Mandelstam's earliest verse to carry a strong whiff of Symbol-
ism — so strong that, when Gumilyov came to review *Stone,* he divided
the collection into an earlier, Symbolist, section and a later, Acmeist,
section. He went on, deploying precision truly Acmeist, to identify the
specific moment when Acmeism began for Mandelstam — with a six-
line lyric of 1912 in which he explicitly dissociates himself from "eter-
nity," so recently invoked by himself.[32] It is the oracular use of that
abstraction (as recorded in an anecdote) by the early-nineteenth-century
poet Batyushkov that Mandelstam deplores, while also rejecting tradi-
tional references to those archetypal stage properties of Symbolism, the
moon and the stars.

No, it is not the moon; a bright clock face
Is beaming at me. Now, am I to blame
If my mind grasps the stars' faint glow as milky?

And I recoil from Batyushkov's conceit.
Asked "What's the time?" by someone hereabouts,
He gave an odd reply: "Eternity."[33]

In his elucidation of this lyric Clarence Brown discusses Mandel-
stam's dethronement of Symbolist references to heavenly bodies and
abstract concepts. He also links the lyric with its author's essay on
François Villon, in which the medieval French poet is applauded for
expelling the moon from his verses in favour of such jolly tangibilities
as roast duck. And Brown quotes for good measure the well-known
lines by the Imagist T. E. Hulme in which the moon, far from sleeping
with Endymion, as in Shakespeare, leans "Over a hedge / Like a red-
faced farmer."[34] But though Mandelstam's short lyric well bears this
interpretation, one highly significant feature of this, arguably his first
venture into the allegedly pellucid atmosphere of Acmeism, must be
noted. Precise as the poem assuredly is, it by no means yields its meaning
to a superficial reading. Mandelstam's work had been more intelligible
in his brief Symbolist phase than it was to become in his mature, Acme-
ist phase — and paradoxically so, since Symbolism stood (broadly
speaking) for obscurity, and Acmeism for clarity. As the poet's career
proceeded, readers of the various Acmeist manifestos, including his
own, must have begun to wonder what had become of the precision and
sharp outlines flown at the masthead of the new movement.

Since architectural balance and harmony were among the qualities cultivated by the Acmeists, it is not surprising that Mandelstam began to specialize in buildings, especially cathedrals — a theme that was to recur throughout his work. One lyric evokes the great temple of St. Sophia in Constantinople, which he had never seen; others commemorate the Cathedral of Notre Dame in Paris and the Kazan Cathedral in St. Petersburg. Of the cunning distribution of thrusts in the Parisian cathedral he writes that

> The secret plan betrays itself from outward:
> Buttressing arches' might has here contrived
> To stop ponderous mass crushing wall.
> Idle is bold vault's battering ram.[35]

Though the three cathedral poems of *Stone* are fairly straightforward, another architectural lyric is characteristic of Mandelstam's more elusive vein. It portrays the Admiralty building in St. Petersburg as discerned through trees, while once again invoking that symbol of Symbolism dethroned, the clock face.

> Dusty poplar pining in northern metropolis;
> Translucent, foliage-entwined clock dial;
> Frigate or acropolis in dark greenery,
> Gleaming from far, water's and sky's brother.
>
> Aerial barque, fastidious mast,
> Serving Peter's heirs as straightedge.
> Its lesson: Beauty is not superman's caprice,
> But simple carpenter's hawk eye.
>
> Benign to us, Four Elements' sovereignty.
> But free man has created a fifth.
> Does it not deny Space's dominion,
> This chastely rigged ark?
>
> Captious jellyfish cling furiously;
> Abandoned like ploughs, anchors rust.
> But see — the Three Dimensions' bonds are split;
> The world's seas all lie open.[36]

The poem contains a complex system of references, many deriving from specific characteristics of the Admiralty building: its historic past as a creation of Peter the Great; its tall, slender spire; the effigy of a three-masted ship on top of it; its Grecian columns; its fourfold clock face; its function as the centre from which the city's streets, and its sailors' voyages, radiate.

Mandelstam's interest in ancient Greece is occasionally reflected in these early poems. Anything but a profound classical scholar, he was yet hypnotized by the sound and look of Greek words — especially by the elaborately inflected forms spawned within so rich a verbal system. One of them particularly captured his imagination: *pepaideukos* ("having trained, taught," the masculine nominative singular of the perfect active participle of the verb *paideuein*). In a lyric of which only two quatrains survive the poet proclaims himself summoned by the "bell" of ancient Greek verbal inflexions to forget his troubles in a "humble philologist's cell" — where, however, two problems continue to plague him.

> Does the aorist require the augment?
> And what voice is *pepaideukos?*[37]

In another lyric Mandelstam compares a long, lazy summer's day to the Homeric hexameter.

> In the woods are orioles, and vowel duration
> Is tonic verse's sole measure.
> But only once a year is Nature
> Lengthiness-saturated like Homeric hexameter.
>
> That day yawns, one long caesura.
> Peace, arduous elongations from dawn.
> Oxen grazing. Golden leisure. Can't bother
> To coax a whole note's richness from the pipe.[38]

Mandelstam's early work offers certain contrasts with Akhmatova's. It is he who speaks with the more authoritative and mature poetic voice from the start. He also lacks the element of creative self-obsession that contributes so much to her first verses. The early Akhmatova is obsessed with herself and her own moods, as also with her tantalizingly delineated relations with her various rejecting and rejected lovers. But such concerns play only a small role in Mandelstam's work. There are no love poems in *Stone,* and very few poems directly focused on his own emotions in his work as a whole. There is, instead, more awareness of the outside world, and of varied cultural manifestations, both Russian and foreign.

Mandelstam also diverges from Akhmatova — increasingly so with the passage of time — in the relative difficulty of his verses. He is said to have had "a sacred horror of telling the reader what he already knows";[39] and it is tempting to add that he also acquired in course of time a sacred horror of telling the reader what he could not conceivably already know. Fortunately numerous commentaries on his work are available. Even with their aid, however, far from all his poems lend themselves to interpretation in terms of a paraphrasable meaning. There is no reason why they should. The true addict of Mandelstam would not even wish to see his work purged of mysteries so profoundly disturbing and exciting — and by no means all resistant to patient investigation and study. But it is an essential working procedure, for those wrestling with his more opaque verses, to assume that they contain layers of discoverable significance. It is never wise to treat them as mere sequences of evocative sounds, and the same is true of the many difficulties and obscurities in the work of the other three poets.

The relatively transparent Akhmatova and the relatively opaque Mandelstam spoke with a different poetic voice from the beginning, despite their common allegiance to Acmeism; and there are few close affinities between either poet and the third major Acmeist, Gumilyov. Yet all three pioneer Acmeists were to remain faithful to the idea of Acmeism to the ends of their days. It was to keep its sentimental importance as a symbol of their reciprocal loyalty that persisted beyond death, unaffected by the degree to which their poetic paths came to diverge.

Besides having been born and bred in Moscow, Tsvetayeva and Pasternak also have other biographical details in common. Not only was each poet's father a professor of the fine arts, but it also happens that their mothers were talented pianists. Both poets began to train for musical careers in youth, but both eventually turned out to lack the necessary vocation.

"Scales poisoned my best years." Such was the verdict, recorded in an early lyric, that the reluctant pianist Marina Tsvetayeva passed on her childhood.[40] As she has also noted, in memoirs of the 1930s, her mother strictly forbade her to use the "loud" pedal when practising. It was a wise precaution, for so turbulent a child would soon have worn the appliance out. Not music, but philological and poetic broodings filled the small Marina's mind during the hours when she was required to do her five-finger exercises. "Pedal" reminded her of "poodle" (both words being almost identical in Russian and English), and also of "beadle" *(pedel)* and "carrion" *(padal)*. "Poor Mother, how I grieved her. Never could she see that my lack of musicality was just *music of a different sort.*"[41]

Tsvetayeva was the most precocious of the four poets. The extensive output of her tenderest years has disappeared, but she was the first member of the quartet to have a volume of verses published. It was entitled *Evening Album* and appeared in 1910, consisting of lyrics that she had been writing since the age of fifteen. Some were addressed to an otherwise unimportant young man, Vladimir Nilender, whom her father had forbidden her to meet. Professor Tsvetayev was so alarmed at the cultivation of bobbed hair, high heels, and cigarette smoking by his fair-haired, short-sighted daughter that he packed her off with her younger sister to Dresden in the summer of 1910 to learn domestic economy while boarding with a pastor's family, just as her first book of verses was appearing in Moscow. But the father's well-meaning attempt was of no avail. Housekeeping was never to become the poet's forte, and her performance at the kitchen sink remained dogged but uninspired throughout life.

Evening Album was brought out at Tsvetayeva's own expense, in five hundred copies that she deposited with a local bookseller, expecting to hear no more of them. Yet the volume chanced to be picked up and praised by several established poets. Gumilyov was the most enthusiastic; others included Valery Bryusov, that eminent Symbolist of the older generation, with whom Tsvetayeva was to conduct a bitter feud until his death in the early 1920s. She was also taken up by another older poet, one widely appreciated as an amiable eccentric: Maksimilian Voloshin, whose motives in visiting the seventeen-year-old girl at her home were misconstrued owing to his insistence on giving her a copy of Casanova's memoirs. As modesty dictated, she decorously returned so compromising a gift;[42] but the friendship blossomed, and she was soon invited to visit Voloshin's famous dacha near Koktebel (now Planyorskoye), a seaside resort in the eastern Crimea. Here he and his no less eccentric mother, the delightfully named Yelena Ottobaldovna, kept open house for holidaying authors, as is described in many literary memoirs, including Tsvetayeva's own reminiscences of Voloshin, and her account of her first meeting with Mandelstam there in summer 1915.

At Koktebel in 1911, shortly after leaving school, Tsvetayeva met Sergey Efron, a schoolboy slightly younger than herself, whom she married in the following year; their daughter Ariadna (Alya) was born shortly afterwards. Efron was to be the least impermanent of the men in the poet's life. She was to bear him three children, she was to leave Russia for Western Europe in 1922 to join him, and she was to return to Russia in 1939 for the same reason. But though she remained attached to her husband, and faithful to him in her fashion for nearly thirty years, there were to be lengthy separations imposed by war and political upheavals. The marriage neither excluded love affairs between the poet and other men nor inhibited the frenzied "crushes" that she conceived for persons of both genders. By contrast with Akhmatova and Mandelstam — whose emotions were tumultuous, but who both cultivated restraint — Tsvetayeva was an active volcano glorying in eruption. She idolized German culture, proudly claiming for herself the characteristics — no less Slavonic than Teutonic — of *Übermass* ("excess of zeal") and *Schwärmerei* ("gush"). Thus fuelled, she fastened her affections throughout life on a succession of individuals many of whom proved too frail to withstand a love that could seem positively vampirical to those of more placid temperament.

This aspect of Tsvetayeva led Pasternak to comment, after her death, that he could never have married her or lived with her. She combined, said he, "every kind of female hysteria in concentrated form." Such she was viewed in isolation from her gifts; of these too — as Pasternak was not slow to affirm — she possessed a superabundance. "Marina's poetic talent could have been divided into ten parts, and each part would have been enough for one man to earn the complete recognition of his contemporaries." Pasternak is also on record as preferring Marina to all other poets throughout his whole life.[43]

Besides being the most precocious and emotionally incontinent of the four poets, Tsvetayeva was to be by far the most prolific. Her abundant productivity helps to explain how nearly four decades could elapse since the death of so fine a poet without her verse ever having been published in anything approaching a comprehensive edition, though the publication of such an edition (by Russica Publishers, New York) began in 1980. How strong a contrast with the outset of the poet's career, when she was easily able to secure the appearance, in quick succession, of three volumes of verse in her native Moscow. After *Evening Album* had appeared, in 1910, *Magic Lantern* followed in 1912; and then came *From Two Books* (1913), containing a selection from the previous volumes. With the advent of world war and revolution the situation changed so radically that Tsvetayeva's fourth book of poems, *Youthful Verses*, had to wait nearly sixty years before being published: it was not brought out until 1976, in Paris.

To review Tsvetayeva's prewar poetic achievements means considering her published work of 1910–13 together with those poems of *Youthful Verses* that were written before the First World War. As all these publications show, her verse is thoroughly saturated with the material of her own life. It is a record far more detailed than can be traced in Akhmatova's coyly unrevealing lyrics. Tsvetayeva has characterized her method as follows: "My verse is a diary, my poetry is a poetry of proper names."[44] These proper names naturally include the numerous individuals who became the successive objects of her all-engulfing enthusiasms. Members of her own family and other contemporaries are among them. Such targets for romantic adoration are often invoked in the affectionate diminutive form of their first names, and it is not always easy to guess which among various competing "Asyas," "Seryozhas," and "Volodyas" the young poet has in mind at a given moment. Much compulsive hero-worship is also concentrated on historical figures, among them the Russian painter and diarist Marie Bashkirtseff, who died of tuberculosis in 1884. They further include Napoleon Bonaparte, and Napoleon's son the Duke of Reichstadt (Napoleon II), whom Tsvetayeva admired as the hero of the play *L'Aiglon* by a French dramatist whom she also idolized, Edmond Rostand; the role had been played in 1910 with transvestite distinction by yet another object of the poet's enthusiasm, Sarah Bernhardt.

In a lyric addressed to her youthful husband, Tsvetayeva threatens to instruct him in the art of remaining childlike, describing herself as a little girl who will never grow up. The intention is confirmed by many allusions to nursery lore and folk tales, as well as by the use of childish vocabulary, including references to her "Mummy," her "dollies," and so on. But though the young poet sometimes suggests that there are fairies at the bottom of her garden, she is elsewhere tearfully conscious that her childhood is over. She prays for that magic period to be restored to her, lamenting its passing.

> "What lies ahead? What failure?
> All is deceit and all, alas, is forbidden."
> Thus, weeping, I took farewell of lovely childhood,
> Aged fifteen.[45]

Elsewhere she bitterly complains of having been born a girl when her fighting temperament would have better fitted her to be a boy. "Woman's lot does not attract me. / I fear boredom, not wounds." Another lyric ends as follows.

> My hand shall hold no sword,
> Pluck no twangling string.
> I'm just a girl, I'm silent.
> Ah, would that I too might
>
> Glance starward, knowing that
> My star too blazed up there;
> Might smile into all others' eyes,
> Not lowering my own.[46]

On the crucial theme of love Tsvetayeva's early verses contain anticipations of her maturity, particularly in maintaining the equation

Love = Pain. Love is "the sweetest of ailments . . . the sweetest of evils."

> Begging a kiss, I got a pike thrust.

Yet she will sacrifice all her happiness in life to love, praying as follows for an unidentified lover. "I need no happiness; give *him* / My happiness, God."[47]
The notion of a heroic premature death, as in the opening stanza of the lyric "Prayer," is perhaps the most striking of all the schoolgirl's early romantic obsessions.

> Christ! God! I crave a miracle.
> Now! This instant! At day's dawn!
> Ah, grant me death
> While life is all a book to me.

"Thou hast given me a fairy-tale childhood," the poet ends. "So grant me death, at age seventeen." In a later poem she expresses a diametrically opposite attitude toward death, but while keeping a similar romantic posture characteristic of a schoolgirl lyricist.

> My future — a mere handful of dust
> Under my grave's cross. I refuse . . . !
>
> To be dead forever! Was it for this
> Fate gave me understanding of all things?[48]

Tsvetayeva's fourth volume, *Youthful Verses,* presents no abrupt change of theme or method, but a refinement of previous procedures combined with shifts of emphasis. Rostand's heroes and the Emperor Napoleon have been largely forgotten by now, though there is a hero-worshipping lyric devoted to Napoleon's conquerors — Russia's army officers of 1812. In place of the obscurer writers commemorated in earlier collections the poet is now more inclined to dwell on a Byron or a Pushkin. Lyrics naming her relatives and intimates continue — there are more poems to her sister and husband. They are now joined by her infant daughter, Ariadna, whom she already imagines herself losing to a future husband and of whom she claims to be jealous. Alya will have everything that her mother can only dream of. But Marina also warns her daughter that

> My unhappy nature
> Is frighteningly evident in you.
> At two years, less one month,
> You are so sad.

Alya will eventually write better poetry than her mother, but will also have cause to clutch her temples in despair, "just as your young mother does."[49]

Other personal invocations include *The Enchanter,* an eleven-lyric cycle in praise of the minor Symbolist poet Lyov Kobylinsky; he had tutored the Tsvetayeva sisters when Marina was fifteen years old, introducing them to the work of Blok, Bely, and other contemporary poets. A further series is dedicated to her brother-in-law Pyotr Efron, who died in 1914, so that the cycle forms an extended obituary elegy. Tsvetayeva was to practise this form extensively over the years, for it conveniently united two of her chief characteristics: her intense devotion to individuals and her obsession with death.

As in the earliest poems, so too in *Youthful Verses* the theme of death is prominent. It is treated less romantically; the poet is no longer so eager to meet a premature picturesque end *à la* Marie Bashkirtseff. She is resigned, rather, to her own death, declaring this resignation in a manner that emphasizes her intense vitality. It is in such material focused on herself, and not in the invocations of relatives and historical figures, that her most impressive poetry of the period is found. Much of it consists of variations on a recurring chain of sentiments: "I am young, I am special, I am full of vitality, I am going to die." All this was true. Other assertions — "I am lonely, I am unappreciated" — are harder to substantiate from the poet's biography of the period.

In a few of these lyrics Tsvetayeva first seems to show her quality as a potential major poet. The opening words of *Youthful Verses* plunge straight into the theme of her own death. "I dedicate these lines / To those who will arrange my funeral." She adds how hurt she is "To think that I too / Must lie encoffined like everyone else." In another lyric she speaks of her unhappiness, of the wasted vitality, of the heroic ardour that she has lavished "on accidental shadows, on a rustle" — all of which helps to explain

> Why my words are brusque
> In my cigarette's eternal smoke,
> And how much sombre, dire anguish
> My fair-haired head contains.

In another poem Tsvetayeva invokes her own paradoxical nature, which — though liable to melt more easily than snow — is yet "Like screech of sand under tooth, / Of steel on glass." There is a "deadly arrow" in her lightest word, and tenderness in her feigned anger.[50]

The most impressive of these self-obsessed lyrics characteristically begins and ends with her own death.

> Ah, how many have fallen into that abyss
> Gaping afar!
> I too shall vanish in my time
> From earth's surface.
>
> Whatever has sung, struggled,
> Gleamed, strained — all shall grow chill:
> My green eyes, my gentle voice,
> My hair's gold.

After begging strangers and friends to trust and love her because she is "Often too sad, / And only twenty years of age," the poet concludes:

> For this, too, love me —
> That I shall die.[51]

Though Tsvetayeva belonged to no poetical school, there are indications that she might have cultivated affinities with Acmeism had she lived in St. Petersburg, the centre of that movement. She shared the Acmeist passion for precision and hard factual detail, extolling these qualities in the preface to *From Two Books:* she advises other writers "not to disdain the *external.* The colour of your eyes is as important as their expression. . . . Be more precise!"[52] But the young Tsvetayeva needed more than clarity and precision if she was to rival her Acmeist colleagues. True, the best of her prewar verses stand comparison with the best of theirs published during the same period. If her average level of excellence is lower, this is partly due to her more prolific output and to the greater incidence of obvious juvenilia in her earliest published work. And so the self-control and vibrant brevity of the early Akhmatova and Mandelstam make some of Tsvetayeva's early lyrics seem too explicit, too insipid, too unrestrained. Besides, she had barely embarked on the daring metrical and other innovations that were eventually to characterize some of her most impressive work.

Tsvetayeva's earliest verses are both mature and immature. The maturity lies in the growing mastery of her chosen form, with its regular rhymes, its regular iambic metres, its by no means regular stanzaic patterns. The immaturity consists in having chosen verse forms too repetitive and regular for her purpose, in an excess of mellifluousness, and in this paradox: that her technique of deploying material so volcanic is the reverse of volcanic, being too tame and conventional to match her surging emotions. In course of time those emotions were to grow still more tumultuous, if possible, and she was to find very different means of turning them into poetry as she floated out of the smooth, placid stream of her youthful verses and began to shoot the foaming, zig-zagging rapids, jagged rocks, and swirling cataracts that lay ahead.

". . . Screech of sand under tooth, / Of steel on glass" — in these lines we hear more of the future Tsvetayeva than in all her consolidated euphonious regrets for her passing childhood and for the dead heroes and heroines of former ages.

Boris Leonidovich Pasternak was a striking young man with an air of evident vitality. He was often compared to a horse because of his long, narrow face, his jutting jaw, and something in the cast of his eye. The point is made in a description by Tsvetayeva in an article of 1922. She had met him casually three or four times over the years, and defined his appearance as magnificent. "There is something in his face both of the Arab and his steed; alertness, keen hearing, the look of one totally poised to take flight at any moment. Immense, no less equine, savage, and timid slant of eye. No eye, that, but an orb."[53]

Boris Leonidovich was the slowest of the four poets to find his literary vocation, and went further than the others in his youthful attempts to pursue other callings. By contrast with the infant Tsvetayeva, that reluctant pianist, he fell under the spell of music in early childhood; and he went on to spend his teenage years studying composition, encouraged by the eminent composer Aleksandr Skriabin, a friend of the family. When the would-be musician was nineteen Skriabin returned to Russia after a long absence, rigorously tested his protégé, and gave a favourable verdict, thus blessing his future career as a composer. Yet no sooner had the antisuggestible Pasternak received this encouragement than he abandoned all attempts to become a professional musician, switching his allegiance to philosophy. After studying at Moscow University he proceeded to Marburg in Germany in 1912, hoping to become a teacher.

The young Russian met the august Professor Hermann Cohen at the University of Marburg, and showed himself so promising a scholar that he soon received an invitation to one of Cohen's famous dinners; this was, in effect, to be licensed as a future professional philosopher. But it was now that Pasternak withdrew, for the second time, from the brink of a potential career. Just as he had abandoned music a few years earlier, so he now gave up the systematic study of philosophy at the very instant when he had achieved a secure foothold in the profession.

Philosophy was not Pasternak's exclusive concern at Marburg in summer 1912: he also found time to propose marriage to a young Russian, Ida Vysotskaya, who was visiting the town. But she turned him down, and this provoked a characteristic reaction from the future poet. Neither plunging into Wertheresque gloom nor proceeding to quarry the experience for Tsvetayevesque intimations of mortality, he experienced a surge of *joie de vivre*. He felt like one reborn, as he recorded a few years after the event.

> I shook. I caught fire, and my fire died away.
> I quivered. I'd just made a marriage proposal,
> But too late. And here am I — rejected, adrift.
> How I pity her tears! In sublime exaltation
>
> I debouch on the square like a man born anew.[54]

To be a rejected lover was, for Pasternak, not only to be resurrected in a torrent of joy, but also to be diverted towards writing poetry. The experience somehow tapped a spring of literary creativity that he had not previously detected in himself: it was after the double rejection at Marburg — of himself by Miss Vysotskaya, of philosophy by himself — that he first took up his life's work. Returning to Russia, he spent the summer of 1913 at his parents' country cottage at Molodi, about forty miles south of Moscow, and wrote his first collection of verses, *Twin in Clouds*.

The volume was published in the following year, but passed almost unnoticed, arousing none of the interest that the first publications of the other three poets all stimulated in some degree. Pasternak himself was later to regret publishing his first book, and has described its title as "idiotically pretentious."[55] He was eventually to discard nearly half the poems, while radically revising the rest for re-publication in a collection of 1929. Was he too severe towards this virgin publication? A recent critic suggests that he was: "Talent and originality of the first rank are visible in practically every poem."[56] This is true, but it is also true that the young poet sometimes strains after originality so eagerly that he all but hides his talent in a thicket of contrivance.

Pasternak's prewar output was meagre. As first published, *Twin in Clouds* contained only twenty-four lyrics, which were supplemented by half a dozen further isolated items scattered in obscure publications of

1913–14. More detailed consideration of his early development will therefore be postponed, and his first book of poems will be considered later, together with the two more substantial collections that were to follow.

Pasternak was exceptional among the four poets, not only because his early product was skimpier than theirs, but also because it was harder to assimilate. Of this his temporary affiliation to Futurism was in part symbol and in part cause. The young Pasternak cultivated angularity, cross-grainedness, obscurity, and disharmony, while the other three poets were — each in his or her own way — exponents of gracefulness, harmony, and clarity. This points ahead to a further contrast, for the late Pasternak was to express himself with striking simplicity, while his three colleagues were all to move in the opposite direction. Pasternak was eventually to emerge as a master of clarity, whereas Mandelstam developed into a poet of supposedly daunting obscurity; Tsvetayeva's work too was to become increasingly difficult to penetrate, as also — in its very different way — was Akhmatova's.

Turning back to the brink of the First World War, when these developments could not be foreseen, one is struck by the level of maturity already attained by the two St. Petersburgers Akhmatova and Mandelstam. These poets of the capital city were more polished and controlled at this stage than their counterparts from the old capital, Moscow. Emotionally undisciplined, less poised, and technically less mature, the early Tsvetayeva and Pasternak might be thought — by St. Petersburgers, at least — to typify the sprawling, slovenly, archetypally "Russian" features of their native habitat, as so often contrasted with the cosmopolitan, sophisticated metropolis on the Neva. The prewar verse of Tsvetayeva and Pasternak is not to be despised, but it was more promise than achievement, whereas Akhmatova and Mandelstam had already made impressive progress towards finding their true poetic voices.

It is also worth noting that the young women were more firmly established in their lives and careers than the young men. By 1914 each had a husband and child to look after or neglect, and each had fairly extensive publications to her credit: Akhmatova and Tsvetayeva had already brought out two and three sizeable volumes of verse, respectively, at a time when Mandelstam and Pasternak had managed only one slim volume apiece.

Another difference between the men and women poets lay in their outlook on life. Whereas the two young matrons were much concerned with death (although alluding to it very differently — Akhmatova with resignation, Tsvetayeva with positive gusto), no such obsession is to be detected in the early Mandelstam and Pasternak. They were more inclined to celebrate the joys of living than to anticipate mortality.

It may also be said of all four poets, at the outbreak of war in 1914, that their finest works, and their greatest sufferings, still lay ahead.

3

CLOUDBURST OF LIGHT

To consider the impact of the First World War on Russia is to marvel that an ordeal so shattering had such a slight influence on the lives and work of four of the country's leading poets.

While Russian soldiers fought and perished at the fronts, Tsvetayeva and Akhmatova lived on, both remarkably undisturbed. The former reared her daughter, the latter neglected her son; each took her summer holiday on the Black Sea coast; each endured a number of love affairs.

Neither of the men was conscripted into the forces, though both were of military age. Mandelstam remained exempt for some reason unknown, undertaking civilian war work as an employee of the Union of Cities, a welfare organization, while Pasternak escaped military service in both world wars owing to a childhood injury that had left him slightly lame: "I broke my leg and avoided two future wars in the course of one evening."[1] During the first conflict Pasternak was employed for brief spells in the Urals, processing the exemptions of others from the call-up. But it was only a temporary post. Meanwhile all four poets retained their metropolitan bases, travelled about Russia, conducted their love affairs — and above all experimented with and improved their verses. None of them became a war poet, since the crisis never eclipsed the personal and private vision of nonmilitary life that their writings of the period predominantly reflect.

Pasternak barely referred to the clash of arms in his verse of the period, though he was to turn to it later as a theme in his novel *Doctor Zhivago*. In 1917 he published his second book of verse, *Over Barriers*. It marks a significant advance on *Twin in Clouds*, and it was better received. But it was to meet a fate similar to that of the earlier book some years later, when the poet once more rejected a high proportion of the lyrics as unfit for re-publication, while subjecting the others to extensive revision.

Over Barriers was in turn put in the shade by Pasternak's third collection, *My Sister Life,* which consists of poems written wholly or chiefly in 1917. This represented so notable an improvement, in his view, that he left the material virtually intact when he later came to edit his work as a whole for comprehensive publication. His high view of *My Sister Life* is shared by many of his admirers, and some rate it the finest of his collections. It established Pasternak's reputation as one of his era's finest poets; but it did so only after a five-year delay, since the volume could not be published until 1922 owing to wartime restrictions. Tsvetayeva was among those who hastened to welcome its appearance, launching the superb, frenzied eulogy of Pasternak contained in her essay *Cloudburst of Light.*

Pasternak entered literature as a loose adherent of Russian Futurism — a movement that embraced a wide variety of poets without combining them on a common platform. So far was it from evolving any cohesive policy that its historian Vladimir Markov can proclaim it as, practically speaking, a synonym for avant-gardism or modernism in general. According to him, Futurism "simply united virtually all those who considered themselves modern at that time." It was "a postsymbolist movement in Russian poetry of 1910–30 which, roughly, put under the same roof all avant-garde forces."[2]

The competing factions within the movement included Cubo-Futurism, as represented by Khlebnikov and Mayakovsky — the two outstanding poets among those who retained long-term Futurist links. There was Ego-Futurism, with Igor Severyanin as its chief champion. And there were also minor Futurist offshoots. They included Centrifuge, which lasted from 1913 until 1917, and to which Pasternak himself belonged; its other most notable adherents were Nikolay Aseyev and Sergey Bobrov.

As conscientious representatives of the literary avant-garde, the Russian Futurists were given to exhibitionist behaviour, cultural iconoclasm, and daring verbal experiment. They strove for novelty, originality, and stridency. They did not speak, they shouted. They posed, they postured, they simpered, they wore weird clothes. They dismissed the consolidated culture of previous ages as worthless and ripe for the junk heap; called for the dynamiting of museums, art galleries, and libraries; mocked Raphael and Velasquez as philistines and "photographers"; demanded that Tolstoy and Dostoyevsky be thrown overboard from the Ship of Modernity; proclaimed Mirra Lokhvitskaya (1869–1905) the superior of Dante, Byron, and Pushkin.

In their writings they paraded deliberate syntactical and orthographical solecisms, and they introduced gross typographical errors into their printed work. They also experimented with the language of what they called Trans-Sense *(zaum)*. Feeling free to create a new vocabulary, and even a new grammar, they believed in the significance of the Word as an autonomously potent force that could override meaning, and evolved ingenious variations on the Russian equivalent of Lewis Carroll's jabberwocky.

Such was Russian Futurism as its opponents might choose to describe it, and one must beware of seeming to disparage a movement that could spawn such creative artists as a Khlebnikov and a Mayakovsky. In any case, the Centrifuge Futurists, including Pasternak, adopted a less provocative stance. They were less brash, less ostentatiously megalomaniac; they showed less hostility to other poetic schools such as Symbolism; and they refrained from urging the wholesale rejection of past culture. Pasternak added to these reservations a distaste for the public strutting and flamboyancy — the carrot buttonholes, the cheeks painted with flowers, the outrageous garb — cultivated by the more strictly orthodox among his fellow Futurists. He was not much given, as many of them were, to that most bourgeois of activities: shocking the bourgeoisie.

Pasternak's main Futurist feature was his determined pursuit of poetical novelty. Of *Twin in Clouds* he remarked: "My constant concern was for each lyric to contain . . . a new thought or a new image."[3] Stunning originality, especially in imagery, was his most Futurist feature, and it was long to outlive his connections with the movement.

Critics have disagreed on the extent to which the young Pasternak strayed beyond the boundaries of meaning into the world of Trans-Sense: Gifford says that he "scarcely ever" did so; Weidlé indicates that he did so occasionally in early poems which he later rejected; Markov implies that he did so quite often and had every right to be proud of the fact.[4] In any case, Pasternak never penetrated as far into Trans-Sense as Khlebnikov, Burlyuk, or Kruchonykh. Nearly all the words in his admittedly recondite vocabulary will be found in one dictionary or another. He did not seek to break, even as he stretched them, the bonds of conventional syntax; he left punctuation and morphology unravished. But there are many occasions when, within these limits, the early Pasternak comes close to offering a medley of meaningless sounds, a verbal "music."

Though the young Pasternak avoided Futurism's wilder extravagances, he so greatly admired the most spectacular of Futurists, Mayakovsky, that he felt compelled to defend his independence by deliberately adopting an approach as distant as possible from the other poet's. According to Pasternak, he and Mayakovsky had too much in common; there were unforeseen technical coincidences, there was a similar structure of images, a similarity in rhyming habits. To avoid mimicking Mayakovsky, "I [Pasternak] began suppressing those elements that corresponded to his — the heroic tone, which in my case would have been false, and the cult of flamboyancy. This narrowed and refined my style."[5]

In accordance with this policy, the militant eccentricities of Futurism gradually disappeared from Pasternak's work over the years. They are more prominent in his first collection than in the second (even though that was actually published under the auspices of Centrifuge), and there are still fewer of them in the third. When *My Sister Life* was written, in 1917, Centrifuge was about to fall apart, and Pasternak had abandoned his affiliations with the Futurists. But he continued to admire Mayakovsky's poetry, though with reservations that increased as the years rolled by. It is tempting to say that Pasternak was never more than an eccentric Futurist. But eccentricity was the very essence of the movement, and his idiosyncrasy within it consisted in avoiding rather than in cultivating rampant unconventionality.

Nature is a basic theme in Pasternak's first three collections — as in all his work — and especially nature perceived in an urban setting. The four seasons; night and day; the transitions between them; thunder, storm, snow, frost, sunshine, flowers, trees: they crowd his verses, threatening to thrust all else aside. His landscapes and townscapes are remarkably devoid of animate beings, despite the occasional bird or person flitting past, usually as part of an ingenious image that conveys the impact of inanimate matter on the poet's psyche.

Far from portraying nature as passive, far from recollecting it in tranquillity, Pasternak endows even the most static natural phenomena with a capacity for frantic hurtling and oscillating. To see the mirrored reflection of one of his many gardens is, for him, to see mirror and vegetation careering madly into each other by turns. In "Looking Glass" the curtain at his back sways, and his mirror "dashes straight into the garden, into fallen timber and chaos."

> Towards background, into gloom, through gate,
> Into steppe, into sleeping herbs' scent
> Streams down path hot quartz,
> Glinting on twigs and snails.

Soon the process is reversed: Pasternak's garden abruptly invades his drawing room, threatens the mirror with its fist, rushes back at the garden swing, tries to catch it, shakes the mirror; "yet doesn't break the glass!"[6]

The poem typifies its author's love of evoking "disorganized mo-

tion within an enclosure which can be so fittingly described by the
nearly untranslatable Russian words *mechetsya* and *tychetsya*" ("thrashes
around," "fidgets," "knocks about").[7] An example of personification on
a grander, less fidgety scale is the invocation with which "First View
of the Urals" begins.

> Without midwife, in gloom, unconscious,
> Groping at night, Urals'
> Stronghold bellowed; slumped in dead faint,
> Agony-blinded; spawned dawn.[8]

For a poet to personify nature is not new; it goes back to Homer's
rosy-fingered or crocus-fingered Dawn arising from the bed of noble
Tithonus. But Homer never aimed at Pasternak's scale of personalizing
the nonpersonal in an atmosphere of violent movement, while he "dislo-
cates reality" (his own phrase) by presenting images calculated to shock
through their unexpectedness. He is so interpenetrated with his own
verse that it is hard to determine whether this is a poet who has written
some poems or some poems that have written a poet. Other bards —
to paraphrase a comment of Tsvetayeva's — write *about* nature, Paster-
nak wrote *it*.[9] In "Stuffy Night," one of his many dripping poems, he
entwines himself in nature's doings with an extra degree of intimacy.

> By fence
> Wet boughs and pale wind,
> Arguing — I froze — about *me!*
>
> It would go on forever, I sensed —
> This ghastly garden chit-chat. . . .
>
> If I'm seen I'll not escape
> Ever, ever — from their spell.[10]

Pasternak likes his scenes moist, damp, soaked, drenched, soggy,
drizzly, glistening, snowy, clammy, and misty. *Twin in Clouds* strikes
this humid note from the first line of the first lyric.

> February. Get ink! Weep!
> Must write of February with sobs,
> While clattering slush
> Burns with black spring.

As for the famous picture, later in the same poem, of thousands of rooks
"like charred pears" poised to "swoop on puddles," that was not given
its final form until the revised text was published in 1929.[11]

Pasternak is almost as obsessed with horticultural settings as with humidity, and he likes to bring the two together. His "Weeping Garden" is "Horrible! It drips, listens: / Is it alone on earth . . . ? / Spongy soil, palpably crushed / By oozings' bulk. . . . / Eerie gulps, / Slipper-shufflings, sighs, sobs."[12] In another, still more stillicide-saturated lyric he speaks of

> Drops collarstud-heavy;
> Garden blinding like river's reach,
> Bespattered, bespluttered
> By a myriad blue tears.[13]

Even these comparatively static references are enough to suggest that Pasternak was no passive, Wordsworthian recorder of the natural scene. His nature is dynamic, flowing "with a violent almost self-conscious energy . . . in rich, enormous overwhelming waves. . . . It forms knots and gathers into violently condensed globules of extreme intensity."[14] Such a globule concludes the lyric about the "July Storm" that

> Reverberates in gloom and silver,
> Swoops down gallery;
>
> Down stairs to porch.
> One, two, three steps. Blindfold me!
> All five mirrors show storm's face
> With mask ripped off.[15]

Not content with his blinding fivefold reflection of lightning, the poet steps up the intensity precisely twenty times in his significantly entitled "Permanently Momentary Storm."

> Doffing its hat,
> Thunder took five score
> Blinding souvenir-snapshots that night.[16]

Such passages inspired Tsvetayeva to single out energy and light as two of Pasternak's most essential features. For her his work contained, above all, "the joy of an explosion, an avalanche, a blow, the purest discharge of all vital veins and forces, a sort of white heat that — at a distance — you might just take for a white page."[17]

Another salient feature of Pasternak's poetry has been indicated by Akhmatova. "His verse was written before the Sixth Day, when God created Man. It lacks human beings, you'll have noticed. He has every-

thing else — storms, forests, chaos — but no people." She admits,
though, that Boris Leonidovich does occasionally appear in person; and
that, when he does, "He portrays himself successfully."[18] Nor are other
individuals absolutely excluded from his verse. For example, the lyric
"Winter Night," together with its variants (it was written in 1913 and
radically rewritten in 1928), introduces no fewer than three sentient
beings. The poet himself appears in the role of resident tutor. "This is
a mansion and I'm here as tutor. / I am alone, having sent my pupil to
bed." The reference is autobiographical, for the young Pasternak often
did obtain temporary employment in this capacity. Autobiographical
too is the poem's dedication, later removed, to "I. V." — in other words,
to Ida Vysotskaya, the young woman who had rejected his marriage
proposal in Marburg. However, in the text originally published in 1914,
the seductive Ida's presence is confined to her initials as invoked in the
epigraph. Only in the revised version does she flit into the body of the
poem, in a line implying that she has struck the author's psyche a "blow"
which has profoundly affected him in a manner unspecified — an Akh-
matovian touch. But the lyric typifies Pasternak in placing so little
emotional weight on this lightly sketched personal crisis, and so much
on an idiosyncratic weather report. Compared with the poem's three
shadowy humans, its meteorological and seasonal manifestations are
vividness itself, especially as polished up in the later version — his street
lamps like buns; his doughnut-roofs, their contours rounded by piled
snow; the unsociable smoke that broods over the proceedings from a
chimney "like feather-drowned owl."[19]

The celebrated lyric "Marburg" was originally written in 1915, but
rewritten at least four times. Here the poet does indeed "portray himself
successfully," for the breathless excitement of being a young Pasternak
is vividly conveyed in all the versions. But what of the young woman
who had inspired the poem, and whom its author had even valued
enough to seek the union of her life with his? She is invoked only
fleetingly — just long enough to be reported as rejecting the poet's
advances. She is then dismissed from the scene, though her ghost briefly
surfaces later when he is found to have learnt her "by heart" like an actor
memorizing a Shakespearian role. But even in these luminous lines we
only hear of her briefly. We do not see her; we see only the poet's
ecstatic reaction to her absence.

> You, all your lines from crest to toe,
> Like touring actor conning Shakespeare,
> That day I bore with me, knew by heart,
> Lurching round town and rehearsing you.[20]

Admitting himself so rarely to his verse, while admitting other human beings more rarely still, Pasternak is the opposite of the creatively self-obsessed Tsvetayeva. He seldom strays further into the poetry of romantic love than in the lyric (from *My Sister Life*) which begins with what is, for the early Pasternak, a sentimental couplet.

> The attempt to separate my spirit
> From thee is plaint of fiddler's bow.

But the quatrain ends with shuddering discord, invoking the absurd appellations of two villages in the Saratov area which the poet had recently visited with his beloved, and where his lament

> Still throbs, anguished,
> In the names Rzhaksa and Muchkap.[21]

Turning to his own vocation, Pasternak defines the nature of poetry in a sequence of startling images: as "butterflies' duel," as "brimful whistle," as "crushed ice hunks' crunch." Poetry is

> All that Night's so bent on winkling out
> From pool's deepest crannies,
> To bring to net as star
> On quivering wet palms.[22]

In one especially striking lyric from *My Sister Life* he combines the themes of love and poetry, for once staking immodest claims more in Mayakovsky's style than his own. His poet is an "unquiet God" whose love plunges the world into chaos "as in the time of fossils," and who despises the rest of mankind: "common frog-spawn dressed up as prime caviar." How different is *he*, the arrogant Poet-Superman!

> One of your women, like amphora Maenad,
> He'll hoist aloft; utilize;
>
> Pour into kiss melted Andes
> And veldt dawn under sway
> Of stars pulverized while night,
> Whitely bleating, blunders round village.[23]

It is instructive to read the young Pasternak while also bearing in mind the differing versions in which some of the more heavily revised poems appeared over the years. One wonders whether any other poet ever generated such a swarm of tropes, images, metaphors, similes, comparisons, conceits. Here is water whining in pincers, like a dirty fingernail. Here are August leaves, asthmatic in every atom. Among the black seams of sledge runners the road surface's frozen abscess has been picked open. February burns like cotton gulping in spirit. Youth floats on happiness like a pillowcase on a child's quiet snore. A storm-cloud dries out while babbling like a laundered apron on a clothesline. Deep roses, covered with blazing wet diamonds, resemble a throatful of tears. Christmas peeps out like a baby jackdaw. Evaporating moisture streams up from balcony panes as from hips and backs of chilly female bathers.[24]

Such daring images can be used to support two diametrically opposed contentions. There is impressively original poetry, more remarkable perhaps than any of the work so far discussed by any of the other three poets. There is, on the other hand, so ingenious and determined a flight from poetical cliché that the less robust reader may occasionally weary of being too relentlessly exposed to the shock of surprise; for where everything is so astonishing, surely nothing is. Pasternak's comparisons are riveting, certainly, but one still wonders whether there are not perhaps too many of them, and whether the word *kak* ("as" or "like") is not overworked to the point — the pun must be excused in this near-Futuristic context — of downright kakophony. A familiar concept is evoked — night, day, snow, winter, summer — and is immediately said to be "like" something far from familiar, so that the comparison by no means sheds light on darkness, but may seem to create obscurity where none need have existed. When Pasterernak says of a harsh winter that it "lays tribute on us," his meaning is clear. But when he adds "like a *baskak,*" his readers need to reach for a dictionary. Not that *baskak* appears in the shorter Russian dictionaries; but the seventeen-volume lexicon of the Soviet Academy of Sciences reveals that it denotes a medieval Tatar tax-collector. The image is original indeed, but it is hardly one of those startlingly *fresh* comparisons — in which the poet's work abounds — that immediately bring a scene to life. Presumably Pasternak wrote 'like a *baskak*' (*kak baskak*) largely for the jingle's sake, and the effect is certainly memorable.[25]

Pasternak can barely speak of anything without immediately remarking, as though by some nervous tic, that it is "like" something else. But in a world where almost everything may resemble almost everything, nothing really resembles anything; and there is even a danger that the sensitive reader's cerebral muscles may go into spasm as he braces himself for the next *kak*. Still, the risk is well worth taking.

One could go on and on quoting Pasternak's images. Some are effective, some are clumsy, and many are strikingly effective through their very clumsiness; some are articulate, others inarticulate; some are quiet and unobtrusive, others strident and exasperating. They swamp his early verse, whether in his anapaests rummaging around like mice in a biscuit tin, or the City of Venice floating on its lagoons like a sodden stone ring-roll; for bakery comparisons are by no means uncommon. There is a vigorous picture of a dawn, dark as autumn and swept by a wind that bears, "Like rain of straw wisps swooping after wagon / String of birch trees swooping down the sky."[26] Another of his wet scenes is that

> Where pond is open secret,
> Where apple trees' tide whispers,
> Where garden hangs like boathouse
> Holding sky out before itself.[27]

To acclaim the poet's exuberance, his effervescent attitude to "life" (one of his favourite words) is also to be struck by an occasional disloyal query: is there not something too undisciplined, hearty, jolly, jaunty — even puppy-like — about all this surging euphoria? With the young Pasternak everything splurges out in all directions in an orgy of affirmation undisciplined and anarchic. This is the glory of his work. But there are times when the glut may seem overwhelming, when one yearns for a poet less radiantly affirmative. True poetry does not always ride on feeling unalloyed; it can also vibrate on the tension between the surrender to emotion and its firm control.

Spring, in Pasternak, is — like everything else — bursting out all over.

> What buds! What viscous slobbered candlestubs
> Stuck to boughs![28]

Superb, at least in the original! But when the fervour spills over into the title of his third volume, *My Sister Life,* he flies a standard of questionable taste at his masthead: the phrase almost has the heavy touch of a Gorky, if not quite of the Russian cliché whereby it is a precondition of any approved person that he should be constantly "saying *yes* to life." Still, the key poem of the volume, which begins with the words of its title, does much to counteract this reservation. It staggers into the arena on a characteristically sodden couplet.

My sister life — in flood today too,
Crashing into everyone as spring rain.

But the poet soon reverts to a drier atmosphere, evoking one of his
favourite settings — a train journey — and the joys of careering
through a countryside which turns the most prosaic of subjects into
magic.

In Maytime when reading your railway timetable
While riding the local Kamyshin line,
You'll find it sublimer than Holy Scripture
Even when conned for the second time.

The lyric ends with characteristic vigour as the steppe swoops off star-
wards from the train while the poet's heart bestrews the landscape with
the compartment doors.[29]

In another lyric Pasternak speaks of the frozen north as a "simula-
crum of lips weighed down by verse." This his own lips often were
— which had its advantages, for his was to be a poetic achievement won
by struggle against the medium. Tsvetayeva once told him that he had
"the inarticulacy of *Greatness.*"[30] And his early writings indeed do
contain passages in which he sounds like someone fighting to express
himself through a mouthful of porridge. "About These Verses" ends
with a sixfold comparison, at one *kak* per line, which would spoil, if
anything could, an otherwise splendid and justifiably renowned lyric.
In the magnificent opening stanzas the poet has been describing a period
of hermit-like isolation in which he has ignored the world around him,
even forgetting "what millennium it is" outside the isolated cottage
where he has been smoking with Byron and carousing with Edgar Allan
Poe. But how he stumbles in his final quatrain, where *as* corresponds
to *kak* in the original.

Free to enter Daryal *as* a friend's home,
As hell, armoury, and arsenal,
I have been dipping life in vermouth,
As my lips, *as* Lermontov's trembling.[31]

That Lermontov was (with Pushkin) *the* Russian poet of the Caucasus,
that the Daryal Gorge is one of the scenic marvels of that spectacular
mountain range — here are pointers, but no more, to whatever Paster-
nak may be struggling to convey. Such passages lead one to question

whether he indeed does reveal in every instance "the power of *inevitably right* comparison" attributed to him by one interpreter.[32]

And yet Pasternak's tied tongue remains a major asset. He resembles a witty stutterer whose choicest felicities are rendered all the more shattering by having to break through a barrier of suspense-creating aphasia. The itch of suspense is not reduced by the reader's constant awareness that any one of the anticipated shafts of genius may prove sublimely bathetic when it eventually pops out.

Confused and exasperated though many readers of the young Pasternak may feel on occasion, the impact of the verses remains exhilarating, electrifying, and creatively tantalizing.

By contrast with Pasternak's verses, which so blithely ignore wartime sufferings, Akhmatova's work of the period reveals profound concern for her fellow citizens' troubles — even though she too was largely spared exposure to dangers and hardships. Her lyrics on the war form only a small section within her writings of the period, but include poignant material. They also typify her tendency to place increasing emphasis on the world about her while drifting away from the self-obsessed mood of her earlier writings.

Akhmatova's poems on the war display her Orthodox Christian faith and intense patriotism together with a profound sympathy for the Russian people's tribulations, past, present, and future. In a lyric composed on the day preceding Germany's declaration of war on Russia in 1914, she describes that summer as a sinister season of intense heat and drought, adding a prophecy of evil and good made by a crippled stranger.

> Bonfire smell. For four weeks
> Dry peat has burned in bogs.
> The very birds sang not today,
> Aspen's quiver is stilled.
>
> The sun has turned God's scourge.
> No shower has sprinkled fields since Easter.
> Came a one-legged wayfarer;
> Spoke alone in yard.
>
> "Dire times are nigh. Soon
> New graves will hem us.
> Expect famine, earthquake, plague,
> Sky's luminaries eclipsed.

"Yet foes shall not divide
Our land for their sport.
On these great griefs Our Lady
Shall spread a white quilt."[33]

In a second poem alluding to the outbreak of war, Akhmatova foresees soldiers' wives groaning over their fatherless children, widows' sobs sounding through the villages, and trampled fields warmly sprinkled with red wetness.[34]

In 1915 the poet looks back on the horrors of the war's early months, comparing Russia's present sufferings with past experiences that can now be seen as blessings.

We thought ourselves bereft, destitute.
But after loss upon loss
Had rendered each day
A Day of Remembrance,
We took to hymning
God's great bounty,
And our own former riches.[35]

In "May Snow" Russia's war losses are symbolically evoked through allusion to spring frost.

Transparent shroud settles
On fresh turf, melts unnoticed;
Cruel, chill spring
Slays swollen buds.[36]

Akhmatova also commemorates the sufferings of wartime Petrograd, a "city of sumptuous parades" that has now become "a camp of savages."

What has happened to our capital?
Who grounded the sun?
Our standard's black eagle
Seemed like a bird in flight.[37]

The poet is eager to sacrifice herself, if only she can alleviate her country's sufferings. "Covering my face, I begged God / To slay me before the first battle."[38] The same theme infuses the moving eight-line "Prayer" in which she again offers herself as a sacrificial victim.

Give me grim years of sickness;
Give me choking, insomnia, fever.

Take my child, my lover,
My mysterious gift of song.
Thus I pray at Thy service
After many weary days:
May the cloud over dark Russia
Become radiant with glory.[39]

In her war poems Akhmatova retains the well-tried method of plain statement combined with cryptic allusion that she had successfully practised from her earliest years, and is content to refine her established style without straining after new techniques. The same is true of the many lyrics of the same period that concentrate on her own and her lovers' tribulations rather than her country's.

Love, usually frustrated or tragic, is still the main theme. Avoiding the riddles, shocks, paradoxes, alarms, and excursions characteristic of Pasternak, Akhmatova yet remains a woman of mystery, continuing to conceal the identity of the various men whom she invokes while merely hinting at the emotional crises that they have provoked, and still writing as if her reader must already have been initiated into all the details of her private life. She still alludes to her lovers as "thou" or "he" as of old; and it is sometimes possible to identify these figures as one or other of the three individuals who probably played the most important part in her life during the war.

The first was her husband, Nikolay Gumilyov, whom — against a background of increasing estrangement — she visited in a Moscow hospital, where he was undergoing treatment in 1915, and whom she also met two years later when they both went to see their infant son at his grandmother's in the village of Slepnyovo in Tver Province. Akhmatova herself spent most of the wartime summers in this rural retreat; it was here too that she composed most of her third collection of lyrics, *White Flock* (published in 1917).

It must have been Gumilyov whom Akhmatova had in mind when she fired off (in summer 1916) one of the earliest among many stinging poetic rebukes that she was to direct, over the years, at various unspecified husbands and lovers who had fallen short of the high standards expected of her consorts. The poem begins in turbulent style.

Ah! You again! Not as some lovesick youth,
But as a husband — bold, unbending, stern —
You come into this house and gaze on me.
My spirit quails before the coming storm.
You ask what I have done to you, by love
And fate to me eternally entrusted.

You call me traitor. And to harp on that!
Oh, will you never weary of such talk?
Thus speaks the ghost that haunts his slayer's dreams.

For once, though, the poet relents and asks her husband (if he it is) to forgive her. She looks back to happier times. "Sweet was the earth while we two were together."[40]

Akhmatova had some reason to ask Gumilyov's forgiveness — he had no doubt given her cause to forgive him in turn — for she had acquired at least two lovers. One, Nikolay Nedobrovo, was a literary critic who had published an article on her that she was to cherish throughout life for its profound insight into her nature. Stressing her preference for tragic love as a theme, he had insisted that this bias reflected no frailty or sentimentality in the poet: her sufferings were those of a strong woman longing to experience emotional extremes at whatever cost. Nedobrovo called her lyrical essence "hard rather than oversoft, cruel rather than tearful, and certainly masterful rather than downtrodden."[41] To the author of this assessment Akhmatova addressed a lyric beginning with unconscious humour in the first word of its second line.

Twelve months we've been together, you and I;
But you're happy and youthful as ever.[42]

The poet evidently found it amazing that a young man could endure an entire year of her company without acquiring any emotional scars.

Not long after having apostrophized Nedobrovo in this fashion Akhmatova had met another lover, the artist Boris Anrep — to whom Nedobrovo had first introduced her. Soon she was addressing a second lyric to Nedobrovo. She implies that their love has always been, or has now become, "platonic," while also claiming an extra degree of intimacy, lying beyond the realm of infatuation or physical desire, for their relations. This special relationship explains "Why my heart / Throbs not at your hand's touch."[43] As for Nedobrovo's heart, that was soon, alas, to cease throbbing altogether; a few years later he died, like so many writers and others of his and earlier generations, of tuberculosis.

A high proportion of Akhmatova's wartime love lyrics are addressed or cryptically allude to Nedobrovo's successor, Boris Anrep: over thirty of them, according to one editor.[44] One verse offers an acrostic of his name in the initial letters of its ten lines. The material also includes some of those enchantingly simple verses to which the Russian language lends itself as aptly as Greek or English.

Ample and yellow is evening's light,
Cool April's caress.
You came many years too late,
Yet I welcome you.

Sit here, near me.
Gaze, happy-eyed.
Here's a blue notebook
With my childhood verses.

Forgive my living so sadly,
And enjoying sunshine so little.
Forgive, forgive my mistaking
Too many others for you.[45]

Two years later, in another fine lyric alluding to Anrep, the note
of farewell is sounded.

We don't know how to part;
Still stroll, shoulders brushing.
Gloaming falls
On you, pensive; on me, silent.

Entering church we glimpse
Burial service, christening, wedding;
We leave, no glance exchanged.
Why is nothing right, for us?

Or we sit on scuffed snow
In graveyard; sigh faintly;
And you sketch, with your stick, pavilions
Where we'll be at one forever.[46]

Akhmatova's love poems cannot always be related to a specific
lover; nor may it be assumed that her thoughts on this topic were
confined to Gumilyov, Nedobrovo, and Anrep. There are many memo-
ries of mysterious past loves, and many anticipatory poems in which she
eagerly awaits an unidentified lover. There is also one set in the present
tense and depicting the poet's beloved as having arrived in person. He
is present here and now, not recalled or hoped for.

On snowdrift's firm crest
To your white, mysterious house,
Both so subdued,
We walk in loving silence.

And sweeter than all songs sung
Is this my dream fulfilled —
Swaying boughs that we brush,
Your spurs' faint jingle.[47]

A dream come true! The reader must make the most of such brief
moments of satisfaction purveyed by the poet of dreams largely un-
fulfilled.

In another lyric of the period Akhmatova expresses an especially
characteristic sentiment: she is content to be discontented. Free to live
a simple life in the country surrounded by picturesque rustics and bees,
she prefers the strains and stresses of St. Petersburg.

Nothing's so precious as this gorgeous
Granite town of triumph and disaster:
Ice floes gleaming on broad streams;
Sunless, gloomy parks;
Muse's voice scarce heard.[48]

Akhmatova's Muse provides consolations that enable her to tolerate the
many disappointments of her life. As she explains in another of her
spring 1915 poems, alluding to yet another unspecified emotional crisis,

I have stopped smiling,
Lips frozen by iced wind.
One hope the poorer, I'll be
One song the richer.

She prizes the poetic vocation itself, not the reward of fame and recogni-
tion. Fame is, to her, "Just a trap, / Where is no joy, no light." Else-
where she remarks: "Earthly fame: puff of smoke. / I never asked for it."
And she adds what it is tempting to regard as a dubious — or ironical
— boast.

To all my lovers
I have brought happiness.[49]

Perhaps she had indeed done so, since cheerfulness was not entirely
outside her range, and she was capable of anticipating the end of winter
with a surge of high morale.

There are such days before spring:
Meadow resting under packed snow;

Dry trees' cheerful rustle;
Warm breeze, gentle and supple;
Your body marvelling, so light it feels;
Your home, so changed you know it not.
And the song you once wearied of
Thrills you afresh as you sing.[50]

As the most obsessed with private emotions of the four poets, Tsvetayeva found few occasions to allude to the war with Germany in her verses of the period, and her rare references to the conflict are typically independent of the pressures of her era. While her contemporaries portrayed the Russian people's sufferings, or hurled defiance at the Kaiser, she was stressing the need for peace on earth.

I know a truth — away with former truths!
Men should not fight each other on this earth.
See, it is evening. See, it will soon be night. . . .

And soon we all shall sleep beneath the soil,
Who would not let each other sleep above it.[51]

Far from filling Tsvetayeva with hatred of Germany, the war only fuelled her enthusiasm for the country and its culture. She is particularly outspoken in the lyric "To Germany," dated 1 December 1914. How, she asks, can she ever abandon or betray a country hounded by innumerable enemies all over the world?

Germany, my infatuation!
Germany, my love. . . !

What land more magical, more wise.
Than thou, O fragrant clime,
Where Lorelei combs golden locks
Above eternal Rhine?[52]

Despite such exceptional glosses on the international situation in Tsvetayeva's wartime verses, her main preoccupation remained herself and the many human objects of her loving admiration. These hero-worshipped individuals, who included both Akhmatova and Mandelstam, increasingly inspired whole cycles of devotional lyrics. Transmuting such enthusiasms into verse during the First World War, while cultivating ever more syncopated rhythms, Tsvetayeva was swiftly advancing towards maturity. Much of her finest work of the period appears in a single volume of lyrics, *Mileposts;* it consists of a poetic diary for the year 1916, and was eventually to be published in 1922. But *Mileposts* by no means exhausts her wartime achievements.

Tsvetayeva's 1914–17 verses include cycles on Akhmatova and Mandelstam. Her personal relations with the two differed widely in their degree of intimacy. It is likely that Mandelstam was briefly in love with her, though she was to deny that; it is also likely, if not fully confirmed, that the two became lovers. As for Akhmatova, Tsvetayeva had never set eyes on her, and they were not to meet until 1940.

It was not necessary for Tsvetayeva to have met someone for her to contract a sense of intense emotional involvement, and her "crush" on Akhmatova dates from 1914, the year in which she first began to read the older poet's lyrics. She at once conceived her usual full-blooded enthusiasm. People might complain that Akhmatova's verse was "all about love," Tsvetayeva commented; she added that it was also "astonishingly about the stag's silver voice; about the misty reaches of Ryazan Province; about the florid cupolas of Khersones Cathedral; about the red maple leaf used as a marker in the Song of Songs; about the 'God-given' air. What a difficult and seductive boon to *poets* Anna Akhmatova is!"[53] These are all references to details of Akhmatova's verse.

In 1915 Tsvetayeva addressed to Akhmatova a lyric recalling the other poet's "slim, un-Russian figure, bowed over folios," and her famous shawl "from Turkic lands, falling like gown." She pithily conveys something of Akhmatova's own oxymoronic mixture with the couplet "Chill in your joy; sultry / In your despondency."[54] In the following year this isolated poem was followed by the cycle in *Mileposts* addressed to Akhmatova, who is invoked as "Muse of Lamentation, loveliest Muse!"

> O thou crazed offspring of white night,
> Unleashing black blizzard on Russia,
> Piercing us with thy wails' arrows. . . .
>
> To tread the earth with thee
> Under one sky is to be crowned.
> He whom thy baleful destiny has wounded
> Goes to his deathbed as death's vanquisher.[55]

Tsvetayeva adds that she is "presenting" her native Moscow, with all its bells, to Akhmatova, together with "my heart for good measure." Akhmatova is "Hooknosed. Her wrath is death; / Lethal, too, her favours." Tsvetayeva also confronts Akhmatova's infant son, Lyov

("Leo") Gumilyov, now aged four, with the following all too accurate diagnosis.

> Red-haired lion cub
> With green eyes,
> You have a terrible heritage to bear.[56]

Other poets apostrophized in Tsvetayeva's wartime lyrics include Aleksandr Blok. Whereas Akhmatova had saluted him in a memorable prewar lyric, Tsvetayeva — that generous soul — bestowed a whole cycle on him. Though she was never to become acquainted with Blok, she was present at two poetry readings that he gave in Moscow in 1920, the year preceding his death. Such near-meetings or non-meetings *(nev-strechi)* between potential soul mates were eventually to become one of her most characteristic themes.

Appropriately enough, Tsvetayeva's verses to the older poet abound in such Blokian themes as snow, mist, swans, daredevil coachmen, and sleigh bells. She also playfully evokes the plopping sound of his surname.

> Stone tossed in still pool
> Gulps — your name.
> Brisk hoof-clop, at night,
> Booms, thunders — your name.
> Cocked pistol's twangy click at temple
> Shall name us — your name.[57]

Besides addressing lyrics to other poets, Tsvetayeva also continued to commemorate members of her own family, including her daughter Alya and her Polish maternal grandmother, who had died in her twenties. So brooding, direct, and imperious yet defensive an expression did Grandmother's portrait wear that Marina Ivanovna was impelled to enquire:

> Young grandmother, who are you . . . ?
>
> This cruel mutiny in my heart —
> Can it be yours, Grandmother?[58]

The cycle *Insomnia* shows Tsvetayeva once more tackling a theme characteristic of Akhmatova. Here Tsvetayeva again provides the lavish measure of a string of linked lyrics where the older poet contents herself with isolated items. In *Insomnia* Tsvetayeva imagines sleeplessness itself lying awake and being put to rest by the poet's lullabies. She also imagines wandering Moscow at night, herself part of her friends' dreams. In another lyric she visualizes the whole world lying awake — the baby crying in his cot, young lovers exchanging kisses, old men brooding on their death.

> If you sleep will you wake again on earth?
> We shall sleep, sleep, sleep our fill in time.[59]

As this cycle illustrates, the wartime Tsvetayeva by no means neglects that favourite prewar theme, her own death. It dominates the fine lyric — remarkable for its tautly sprung, eerie rhythm, such as metrical experiment was increasingly conferring on her verse — that begins "My soul, make merry: drink, eat!" The poet will soon be buried in a nameless grave in the raven-haunted, wolf-infested steppe where the signpost by a deserted road fork shall be the cross over her grave.

> Light for me no candle,
> In church's gloom.
> I want no eternal memory
> On my native earth.[60]

This key theme of the young Tsvetayeva — the simultaneous consciousness of irrepressible vitality and inevitable death — also figures in the cycle of nine robust lyrics, *Moscow Verses*, which is addressed to her native city. The combination is well summed up in the couplet in which she sees herself laid out for burial with her

> Eyes, mobile as flame,
> Chilled by strangers' five-copeck pieces.

Tsvetayeva, who repeatedly spoke of presenting Moscow to someone, now speaks of the time when her four-year-old daughter will have grown up and bestowed that city on *her* daughter. As for Marina herself, her fate will be

> Sleep galore, bells' tolling,
> Early dawns
> In Vagankov Graveyard.[61]

The Moscow poems abound in details of the city incantationally repeated — its five cathedrals, its seven hills, its forty-times-forty churches. Once again the varied, unexpected, ingenious rhythms give her verse a strength that it had not known in her prewar period. She now begins to make her mark as one of the most metrically creative Russian poets, but this creativity does not exclude devastating simplicity such as all four poets have triumphantly achieved on many occasions. *Moscow Verses* ends with such a lyric, a favourite of her own: "one of those that is most Me."[62]

> Crimson-clustered
> Rowan flared.
> Leaves fell,
> I was born.
>
> Wrangle of hundred
> Bells.
> Saturday.
> St. John's Day.
>
> Still I
> Want to chew
> Hot rowanberry's
> Bitter bunch.[63]

Not long after their first meeting at Koktebel, Tsvetayeva and Mandelstam embarked on their brief love affair: the only passion to be physically consummated — it seems probable — within the quartet of poets studied here. Osip Emilyevich took to visiting Marina Ivanovna in Moscow, and he spent part of the early summer of 1916 staying with her in the small, historic provincial town of Aleksandrovskaya Sloboda (now Aleksandrov) in Vladimir Province.

Mandelstam was one among several individuals on whom Tsvetayeva claimed to have bestowed her native Moscow, and it is in this capacity that he figures in her *Moscow Verses*.

> From my hands this city not made by hands
> Accept, my strange, my splendid brother.[64]

No fewer than nine of *Mileposts'* lyrics are known to be addressed to Mandelstam,[65] though his name does not appear in the text. He is the young man "with the longest eyelashes in the world," for whom she feels a strange tenderness, though she "has known darker lips," and his are not the only curls that she has stroked. His characteristic posture is also recognizable, in the lines "You throw back your head / Because you are proud and like talking nonsense." She thinks of him as a "heavenly,

ten-year-old boy," and is referring to their joint Moscow excursions
when she writes

> Let us linger by the stream that rinses
> Street lamps' coloured beads.
> I'll take you to the square
> That witnessed our Boy-Tsars.[66]

Surrounded, as Tsvetayeva's guest in summer 1916, by children,
cows, an aged nanny, and the gently undulating pastoral landscape of
Vladimir Province, Mandelstam — that St. Petersburger and Crimean
— grew bored. He quickly tired of too many country strolls; he was
always the first who wanted to return home. He would grow especially
restive whenever Marina Ivanovna — no doubt in search of copy —
gravitated to the local cemetery, where she would brood interminably
on the inscriptions, hardly having eyes for her lover at all. One morning,
in the middle of breakfast, Osip abruptly announced "in lordly fashion"
that he was leaving. "I, er, can't cope with this place. Anyway, it's time
we put a stop to all this." Soon he was on a local train, Crimea-bound.[67]

It was the end of their affair, but not of the verses that sprang from
it, especially as the young man had just taken farewell of a specialist in
the poetry of lovers' partings. She wrote of their separation in a lyric
that modestly rates her own talents lower than his, while comparing him
to the sonorous eighteenth-century Russian poet Derzhavin. It is sur-
prising that she should call her own voice "quiet," though it indeed can
possess that dimension, as the lyric illustrates.

> Neither has robbed the other!
> I'm glad we are apart.
> I kiss you through hundreds
> Of intervening versts.
>
> I know our gifts are unequal.
> My voice is above all quiet.
> What use, young Derzhavin,
> To you, my untutored verse?
>
> I bless your awesome flight:
> Soar, young eagle!
> You have faced the sun unblinking —
> Can my young eyes daunt you?
>
> More tenderly, more irrevocably
> No one ever gazed after you.
> I kiss you through hundreds
> Of intervening versts.[68]

Though Tsvetayeva has justifiably denounced those who "would rather gossip about poets than read them," and has questioned the value of "cribs from everyday life" (the study of a poet's biography) as a key to understanding verse,[69] the temptation to speculate irresponsibly on the inner relationship between her and Mandelstam has not always been resisted. In 1930 the émigré Russian poet Georgy Ivanov published a memoir of the Mandelstam-Tsvetayeva *affaire* that has been universally rejected as grossly inaccurate. He claimed Osip as "madly infatuated" with Marina, and described her as "a very pretty, rather vulgar brunette" — a lady doctor by profession and the former mistress of some businessman or merchant. This highly spiced fantasy provoked Tsvetayeva into rebutting his memoir with her own description of her encounters with Mandelstam, and she did it in her usual forthright manner. Peppering her quotations from the memoirist with derisive asides and interspersed question marks, she explains that Ivanov's account is inaccurate down to the colour of her hair. As for her being "very pretty," she scouts the flaccid compliment with blistering scorn. "I was never *very pretty*, or even pretty without the *very*. I was never slightly or excessively vulgar. I have not been a lady doctor. I have not been the kept mistress of a merchant." And as for Mandelstam's alleged infatuation: "He wasn't even capable of love."[70]

Beside the nine poems addressed by Marina to Osip there are three by him in which he alludes, more or less cryptically, to her. She appears most clearly in "Not Believing the Miracle of Resurrection." It directly refers (without naming her) to their time spent together at Aleksandrovskaya Sloboda, as well as to their strolls in the cemetery and on the broad meadow near the local convent. Mandelstam goes on to record the great reluctance with which he had taken his departure for the south.

> But to stay in this dark, wooden
> Crackpots' abode,
> With so nebulous a nun,
> Could only mean trouble.

It had been better to leave, even if Marina had

> Never stopped kissing him,
> Though disdainful in Moscow.[71]

This is even further from a conventional love poem than are Tsvetayeva's verses addressed to Mandelstam. But Mandelstam rarely attempted anything approaching that genre, and certainly did not do so in his two other poems of 1916 written with Tsvetayeva in mind. In these his poet-mistress lies buried so deeply that her presence would remain unsuspected without the aid of literary scholarship. Both are set in Moscow, the city that Tsvetayeva had "bestowed" on Mandelstam, and the first is largely architectural, retaining no more of the explosive Marina than her eyebrows.

> In Uspensky Cathedral's stone arches
> I discern lofty, arched eyebrows.[72]

"Straw-Strewn Sledge," Mandelstam's second poem combining the themes of Moscow and Tsvetayeva, already shows him capable of writing verses as difficult as any of Pasternak's; the two poets are now united in opposing masculine opacity to feminine clarity, as still exemplified by Akhmatova and Tsvetayeva. Evocative, eerie, macabre, and ill-adapted for summary elucidation, Mandelstam's sledge poem bears the dimly discerned Marina and himself back into Moscow's past. The historical echoes include an evocation of the second most notable Marina in Russia's history, Marina Mniszek (consort of the early-seventeenth-century Pretender to the Russian throne False Dmitry), with whom Tsvetayeva often identifies herself in her verse.[73]

Another famous woman to adorn Mandelstam's verses of these years is that noted beauty of his own period Princess Salomeya Andronikova, who has since described the poet as "more than merely ugly." Mandelstam's two-tier poem to her, "The Straw" (*"Solominka"*), is one of his best known, and is based on an incantational repetition of the diminutive forms of the word for straw *(solomka, solominka)* as echoes of the name Salomeya. Though the Princess happens to have survived her admirer for over forty years, she is here portrayed as dying or partly dying — or perhaps as just falling asleep, for the lyric is again enchantingly vague — while lying in her bed in her Petrograd home on the banks of the Neva. It is winter and the river itself, frozen or half frozen, has somehow invaded and filled the bedroom.

> In huge room above black Neva . . .
> Pale blue ice streams in air.

Solemn December sends its breath streaming,
As if heavy Neva were in the room.[74]

This mesmeric, intricately punning poem, vibrant with assonance
and intertwining re-echoed motifs, has two themes — insomnia and the
room mysteriously filled with water — in common with another superb
lyric of the period. It is one of the many in which Mandelstam conjures
up ancient Greece: a poem poised on the tension between wakefulness
and sleep, between poetry and life. Here it is the poet's own bedroom
which suffers symbolic flooding.

Insomnia. Homer. Taut sails.
I have half read the Catalogue of Ships:
That long litter, that crane train
Which soared, once, over Hellas.

Like wedge of cranes to foreign climes
With foam celestial on your Tsars' beards —
Whither sail you? What, but for Helen,
Could Troy alone mean to Achaea's heroes?

Sea, Homer: all is moved by love.
To which, then, should I hearken? Now Homer speaks no more,
And the swart ocean booms — rhetorical,
Crashing, ponderous at my bed-head.[75]

Advancing three thousand years from the Trojan War to the First
World War, Mandelstam returns to a favourite theme, monumental
church architecture, as he denounces the destruction of Reims Cathe-
dral by German bombardment. The poet points out that Cologne too
has its cathedral, and claims that its bells are ringing out in protest to
ask "What have you done to my brother of Reims?"[76]

In a longer wartime poem, "The Menagerie," Mandelstam makes
a general call for peace more elaborate than that of Tsvetayeva, quoted
above. Various emblematic animals — the German eagle, the French
cock, the British lion, and the Russian bear — have started an unseemly
quarrel, and Mandelstam proposes confining them all in a cage so that de-
cent people can live in peace. In the following lines he expresses his cos-
mopolitan cultural and historical feelings as a pan-European of his day.

I hymn wine immemorial,
Italic speech's springs;
I hymn in ancient Aryan cradle
Slavonic and Germanic flax.

The poem evokes a golden age of universal harmony, a theme to which Mandelstam was to return more movingly in later lyrics. It ends as follows.

> Having locked beasts in zoo,
> We shall long enjoy peace.
> Volga's water shall flood higher,
> Rhine's stream flow brighter.
> And Man, grown wiser, shall
> Unbidden honour outlanders
> Like demigods, with wild dancing
> On great rivers' banks.[77]

4

MY CRAFT ADRIFT

THE war against Germany was halfway through its third year when the first successful Russian revolution took place in February 1917 after outbreaks of popular disorder in the capital. The collapse of the monarchy introduced eight months of ineffectual semi-rule by the so-called Provisional Government, and then the October Revolution occurred through a Bolshevik coup d'état. In the following March the Treaty of Brest-Litovsk established peace with Germany at the price of sizeable Russian territorial concessions. The seat of government was transferred from Petrograd to Moscow, which had been the Russian capital over two hundred years earlier.

The Soviet epoch had begun, but the immediate effect of the 1917 revolutions on the four poets was far from catastrophic. This was partly because each upheaval accomplished a transfer of power within a few days without involving widespread military operations such as were to follow in 1918–21.

While the Provisional Government was unsuccessfully attempting to control the mobs of revolutionary Petrograd and to contain Bolshevik agitation in summer 1917, Mandelstam was sunning himself at a friend's dacha at the Crimean coastal resort of Alushta. Outwardly unaffected by the problems besetting Aleksandr Kerensky, who had become Russia's Prime Minister in July, the poet was still brooding on matters Mediterranean and on myths from the dawn of Greek history. These preoccupations inspired the idyllic summer scene — remote from the roar of German guns and the screams of Russian revolutionary agitators — conjured up in his incandescent lyric "Golden Honey Streams from Bottle."

> Like heavy barrels peaceful days roll on. . . .
>
> After tea we went into huge brown garden.
> Window blinds' dark lashes were down.

We passed white columns, inspected vineyard
Where drowsy hills were glazed with spilled air.

The golden hectares' noble, rust-coloured plantings display the lore of
Hellas in stony Tauris, evoking confused memories of the Golden
Fleece, Helen of Troy, and Penelope, as also of Odysseus — who, after
the roaring of the heavy seas in which he had put to work the canvas
of his sails, "Abandoned ship, / Returned home, replete with space and
time."[1]

The lyric is an outstanding example of Mandelstam's art, and an
extreme instance of a poet turning his back on current events. But there
are other, no less admirable, poems in which he vividly reacts to contem-
porary pressures, and which include certain vague but poetically im-
pressive premonitions of impending doom.

Buried deep in a moving lyric of early 1918, "Clock-Grasshopper's
Song," is the poet's awareness that he is fated to perish, and that his
poetry will cause his death. He senses that mice are gnawing the frail
bottom of his boat of life, which has been cast adrift by his Muse —
here personified as a swallow, and also as his daughter.

Why do mouse teeth gnaw
Life's frail keel?
Because Swallow-Daughter
Has cast my craft adrift.

This is the lyric in which Mandelstam invokes Nightingale Fever, the
sickness which will not let him stop writing poetry.

For death is blameless;
And there is no hope
For heart still flushed
With Nightingale Fever.[2]

Shortly before writing this, Mandelstam had linked his sense of
impending catastrophe with a specific locality. In two remarkable short
poems of 1916 he addresses his native St. Petersburg/Petrograd, giving
the city a Greek flavour by calling it Petropolis — as had Pushkin and
Tyutchev before him. These are both poems of foreboding. In the
earlier of them the note of menace is muted, and is conveyed by the
references to "dragonflies" and "transparency": both established sym-
bols of death in his work as a whole.

I am cold. Transparent spring
Decks Petropolis with green fluff;

But Neva's wave, gelatinous,
Induces mild disgust.
Along northern river's embankment
Automobiles' fireflies dart;
Dragonflies swoop, and steel beetles;
Stars' gold pins sparkle.
But no stars can quell
Sea wave's cumbrous emerald.[3]

In the second Petropolis poem the notes of looming disaster are made explicit by the reference to death in the first line, and then by the dehelmeting of Athene, goddess of wisdom (whose stone statue was to be found in the vestibule of the city's Admiralty) in favour of Proserpine, goddess of death. The poet invokes her in her Latin form as "Proserpina," instead of Persephone, partly in order to echo *prozrachny* ("transparent").

In transparent Petropolis we shall die,
Where over us Proserpina holds sway.
With every sigh we sup deadly air,
And every hour's our hour of death.

Sea goddess, dread Athene,
Doff thy mighty stone helm.
In transparent Petropolis we shall die —
Proserpina's domain, not thine.[4]

What terrible fate had Mandelstam in mind for Petrograd in these lyrics, both written shortly before the revolutions? Alert to the future's vibrations, did he sense that the city would cease to be the country's capital, and be ravaged by its own citizens? That prospect was becoming apparent by the year 1918, when he wrote his third, still more doom-laden, Petropolis lyric — celebrated, obscure, haunting, of disputed punctuation — in which he again uses transparency as a symbol for death. No longer merely threatened by extinction, the city is already in its death throes as the poet hails a strange, glittering light high aloft in the night sky. It is no star, but a will o' the wisp that later changes into a winged ship; and yet it is, perhaps, a star after all. He ends with the following quatrain.

Transparent spring over black Neva
Is broken. Immortality's wax melts.
Ah, if a star thou art, Petropolis, thy city —
Thy brother, Petropolis — is dying.[5]

So much for Mandelstam the messenger of generalized doom. What of his more detailed involvement in the march of events? By July 1917 he had "conceived an intense dislike for the Bolsheviks." It was now, a month or two before their eventual assumption of power had even begun to seem probable, that the poet chanced to meet two senior Bolshevik leaders, Kamenev and Zinovyev, and seized the opportunity to tell them how low an opinion he held of their political faith. He called it an "upside-down church."[6]

The Bolshevik Revolution of October 1917, and the consequent establishment of Soviet rule, did little to modify Mandelstam's disapproval of the inverted church. He was so hostile to the upheaval that he referred to its main instigator, Lenin, as "October's Upstart." The term occurs in a forthright lyric published in a newspaper on 15 November 1917 — shortly after the change of government, but before the imposition of effective political censorship by the new rulers.

> When October's Upstart was preparing
> Our yoke of violence and rancour;
> When murderous armoured car bristled,
> And low-browed machine-gunner —
>
> "Crucify Kerensky!" demanded the soldier
> While the vicious rabble clapped.[7]

Vicious rabble! Such was Mandelstam's view of the "heroic" armed workers whom the Bolsheviks had mobilized to overthrow Kerensky's government only a few weeks earlier. We also note that the same couplet equates the ousted Prime Minister of the Provisional Government with Jesus Christ; and Kerensky is further epitomized as the prototype of "the free citizen" in a later line of the poem, which ends with Russia descending into hell.

This outspoken lyric is not one of Mandelstam's best. In a finer sample of his work, published on 24 May 1918 and also devoted to the October Revolution, he is less antagonistic towards that event. This is reflected in the title, *Sumerki svobody* — best translated as "Freedom's Half-Light," since *sumerki* denotes the crepuscular gloaming that can accompany either the onset of morning or the onset of night. Lenin is no longer October's Upstart now, but the acknowledged leader of his people. Yet the poet is far from acclaiming either the Leader or the prospects for the Led with glowing optimism.

Let us laud the fateful load
Tearfully assumed by the People's Leader.
Let us praise power's sombre burden,
Its unbearable pressure.
No man of feeling but can sense
The sinking of thy ship, O Time.

By the end of the poem Mandelstam has sufficiently recovered to plead
that the new régime, still so tentatively established, should be given a
chance. In the following lines the entire earth has become a Ship of
State, his tribute to the global impact of Russia's recent history.

Let's try it then: a great, clumsy,
Creaking turn of helm.
Earth's under way. Show manhood, men!
Cleaving ocean as with plough,
We shall recall, even in Lethe's chill,
That Earth cost us ten heavens.[8]

Predicting doom both for himself and for Petrograd, Mandelstam
paid the same high compliment to one of the city's leading citizens,
Anna Akhmatova. He equated her with Cassandra — that earlier proph-
etess of woe who also foretold her own downfall.

Some time in crazed metropolis,
At Scythian orgy on Neva's banks,
To grisly revelry's roar,
They'll snatch the kerchief from that lovely head.[9]

In another poem of the same period Mandelstam playfully alluded to
Akhmatova's famous speech defect. It consisted, technically speaking,
of a tendency to confuse her affricates, and in practical terms of sound-
ing the Russian word *chto* ("what") as *tso;* this form of mispronuncia-
tion is faithfully reflected in recordings of her reading her own poems.

Your wondrous accent —
Hot whistle of birds of prey. . . .

How much air, silk,
Breeze in your whisper.[10]

The growing friendship of Akhmatova and Mandelstam was tem-
porarily impaired, shortly after he had written the lyrics quoted above,

through her tactlessness in showing that she thought him in danger of becoming infatuated with her. As she has primly recorded in her memoirs, "I had to explain to Osip that we should not meet so often: that it might expose our relationship to an invidious interpretation." Soon after this, she continues, Mandelstam suddenly disappeared from her horizon — in March 1918. And no wonder, for he was gravely offended by an impertinent assumption which incidentally suggested that she had not read the opening lines of his lyric "To Cassandra" with proper attention.

> Not in my lustier moments have I sought
> Your lips, Cassandra, or your eyes.[11]

In view of the free-and-easy morals of early-twentieth-century Russian literary society — and standards had not become more rigorous in Revolutionary Petrograd — Akhmatova had behaved absurdly in creating such a fuss about sexual advances that had never even been made. Mandelstam was later to explain how much the episode rankled, and added that it typified Akhmatova's maniacal obsession with the notion that all men were in love with her.[12] She was to retain this understandable fixation into her eighth decade; fortunately its damaging effect on her friendship with Mandelstam was only temporary.

Akhmatova came closest of all the four poets to equating her country's destiny with her own. Long before emigration from Soviet Russia became an acute issue, she firmly resolved never to desert her motherland in its agony, painful though the cost might be. Refusing to leave Russia to its fate, she did not lightly tolerate such defections in others, and was apt to express her indignation in the lyrical rebukes to which she was much given. One of these, dated July 1917, is addressed to her lover Boris Anrep, who had contrived to leave wartime Russia for England.

> Apostate! For green island
> Renouncing homeland; renouncing
> Our songs, our icons,
> Pine tree over calm lake.[13]

The most outspoken of Akhmatova's denunciations of exile occurs in the famous lyric, first published in April 1918, in which she sternly

maintains her determination never to abandon Russia, despite the ap-
palling degradation into which the country has sunk during the war
years.

> When, in suicidal anguish,
> Our folk awaited German guests,
> And Byzantium's stern spirit
> Fled Russia's Church;
> When the Capital on the Neva
> Forgot her majesty
> Like drunken whore,
> Not knowing who was taking her —
> I heard a voice that called, soothed,
> Said: "Come to me.
> Leave thy dim, sinful land —
> Leave Russia for ever.
> Thy hands of blood shall I rinse clean,
> Banish heart's black shame;
> With new name shall I cover
> Defeats' and abuses' hurt."
> Equably, calmly
> I closed ears with hands,
> That those unworthy words
> Might not pollute my spirit's grief.

As this remarkable lyric emphasizes, Akhmatova had decided that it was
more difficult and important to die *with* one's country than *for* it.[14]

It has been said of Pasternak's verses of 1914–24 that they utterly neglect
the epoch-making events of those years, and that, were they not dated,
"you would never suppose them to have been written at a time of war
and revolution."[15] But revolutionary themes do occasionally flicker in
his lyrics of the era. Vaguely sympathizing with revolution in the ab-
stract, like so many other young Russian intellectuals of his age, he had
become sufficiently involved in the abortive upheaval of 1905 to take
part in a street demonstration, during which a Cossack had struck him
a glancing blow. He also went on to commemorate an important revolu-
tionary event of December 1905 — the workers' revolt in the Presnya
District of Moscow — in a lyric written ten years later.

> Alarm blew from the future,
> Like sirocco from the south.

Hurling saffron torches
From palaces' pedestals,
With burning tow
It lashed foul weather's murk.[16]

When the poem was published, in *Over Barriers* in 1917, the more subversive passages had been removed by the Tsarist censor. In these the poet speaks of the fateful December as a permanent memorial to its revolutionary heroes, and refers to the aftermath of the Presnya rising as follows. "The promise / Of freedoms passed, and in the strikers' camp / For years gun barrels reared."[17] If this item had been offered for publication a month or two later, it would have escaped the censorship controls that removed the above lines, for Pasternak's "promise of freedoms," including freedom of speech, was almost too abundantly fulfilled through the February Revolution.

While war-ravaged Russia lurched from incompetently imposed regimentation into mounting chaos, anarchy, and licence during the interval between the two 1917 revolutions, Pasternak was blithely touring the Saratov area with a woman friend. He was also writing his third volume of verse, *My Sister Life,* which offers an occasional muffled echo of the revolutionary events of 1917. In "Spring Rain" Pasternak refers to the Revolution as a

Dazzling debouching into Forum
From catacombs yesterday sealed.[18]

Another lyric has the punning title *"Raspad,"* which not only means "break up" or "dissolution," but is also the name of a railway halt visited by the poet on the lower Volga. Here he speaks of "prairie drought / Shrouded in mist, whirling up / Like revolutionary haystack." He also refers to the soldiers' and peasants' mutinies of the era, and to the glow of manor houses put to the torch by mobs of *muzhiks.*[19]

Though these and other revolutionary motifs briefly surface, they are all but drowned in details of landscape. As Andrey Sinyavsky puts it, "Pasternak is more likely to tell us what the weather was like at a certain moment in history than to give a consistent exposition of the order and movement of events."[20] Similarly, Tsvetayeva has pointed out that the Revolution was apprehended by Pasternak, like everything else, through nature. She added (writing in 1922) that his real message about the Revolution had still to be pronounced; in summer 1917 he had just been "walking in step with Revolution, ears cocked."[21]

Pasternak's readers had to wait forty years for a full-scale study of the 1917 revolutions: the novel *Doctor Zhivago*. Its hero refers to the February upheaval as a liberating experience. "Revolution erupted forcibly, like a breath held too long. Everyone revived, became transformed, transfigured, changed. Each individual seemed to experience two revolutions: his own personal upheaval, and a second one common to all." It was a time when — the passage executes a typical skid into the world of nonsentient phenomena — "Stars and trees came together and conversed, flowers talked philosophy . . . stone buildings held political meetings."[22]

It seems safe to assume that these thoughts of Yury Zhivago express his creator's own feelings in February 1917. So too, in all probability, do Zhivago's enthusiastic comments on the October Revolution: "What magnificent surgery! What artistry! To cut out all the old stinking sores at one fell swoop. A straightforward, no-nonsense sentence of death on age-old injustice." However, if this indeed was Pasternak's immediate reaction to October 1917, he was to modify it radically in later years — as does Yury Zhivago in the novel, for he soon comes to deplore Bolshevik ruthlessness, also realizing from the outset that "he and his own circle are doomed."[23]

Zhivago's ruminations on revolution also include, as a general conclusion, the thesis that he and his generation, surrounded though they were by slaughter and death, had at least experienced more in five or ten years than others had in an entire century.[24]

Since Tsvetayeva was so fond of incorporating autobiographical material in her verse, it is no surprise to find the February and October revolutions — together with the Russian Civil War and attendant events — more fully reflected in her writings of the period than in those of Akhmatova, Mandelstam, and Pasternak. What is more remarkable, and new to Tsvetayeva's work, is the sharp political slant given to those topics by one who had hitherto avoided such themes. Even more astonishing — and richly typical of her antisuggestibility — is the ideological stance which she adopted in 1917: violent opposition to revolution, whether of the February or October variety.

In one lyric, written within two weeks of the abdication of the last Tsar-Emperor, Tsvetayeva disgustedly dismisses the revolutionary troops of the period as "ash-coloured, sand-hued . . . faceless, nameless, songless." In the second she offers an Easter kiss to the fallen Tsar, now under arrest. "The two-headed eagle / Has fallen ingloriously. . . . / God, not man, O Tsar, / Has called thee to account." But now that it is Easter, Tsvetayeva hopes that the fallen monarch will sleep peacefully. "See no red / Banners in dreams." A third poem uses the stately, archaic language of the Russian Church to intercede for the Heir to the Throne, the Tsarevich Alexis, and prays — all too ineffectually — that the father's sins may not be visited on the son. In another lyric of the period between the two revolutions Tsvetayeva speaks admiringly of Kerensky — hailing him as a "young dictator" in the style of Bonaparte, whom she so admired.[25]

Far from welcoming the Century of the Common Man, Tsvetayeva disparages the mutinous masses — especially the revolutionary soldiers. She complains that freedom has been degraded, resembling a street whore hanging on a soldier's neck. Nor, it seems, was her four-year-old daughter greatly impressed by the spectacle of armed starvelings arisen from their slumbers.

> With snow leopard's icy eyes
> You gazed at that scum.
>
> Your countenance, amid those dark ones,
> Was dazzling, shining white.[26]

After spending most of 1917 in Moscow, Tsvetayeva chanced to be in the Crimean resort of Feodosiya when the October Revolution erupted, the country passing — precariously, it seemed — into Bolshevik hands through the coup staged in Petrograd at Lenin's insistence. This event was not directly recorded by Tsvetayeva, but is obliquely reflected in a lyric of late October 1917 that describes a mob of howling soldiers looting a Feodosiya wine store.

> The whole town, stamping like bull,
> Stumbling in muddy puddle, tipples. . . .
>
> And round the merry rumour flies:
> Somewhere two men have drowned in wine.[27]

In the chaos of late 1917, when the Bolsheviks held power without having fully consolidated their hold on the country, Tsvetayeva became separated from Sergey Efron, her husband. He left her to join the White Volunteer Army in the south, while she was accidentally stranded in Moscow. In March 1918, with the Russian capital now transferred to that city, and the Peace of Brest-Litovsk signed with Germany, she was still denouncing those who harnessed pedigree horses to peasant sledges; drank the wines of the nobility from puddles; burst into churches on horseback; stabled their horses in cathedrals; impiously jolted the calendar forward by a baker's dozen of days, through adopting the calendar used in Western Europe; were ready to execute anyone for using the word "Tsar." In March, too, she wrote a poem praising the White Guards of the River Don, in the southeast of European Russia, where resistance to Bolshevik Moscow was now being consolidated. Easter brought her thoughts back to the Tsar again, and she wrote a short lyric claiming that he would reascend his throne; in fact, however, the abdicated Emperor and his family were to be put to death by the Bolsheviks at Yekaterinburg in the Urals within a few months.[28]

Though Tsvetayeva's eulogies of the Whites are outspoken and ideologically militant, it would be misleading to dismiss them as mere propaganda or to assume that they are inferior to her many nonideological lyrics of the period. Mayakovsky could write magnificent poetry (though not perhaps his best) floating the Reddest of Red ideology; and there was no reason why Tsvetayeva should not have excelled while presenting herself as Whiter than White. She continued to applaud the anti-Bolshevik cause throughout the Civil War and after it — naturally without any hope of publishing these particular items in Soviet Russia. Not until 1957, and in Munich, were they first issued as a collection, as she had all along intended, having carefully prepared them for the press. Entitled *Swan Encampment* — she alludes to members of the idolized White forces as "swans" — the edition is based on the original manuscript, deposited by the author in Basle in 1939. The editors have respected her wishes by preserving the old Russian orthography that she had stubbornly continued to use in defiance of the spelling reform of October 1918. The edition also preserves the poet's own dating, inscribed under each lyric in her own hand in accordance with the Old Style calendar abandoned in Russia earlier in 1918.

These minor details reflect Tsvetayeva's intransigent opposition to Bolshevism, the theme to which so much of *Swan Encampment* is devoted. But a survey of her writings and attitudes as a whole suggests that her fervent support of the White cause was inspired less by ideological conviction — such as she was barely capable of entertaining — than by a craving to attach herself to *any* cause, provided always that it was lost. The White armies, whose Swan Song she sang, appealed to her because she believed them romantically doomed, not because they stood for certain political principles — which, indeed, they barely did, beyond the generalized hostility towards Bolshevism that they had in common.

Though *Swan Encampment* is principally a comment on the world from 1917 onwards, it also abounds in telling historical allusions. Modern Russia's plight is likened to that of twelfth-century Kievan Russia, as recorded in that monument of medieval Russian literature *The Lay of Igor's Raid.* Championing her native Moscow, Tsvetayeva boasts that the early-seventeenth-century Pretender False Dmitry did not succeed in Polonizing the city, any more than Peter the Great managed to Germanize it. In another striking poem, devoted exclusively to the latter sovereign, Tsvetayeva holds him responsible for all the country's ills. The great Tsar-Emperor had been, says she, the original "Founder of the Soviets."[29]

5

BLACK VELVET

In contrast with the two revolutionary upheavals of 1917, which had little immediate impact on the four poets, the Civil War of 1918–21 inflicted acute privations and hazards for which their comparatively sheltered early years had done little to prepare them.

In its wider aspects the Civil War represented the successful defence of Bolshevism and of Lenin's Soviet government — which held Moscow, Petrograd, and central Russia — against a miscellaneous array of White armies as they advanced or retreated from the vast country's periphery. The Whites were chiefly based on the south and southwest of European Russia — especially on the Ukraine, the Don, and the Crimea; and their forces also threatened the Soviet heartland from Siberia in the east, from the Baltic countries in the west, and from the Murmansk-Arkhangelsk area in the north. Aid given to the Whites by the French, the British, the Americans, and other foreigners mobilized collective Russian resistance against the intruding alien, and may have contributed to the eventual victory of the Reds.

Already drained by three and a half years of foreign conflict, the country's resources were to be still more drastically depleted by three and a half years of a civil war that added widespread losses from famine, exposure, and disease to the huge military and civilian casualties now inflicted by Russians on Russians.

Under these conditions the four poets all suffered from 1918 onwards the precipitous descent from privilege to adversity that world war and revolution had so far failed to impose on them. Modest sufficiency gave way to dire poverty, relative safety to extreme danger. In Akhmatova's brief memoir of Mandelstam these conditions are spelled out baldly, almost in telegraphese, when she comes to describe Petrograd in 1920. Except for one relieving feature — that "poetry was still popular, especially with the young" — Petrograd's condition was disastrous. "Dust, gloom, yawning voids ... typhus, famine, shootings, unlit living quarters, damp firewood, people swollen out of all recognition . . . all the cemeteries looted." The city had not merely changed, Akhmatova adds; it had turned into the opposite of itself.[1] What she says of Petrograd during these terrible years is echoed by what Pasternak has to say in *Doctor Zhivago* of Moscow and the provinces.

During the Civil War all four poets bravely faced the sudden plunge into disaster. They were not prevented from practising their craft by one aspect of these years that — given the appalling calamities occurring on all hands — can only seem of minor significance: the severe curtailment of book publishing. In 1918 the issue of new literary works virtually ceased owing to the paper shortage and other inconveniences of the period. But the poets continued to write — except for Akhmatova, who had very little to say during the Civil War — and so a large quantity of their unpublished lyrics quickly accumulated. Much of the material could not become widely known until 1922, when large-scale publication was resumed. Against this may be set the continuing publication of isolated lyrics in periodicals, the circulation of verses in manuscript, and the recitals of new work that could still be given in cafés and lecture halls. As has often been noted, poetry of the Civil War years was less handicapped than prose literature, being more suitable for public declamation and private circulation.

Since the four poets were all civilians, their work of the Civil War period reflects the considerable hazards of the home front without attempting to chronicle the fighting. Military episodes were, however, to figure many years later in Tsvetayeva's poem *Perekop*, depicting action on the southern front in 1920, while Pasternak's *Doctor Zhivago* was to portray the activities of Red partisans in Siberia during the same period.

During the Civil War Tsvetayeva resided in the Red capital, suffering privations that even exceeded the Muscovite norm. On one occasion a burglar who had broken into her quarters was so horrified by the spectacle of her poverty that he offered her money of his own.[2] How terrible these years indeed were for the poet, as for the population at large, is illustrated by the fate of her younger daughter Irina, born in 1917. Barely able to keep herself and Alya, Tsvetayeva sent Irina to a Muscovite orphanage, hoping that the child might fare better there, but the result was that she died of starvation at the age of three. She is commemorated by her mother in the touching lyric that ends

Bright, slender-necked
Dandelion on stalk —
I can't yet fully grasp
That my child is in earth.[3]

Harsh though her living conditions were, Tsvetayeva continued to write verse in quantity, most of it devoid of public and political implications. But she also maintained the output of militantly pro-White poems. One of her finest lyrics of the period celebrates the anniversary of the Bolshevik Revolution. The date happened to coincide with a crisis in the Civil War — the approach of a White army that seemed poised to capture Moscow from the south. But the verses do not directly allude to this development, being devoted to a historical figure: Stenka Razin, leader of a full-scale seventeenth-century Russian peasant revolt. Eloquently appealing for that captured rebel chieftain to be spared, Tsvetayeva was several centuries too late, since he had already been executed by quartering back in 1671. The interest of the poem lies in its thunderous language, but also in its status as a passionate appeal to the White forces, seemingly victorious for the moment, to spare the Reds, who were thought to face imminent defeat at this low point in their fortunes. How typical of Tsvetayeva that she was poised to switch her allegiance from White to Red instantaneously, just as soon as the Reds momentarily appeared to be on the losing side.

> Razin! Razin! Told is thy tale!
> Tamed, bound is Red Beast.
> Dread teeth are broken.
> Yet, for his dark, dim life's sake —
>
> Aye, for his reckless prowess —
> Unbind Stenka Razin![4]

Since the White armies were soon driven back, Tsvetayeva's appeal for clemency towards the Reds was pointless. In any case the Whites would not have retained her support had they gone on to win the Civil War; never could any victorious cause long have held the poet's sympathies.

Tsvetayeva's main cultural and social activities of 1918–19 revolved around the Third Studio, a small experimental stage company affiliated to the Moscow Art Theatre. For several members of this enterprise — young people a year or two her juniors — she conceived powerful emotional attachments: the poet-actor Pavel Antokolsky, the actor-producer Yury Zavadsky, and a tiny Russian actress with an English surname, Sonechka Holliday. These contacts are commemorated in her verses of the period, also figuring in a memoir written nearly twenty years later, *Tale of Sonechka*. Here the poet has reconstructed, with the aid of old diaries and notebooks, the heady days when she had been simultaneously in love with the theatre and — it seemed — with almost everyone in it.

From becoming stage-struck to turning playwright was only a short step. "The urge was irresistible. My voice had simply outgrown lyric poetry. I had too much puff in my chest for a flute."[5] The outcome was a series of no fewer than seven verse plays written in 1918–19 for her theatrical friends. But though readings took place at which the texts were eagerly applauded, none of the poet's dramas was to be produced on this or (it seems) any other stage. They are more poems than plays. Not that they are overwhelmingly impressive as poetry either, despite the presence of some memorable lines and passages. The neatly turned iambics, the style too often reminiscent of the early-nineteenth-century playwright Griboyedov — here was a medium too orthodox, too tame for a poet who was already displaying her power along far less conventional lines in *Mileposts* and *Swan Encampment.*

All romantic excursions into the past, the plays of 1918–19 collectively span time and space from sixteenth-century Germany *(Stone Angel)* to early-nineteenth-century Bohemia *(Snowstorm),* also taking in Austria, Poland, and France. Three of them *(Death of Casanova, Phoenix, Adventure)* are loosely based on the memoirs of the late-eighteenth-century memoirist Casanova, in whom Maksimilian Voloshin had once sought to interest Tsvetayeva as a schoolgirl. Other sexually irresistible heroes — the Stone Angel in the play of that title, the Duc de Lauzun in *Fortune* — were intended as vehicles for the handsome young actor Zavadsky, with whom both Tsvetayeva and her bosom friend Sonechka were infatuated. The plays are hyperbolically romantic in content, most of the minor characters being depicted as reeling before the devastating attractiveness of various supermen and superwomen, but also (in *Adventure*) of the heroically stunning hermaphrodite Henri-Henriette.

As poetry this group of romantic plays yields not only to the lyrics of the same period, but also to the two dramas that Tsvetayeva was to write in the 1920s on ancient Greek themes, *Ariadne* and *Phaedra.* And so her theatrical excursions of 1918–19 have more biographical than literary interest. They did little to advance her progress as an artist.

In late 1918 Tsvetayeva plunged into a segment of Moscow as far removed as possible from the Bohemian atmosphere of the early post-Revolutionary theatre: she obtained employment as a clerk in the People's Commissariat for Nationalities, which happened to be headed by Stalin. Her task consisted of pasting up newspaper cuttings, and she performed it with anecdotal incompetence, according to her own account in the amusing article *My Jobs.* She obstinately refused to modify her spelling in accordance with the New Orthography introduced in

October 1918, particularly insisting on retaining the time-hallowed let-ter *yat* (suddenly declared obsolete), no matter how often her colleagues tried to induce 'Comrade Efron' to abandon such counter-revolutionary habits. In the end she resigned her post after five and a half months, swearing that she would never again take an office job even if her life depended on it.[6]

During the Civil War Tsvetayeva continued to write lyrics on personal themes: her family and friends; love, death, insomnia, loneli-ness; her own mutinous and perennially fascinating nature. In a striking lyric of 1920 she revives the image of her maternal grandmother, a turbulent fellow spirit who had already figured in an earlier lyric in-spired by her portrait.[7] The long-deceased Polish gentlewoman is now seen playing her piano with hands that have been kissed over and over again, for she has the entire nobility of her native Poland at her feet. With this upper-class Polish beauty Tsvetayeva effectively contrasts her paternal grandmother: wife to a poor Russian priest, she had reared her four sons, including the poet's father, in dire poverty in a primitive village hut. The poet claims herself the true descendant of both her grandmothers, since she is simultaneously a plebeian and an aristocrat.[8] As the poem illustrates, Tsvetayeva saw herself as the fusion of extremes; she could never tolerate being classed as a bourgeois, intellectual, mid-dle-class, or otherwise middling sort of person.

In another lyric the poet varies the grandmaternal theme by ima-gining herself in the distant future — a naughty, dynamic, dancing grannie whose granddaughter will take after her, to the dismay of the female parent of the intervening generation, and who will also exem-plify the truth that "a nimble dancer is also nimble on feather bed."[9] This is one of several references in lyrics of the period to sensual proclivities such as the poet sometimes paraded and sometimes ostenta-tiously renounced.

Tsvetayeva's surviving daughter Alya remained prominent in her mother's verse. She is the recipient of a cycle of eleven lyrics, written between 1916 and 1919, in which the mother blesses the little girl's good influence on herself. Alya, here addressed as "Consuela," has driven all the squalor of former love affairs out of Marina's life.

> O my Golden Age!
> O swarm of fabulous transgressions,
> All brushed away
> By Consuela, my consolation . . . !
>
> I could meet death this instant.
> No amorous speck is left![10]

Here Tsvetayeva invokes the theme of sexual renunciation which was shortly to become prominent in her work. Subject to competing sensual and ascetic urges, she oscillates from one to the other while increasingly gravitating towards the second. It is this second, self-denying Tsvetayeva that thoughts of her daughter seem to evoke. Indeed, one of her addresses to Alya even seems to suggest that the little girl had been conceived immaculately, or at least supernaturally.

> I must have slept with an angel,
> Taken God in my embrace.
> Every hour I bless
> Thy conception's midnight.

But Alya makes her mother think of death as well as birth. One day Marina will be no more than a dim memory to her daughter.

> You'll forget my aquiline profile;
> My forehead, cigarette-enhaloed;
> My perpetual laughter that fools everyone.[11]

Still obsessed with death and love, Tsvetayeva fuses these motifs in the remarkable lyric "To You — in a Hundred Years." Here she imagines a lover of the future who is to be born exactly a century after her own decease, at a time when

> Old men, even, have forgotten me.
> Lips cannot reach! Over Lethe's waters
> I stretch my hands. . . .
>
> And when you meet other women — living, happy —
> When you gaze at them, I catch your words with pride:
> "O rabble of impostors. You're all dead.
> She, she alone, lives."[12]

In one of her own favourite short poems of the period Tsvetayeva claims a talent for extreme submissiveness such as she did not regularly cultivate in life. She is a white page waiting to be written on by her lover's pen, and she is the fruitful soil waiting for him to shine and rain on her. "You are Lord and Master, I / Am black earth, white paper."[13] There is a similar streak of tractability in Akhmatova's verse — a reminder that the most masterful and tempestuous woman may occasionally choose to submerge her personality in a lover's.

A sense of isolation remains a basic theme of Tsvetayeva's lyrics. It is poignantly expressed in "Roland's Horn," where she hymns her own loneliness, by contrast with others who belong to a collective.

> The soldier boasts a regiment, Satan his legions;
> Thieves have riff-raff, jesters humps.

Lacking this kind of corporate backing, mocked and jeered by morons and vulgarians, Tsvetayeva stands and sends a "loud summons into heaven's void."

> And this fire blazing in my breast ensures
> That thee, O horn, some Charlemagne shall hear.[14]

Tsvetayeva was the first of the four poets to attempt a long narrative work in verse: *Tsar-Maiden*, written in 1920 and in the idiom of Russian folk tales. Akhmatova and Tsvetayeva had already exploited peasant language in their lyrics, but *Tsar-Maiden* eclipses all their efforts by creating so saturated a solution of folk elements. The poem is based on a fable contained in the celebrated *Russian Folk Tales* compiled by Afanasyev, and represents a triumph of creative versatility, the fusion of metrical ingenuity and popular motifs being accomplished with colossal verve and style. The plot revolves around the attempts by two rivals — an amorous Stepmother-Tsaritsa (the villainess) and the heroic Tsar-Maiden (a more than Amazonian heroine) — to win, by various magical and incantational means, the love of a young Tsarevich. This paltry, psaltery-playing youth is rendered sexually irresistible by his narrow shoulders, general feebleness, and debilitated condition. As he reflects of himself,

> Can't see why my nature
> Pleases women so.
> My arms and legs are frail —
> Regular noodles.[15]

Tsvetayeva has infused into this fascinating poem many basic ideas that can also be traced in her other work. There is the primacy of creative art over love, power, and all other considerations, as incarnated in the Tsarevich's mastery of the psaltery. There is the psycho-sexual relationship between two opposites: the all-powerful Tsar-Maiden, whose head reaches the skies, whose tresses are like a horse's mane, who wears the moon as an earring, and who represents the spirit of action and aggressiveness. And there is the feeble yet irresistible Tsarevich, who is not only pursued by this prodigy of rampant femininity, but who also has to fight off his stepmother's determined attempts to lead him astray. The antics of that seductress include the striptease lovingly described towards the end of the poem. A Beardsley-like illustration of this, complete with full frontal exposure, embellishes the Moscow (1922) edition[16] — an indication of how far Soviet censorship then was from the militant prudishness of later years.

In the Tsar-Maiden's quest for the Tsarevich we sense echoes of Tsvetayeva's own life. Though not built on so heroic a physical scale as her folk heroine, she herself was a strong, masterful woman, and was prone to fasten her emotions on some younger, weaker, less decisive male. One among many such was her now absent husband, Sergey, whom neither years of separation nor her emotional involvements with others could cause her to forget.

A third motif running through *Tsar-Maiden* creates a tension of its own, in opposition to the many outspokenly voluptuous passages — love unfulfilled, such as was to dominate its author increasingly during the early 1920s. This theme pervades the poem as a whole, and is reflected in Tsvetayeva's rejection of Afanasyev's happy ending, which blissfully unites the hero and the heroine. She herself defined the work as a tragedy of missed opportunities. "All the loves misfire, you see. . . . [The Tsarevich] loves no one, he loves only his psaltery." She goes on to compare him with Hippolytus,[17] that hero from ancient Greek legend whom Euripides and later dramatists have portrayed as a very paragon of compulsive chastity, and whose image was to inspire some of Tsvetayeva's most powerful verse of the next few years.

The year 1917 marked a revolution in Akhmatova's personal life — the final break with her poet-husband Gumilyov, from whom she had already been long separated by his travels and war service. She now left the home in Tsarskoye Selo that they had so rarely shared, and embarked on four decades of residence in what always seemed temporary quarters, chiefly in Petrograd/Leningrad. Not until she was eventually granted a dacha at Komarovo near that city, when she was in her late sixties, could she again feel that she possessed anything approaching a home.

In 1918 Akhmatova received a divorce from Gumilyov, and married her second husband — Vladimir Shileyko, a distinguished Assyriologist. This second marriage had a catastrophic effect on her creative life, for the specialist in cuneiform proved a masterful, ogre-like husband who forbade his wife to write poetry; he is even reported as fuelling their samovar with such verse as she contrived to compose in defiance of this interdiction. Consequently she wrote hardly any poems — barely half a dozen in all — during the three-year period 1918–20. This can be concluded from the dates that she habitually appended to individual published items. Not that we should take these entries too seriously, for she was prone to err, whether through forgetfulness or a wish to tease her biographers.

In December 1917, at an early stage in her relationship with Shileyko, Akhmatova wrote of him ambivalently.

> You are always mysterious and new.
> I submit to you more each day.
> But your love, my stern darling,
> Is ordeal by iron and fire.
>
> You forbid singing and smiling.
> My prayers you have long banned.
> But may I never part from you —
> Nothing else matters.
>
> Thus, a stranger to earth and sky,
> I live and sing no more,
> As if you'd cheated hell and heaven
> Of my free spirit.[18]

To Shileyko the poet also wrote, in April 1918, protesting "You don't want children from me, / You dislike my verse." By July of the same year his love has made her yellow, prone to fainting, and so desperate that she begs him to claw her tubercular chest until she dies of a haemorrhage.[19]

In June 1921, at the time of the final rupture with Shileyko, Akhmatova wrote that marriage to him was like being in the clutches of a dragon, "With whip hanging on wall, / To stop me singing songs." In another lyric she complains "My husband's a hangman, his house a prison." Finally, in one of her many splendid wrathful poems, Akhmatova pronounces a curse on Shileyko. Does he think her a weakling who will kill herself because she is separated from him? Or that she will stoop to seeking influence over him through love potions?

> I swear by the gardens of paradise,
> By miracle-working icon,
> By our nights' flaming fumes:
> I'll never go back to you.[20]

Akhmatova felt no less harassed by the privations of Petrograd during the Civil War than by her husband's despotic temper, but had already begun to develop the formidable stoicism that was to distinguish her during many years of future suffering. In verse, as in life, she could turn catastrophe into triumph.

All is looted, betrayed, sold;
Black death's wing has flashed;
All is gnawed by ravenous anguish.
Why, then, is our vista so bright?

Drift of cherry-blossom's scent by day,
Woods near city beyond compare,
New constellations glinting at night
In July skies' pellucid depths.

And the miracle comes so close
To dirty, tumbledown houses —
Miracle beyond all ken,
Yet so long our hearts' desire.[21]

Despite his dislike of Bolshevism and his poetical denunciation of Lenin as October's Upstart, Mandelstam managed to obtain temporary employment at the People's Commissariat for Enlightenment, the new education ministry, and in March 1918 he was transferred from Petrograd to Moscow along with the seat of government as a whole. What function he performed at the commissariat remains obscure, but he is reported as intervening to save a church choir from dissolution, and as going in terror of his own typist. He is also known to have resided briefly in the Kremlin as the guest of a senior official of his commissariat. One morning, as he was breakfasting in the dining hall, he chanced to learn that Trotsky was expected to join the company at any moment. But the young poet was so acutely sensitized by his dread of power that he would not risk allowing his eyes to rest on the world's second most influential Bolshevik, and swiftly fled the premises.

Here was the Rabbit in Mandelstam that had helped to earn him the nickname "Rabbit-Leopard." But the second of these beasts sometimes found occasion to pounce, as in the poet's famous clash with Yakov Blyumkin, a pistol-toting officer of the Cheka (security police). Blyumkin was apt to boast publicly of his power of life and death over the many political prisoners languishing in the Cheka's dungeons. He was once proclaiming publicly — in a café, according to one account — his intention of having a certain art historian shot, when Mandelstam snatched the execution warrant from him and tore it up. Then the poet somehow contrived to take the case straight to the Cheka head, Feliks Dzerzhinsky, in person, with the result that the death sentence was rescinded. Suspended from duty, Blyumkin used the imposed period of leisure to assassinate the German Ambassador, Count Mirbach, in his embassy in Moscow on 6 July 1918. Blyumkin is also reported as seeking to recruit Mandelstam, of all people, to the Cheka. He would point his loaded revolver at the poet whenever they met; and who could doubt the proven killer's readiness to pull the trigger if the whim should seize him?

When Blyumkin was eventually executed, on the meaningless charge of "Trotskyism" in 1929, Mandelstam was horrified, being so passionately opposed to capital punishment as to deplore it even when applied to this atrocious desperado. Despite his own reported youthful wish to join a political assassination squad, he also deplored the slaughter of the Petrograd Cheka chief, Uritsky, by a Socialist revolutionary, which took place in August 1918.[22]

Tiring of Blyumkin, of the People's Commissariat for Enlightenment, and of revolutionary Moscow in general, Mandelstam headed for the south in summer 1918: a prelude to two years' desultory and dangerous peregrinations through the Ukraine, the Crimea, and the Caucasus. The following spring found him in Kiev at a time when the city was precariously held by Reds and menaced by Whites. Here the poet first met his future wife: Nadezhda Yakovlevna Khazina, an art student who was about ten years younger than he, and of Jewish descent. Their association was eventually to develop into the most stable marital union enjoyed by any of the four poets.

According to Nadezhda Yakovlevna's memoirs they became lovers on 1 May 1919. On the following day Mandelstam wrote "On Pieria's Stony Spurs," one of his most enchanting lyrics, and one of many commemorating his vocation as a man of the Mediterranean. It invokes the birth of poetry in ancient Greece, and ends by offering what so many Greek and Roman poets had already provided in their time — the vision of a Golden Age.

> On Pieria's stony spurs
> Muses danced their primal dance,
> That blind lyrists, bee-like, might
> Bestow on us Ionian honey. . . .

Spring flits to trample Hellas' leas,
Sappho's bright boot is donned.
With tiny hammers cicadas
Forge their storied ring. . . .

Leisurely is tortoise-lyre.
Unfingered, she scarce crawls;
Sunbathes in Epirus,
Softly warms golden belly.
Now, who will fondle such a one?
Who'll turn the sleeper over?
Adreamed, she awaits Terpander,
Senses dry fingers' flurry.

Cold spring waters oaks,
Grass hair rustles unconfined,
Lungwort's scent gladdens wasps.
O Holy Isles, where are ye —
Where broken bread is not eaten:
Land of honey, wine, milk,
Where creaking toil not darkens sky;
Wheel turns smoothly.[23]

Nothing could have been further in spirit from this delicious idyll than Kiev in mid-1919, where the poet and his future wife were overtaken by the horrors of the Civil War. The city changed hands between competing factions so frequently that the inhabitants could not agree, when it was all over, whether the number of these occasions was as low as fourteen or as high as nineteen.

Nadezhda Yakovlevna's memoirs preserve nightmare glimpses from the years of Kiev's agony, to which many contending parties — Reds, Whites, Ukrainian nationalists, and honest, straightforward bandits — made their contribution. There was the squad of Red troops that suddenly halted in front of a desirable four-storey residence, and began blazing away at the windows, hoping to slaughter the "bourgeois" lurking inside. When the White General Denikin captured the town it was the turn of those suspected of Bolshevik sympathies to suffer violence. Mandelstam himself was endangered both as a Jew in this era of pogroms, and even as a suspected Bolshevik. He is rumoured to have been arrested by the White authorities in Kiev, but to have been released unscathed against the probabilities — unlike the unfortunates whom he and Nadezhda Yakovlevna could see lynched before their eyes from the windows of her parents' home in the fashionable Lipki district. "Streams of blood flowed on the very street, in front of every window.

We all saw dead and wounded on the pavements and roadway, and it was less a stray bullet that we feared than the degradations and tortures inflicted before death."[24]

The poet fled from these outrages, becoming separated from his future wife for some eighteen months and resuming his southern travels in territory now held by the Whites. In November 1919 he surfaced in Feodosiya, exactly two years after Tsvetayeva had described drunken mobs looting the wine cellars of that high-class east Crimean coastal resort.[25] It is a very different Feodosiya — idyllic, exotic, oriental — that Mandelstam conjures up in his own lyrical address to the little port.

> Upland-girt,
> You pelt downhill like sheep flock;
> Your stones — pink, white —
> Gleam in dry, limpid air.
> Pirate feluccas bob,
> Turkish flags' poppies burn in port;
> Cane-masts, waves' tensile crystal;
> Hammock-dinghies, rope-slung.[26]

Feodosiya proved by no means as paradisical a haven as Mandelstam's lyric may suggest. By January 1920 he was enduring a winter bleaker than anyone could remember in this subtropical latitude, while heavy artillery was being hauled over the frozen sea near the closest theatre of war, the Perekop Isthmus. There were English troops — Mandelstam calls them "Bobbies" in his memoirs — stationed in the town and annoying everyone by singing Scottish songs. Altogether Feodosiya had become such a hell on earth that the very town idiot had stopped wandering the streets and being followed everywhere by his train of urchins. Soon Mandelstam too had disappeared from circulation, when he was arrested — again as a suspected Bolshevik agent — by the political police of General Wrangel's White administration. He might easily have been shot in those days when "the chance to murder unpunished affected some people like a bath in fresh mineral water,"[27] had not a friendly Colonel interceded on his behalf; that benefactor is described, with other associates of these months, in the poet's scintillating prose memoir *Feodosiya*.

Mandelstam proceeded from Feodosiya to Tiflis, to which city (now the capital of briefly independent Georgia) he addressed an effervescent lyric.[28] He also narrowly escaped being forcibly returned — and to certain death in the context — to White-occupied Crimea. Eventually he contrived, after many adventures, to make his way back to Moscow, where he reverted to Soviet domicile in the summer of 1920 after his two-year absence. He went on to spend the winter in his native Petrograd.

Once again Mandelstam saluted his native city in a haunting lyric, "In Petersburg We'll Meet Again." It emphasizes the former capital's baleful potentialities, evoking the image of an executioner's block (described as "draped with black velvet" in other verses of the same year) with the lines

> In Soviet night's black velvet,
> Velvet of universal void.

Yet he feels mysteriously immune from these dangers.

> Metropolis humped like wild cat,
> Patrol guarding bridge;
> Vicious truck swoops through gloaming,
> Hoots cuckoo-like.
> I need no night pass,
> Fear no sentries.

The poet's safety is ensured, he suggests, by some "blessed, meaningless word," for which "I shall pray in the Soviet night."[29]

Mandelstam celebrated this Petrograd winter of 1920–21 by conducting a love affair with an actress, Olga Arbenina, to whom several lyrics of the period are addressed. Two of them are relatively simple, and are among Mandelstam's few approximations to the conventional love poem.[30] In the third, more difficult, lyric the poet offers his actress a gift of sunshine and honey, only to fall victim to some ill-defined fear inspired by a shadow or ghost approaching him soundlessly in fur slippers. His gift of honey and sunshine is transformed into an "ugly, dry necklace / Of dead bees that have converted honey into sun."[31]

Another famous lyric commemorates Mandelstam's break with Arbenina — she had run away from him in the middle of the night, ignoring the curfew then in force, after they had returned from attending a ballet performance.[32] Brooding on his loss, the poet recalls the Trojan Horse and the sack of Troy as preserved in Greek legend — yet another sample of his creative obsession with matters Hellenic. The first half of the poem presents the interplay of these themes.

> For letting your arms go,
> For betraying your tender, salty lips

I must await dawn in thickset acropolis.
How I loathe the ancient, scented timbers.

Achaean heroes equip horse in darkness,
Gnaw hard into walls with toothed saws.
Blood's dry fluster not abates;
No name, no sound, no mould can express you.

How could I suppose you'd return, how dared I?
Why was I torn from you too soon —
Murk still undispersed, ere cock-crow,
Before hot axes' slicing into timber.[33]

After vibrating in response to the revolutionary fervour of 1917, while also writing the lyrics of *My Sister Life*, Pasternak entered a less exuberant phase in the Civil War years. He spent them in Moscow, sharing the extreme privations of the times. Though Tsvetayeva remembered meeting him in the street in winter 1919, when he was on his way to sell books because he had "no bread in the house,"[34] the period remains something of a lacuna in his life. He says little of it in his two autobiographical essays, and for a fuller picture of his reaction to Russia's agony of the Civil War years his readers must again turn to *Doctor Zhivago*. The novel contains memorable pictures of the dangers and tribulations suffered in Moscow and the provinces: the battle to steal or scrounge firewood, and to obtain food by barter or intrigue at a time when sudden death might come through such causes as typhus and trigger-happy sailors as well as from freezing, exposure, and starvation.

Since these conditions were barely conducive to survival, let alone to authorship, it is not surprising that Pasternak wrote less verse in the five years 1918–22 combined than he had in 1917 alone; his leanest twelvemonth was 1920, when his Muse — like Akhmatova's — appears to have preserved total silence.

Most of Pasternak's lyrics of the Civil War years appeared in the collection *Themes and Variations*, published in Berlin in 1923. Among the freshly orchestrated topics is the depopulated townscape that figures in "A Meeting." Here is an encounter quintessentially Pasternakian; for though the poet himself surfaces early he comes no nearer to "meeting" any human being than when he is found departing from some vaguely adumbrated gathering in a Moscow flat before six o'clock in the morning.

Like lump of scenery
From suddenly soaked stairway

Flopped into water, crashed
A weary "See you tomorrow."

Water streams from pipes, gutters, puddles, hedges, roofs; pavements
are slippery; wind rips wetness like an old rag. One could walk to
Podolsk, twenty-five miles to the south, without setting eyes on a soul.
But the poet has soon found companions; need one say that they are
inanimate?

March night and author
Walked side by side, arguing,
As landscape's chill hand
Led them home, led them from the gathering.

Soon these two have met a third companion: a personified Tomorrow
who walks along carrying some picture-framer's moulding while pre-
paring to present trees, buildings, and churches to the poet in a series
of isolated "takes."[35]

Less dehumanized is the fascinating lyric "Shakespeare." Even
here the animate characters tend to be elbowed out by the clumsily
spiralling snow, frowsty like a slipped stomach-band, which starts fall-
ing when half asleep, lulling the drowsy wilderness. Inside a tavern the
intoxicated bard wearily smokes his pipe, and is harangued by one of
his own newly written sonnets, which demands to be read out to the
company. "You must be mad," Shakespeare tells the sonnet as he pays
his bill and leaves, hurling a napkin at the apparition.[36] This Browning-
esque effusion has all Pasternak's intense verve, and underlines the
interest in Shakespeare that was eventually to inspire translations of
eight of the plays into Russian.

The most urgent poetry in the collection *Themes and Variations* is
in the sequence of seven lyrics addressed to Pushkin. They evoke
Russia's poet of poets standing on a cliff in a storm, and stress the sweep
of historical time and global geography comprehended in the phenome-
non of Pushkin. Pasternak emphasizes the other poet's African ancestry
as a one-eighth Ethiopian descended from a black great-grandfather
imported into Russia in Peter the Great's day. Pasternak's Pushkin

Stands, eyes shut, and sees in Sphinx
Not our nonsense; not some baffled
Greek's conjectures; no enigma —
But forbear; flat-lipped Hamite . . .
Pox-rutted by sands.

Brewery images predominate in Pasternak's stormscape as frothing beer frenziedly slops off cliffs', capes', rocks', spits', and sandbanks' whiskers.

> Anchors, ports,
> Jetsam, swollen
> Corpses, grey
> Plankways have ears rammed
> With tufty Pilsen's smoke. . . .
>
> Where loops' white raging,
> Where squashed storms' rumbling
> Sucks sand dry,
> As ale or chewed betel.[37]

After this splendid excursion into the meteorological area, Pasternak is briefly brought back to Pushkin and Africa by his betel nut to ask a question arising from the earlier poet's ancestry and from his upbringing at the Tsarskoye Selo *lycée* near St. Petersburg.

> What was his Kaffir heritage?
> What did Tsarskoye Selo's *lycée* give him?

Before this query can be answered the sea is at it again.

> Squall raged. Sand-thickened
> Purple breaker grew bloodshot.[38]

In one particularly impressive sequence, competing themes — time, geography (arctic and tropical), the Sphinx, and Pushkin's own most famous lyric, "The Prophet" — are united to produce some of the most resoundingly authoritative lines in Russian poetry. The brew of hurtling stars, sea-washed headlands, blinded salt, dried tears, wax-drowned candles makes an enchanting and potent medley.

> Blood of colossus
> Seeming to cool. Lips swollen
> In desert's blue smile.
> Night waning at ebb-tide's hour.
>
> Sea brushed by Moroccan breeze.
> Sand storm. Arkhangelsk snoring in snow.
> Candles guttering. Prophet's draft
> Drying. Dawn glimmering on Ganges.[39]

So much for the global sweep of genius and of history. What of the Russian scene in the poet's own day? That flickers momentarily in two adjacent lyrics — the one written just before 1 January 1919, and the other just after. The earlier verses are, once again, heavily meteorological, as the title indicates: "Kremlin in Blizzard, End of 1918." Here is a symbolic storm, like so many of Blok's; but whereas Blok largely dealt in intimations of imminent calamity, Pasternak is surrounded by doom in process of implementation. Lost in a blizzard at midnight, he appeals to the raging elements with his last gasp, like some storm-buffeted dispatch bearer, who

> Cuff-gripped
> By chortling blizzard
> Greeting him in manacles,
> Fumbles hood's tassels.

The grandiose typhoon seems to be lurching headlong straight through the end of expiring 1918 into unbroached 1919; but the lyric ends calmly, while anticipating further storms in the future.

> Beyond these squalls' ocean,
> I feel, this year not yet arrived
> Will take me, shattered as I am,
> And tackle my re-education.

The poet's re-education is already being tackled in the second of the two linked lyrics, "January 1919," in which he admits having entertained thoughts of suicide, but puts them aside as he faces the future with typical resilience.

> That year! How often at my window
> The old one whispered "Jump!"
> But this new one's blown all that away,
> Like a Christmas tale in Dickens.[40]

In *The Breach,* a cycle of nine lyrics mourning a terminated love affair, Pasternak explores a new dimension of feeling. The emotional context — rejection of the poet by his beloved — resembles that of the earlier "Marburg." But whereas the previous rebuff had led, however paradoxically, to a surge of high morale, this later rupture proves deeply traumatic. It has covered the poet's heart with eczema, as he complains, offering yet another "dislocation of reality." Had he only been a human being, and not just an empty collection of temples, lips, eyes, palms, shoulders, and cheeks, he would have mobilized the whistle of his verses and led them into the attack to overcome the shame generated by his hazily sketched predicament. Addressing his beloved in the final stanza, he allows himself another of his rare glimpses into the dangers of the era.

> I won't keep you. Go. Do good works.
> Go to others. *Werther*'s been written already,
> And nowadays the very air smells of death:
> To open a window is to open your veins.[41]

Other items in the collection *Themes and Variations* include the much-quoted lyric "Poetry." As a call for verse to treat mundane topics in a straightforward manner the poem looks forward to the post-1940 Pasternak, but it does so in a sequence of conceits in the complex manner of his youth. Poetry is not "the euphuists's pomposity," but "summer with a third-class seat; / Suburb, not refrain." Poetry is also the stuffy Yamskaya (Moscow's red-light district) and the nocturnal Shevardino Redoubt (a feature of the battlefield at Borodino in 1812). Above all, poetry is the essence of simplicity, an idea that Pasternak quirkily expresses in his reality-dislocating final stanza.

> O Poetry, when under tap
> Stands truism empty as zinc bucket,
> Yet still the stream remains intact
> With notebook under it — so flow![42]

Part Two

For comets' path is

Poet's path. Disbonded links between
Cause and effect — they are his glue! Scanning the skies
Will get you nowhere: bards' eclipses are
Unscheduled in your almanacs.

MARINA TSVETAYEVA, 1923

6

HERBS FOR ALIEN TRIBE

By early 1921 Russia was at peace after nearly seven years of foreign and civil war, but future prospects remained disquieting. Outbreaks of resistance to Red authority — including the Kronstadt sailors' mutiny and peasant revolts — helped to aggravate the privations inflicted by years of fighting, as did the devastating famine that continued into 1922. Yet even opponents of Bolshevism were relieved to find themselves living under a government no longer exposed to effective challenge, for by now almost any form of rule appeared preferable to the anarchy and massacres of recent years. That the worst sufferings were over seemed confirmed by a major change of policy in 1921: the suspension of War Communism — the ruthless command economy of recent years — and its replacement by a modified and restricted form of restored capitalism, the New Economic Policy (NEP).

The prospects for intellectual life now appeared especially favourable. Book publishing was resumed at home, no steps yet being taken by the authorities to prevent Russia-based writers from issuing their work abroad. They availed themselves of this opportunity so freely that Berlin, and later Paris, became centres of comparable importance to Petrograd and Moscow for the publication of new Russian literary works. A book might even be brought out independently in Russia and abroad in the same year — as was Tsvetayeva's *Tsar-Maiden,* separately issued in Moscow and Berlin in 1922.

For a few years home-based Russians were also permitted to travel abroad, sampling emigration without committing themselves to it, while the self-expatriated could freely return to their native country — officially designated, from December 1922, as the USSR or Soviet Union. Future émigrés and future Soviet citizens could now confer in Berlin cafés without even knowing, or yet being obliged to decide, where they would eventually choose to live. Some authors who seemed to have embraced emigration — for example, Aleksey Tolstoy and Andrey Bely — decided to return home after a few years; others, including Tsvetayeva, expatriated themselves on a long-term basis; while members of a third category (Pasternak among them) seized the opportunity to make brief sallies from their homeland into Western countries.

Freedom to travel and publish helped to make the first years of peacetime Soviet rule remarkably mild by comparison with former rigours and future horrors. But the period had its harsher aspects too, and the temptation to regard it as a cultural utopia must be resisted. Any such impression was brutally dispelled in summer 1921 with the execution of Akhmatova's divorced husband, Nikolay Gumilyov, on political charges. Himself a considerable poet and the leading spirit of the Acmeist group, Gumilyov had been arrested by the Petrograd Cheka for complicity in the Tagantsev affair — an alleged counter-revolutionary conspiracy organized by a professor at the city's university. After the poet had been in custody for a few weeks an announcement appeared in the press to the effect that he had been shot, together with sixty others. Part of the announcement read "Gumilyov, Nikolay Stepanovich, aged thirty-three, former member of the gentry, philologian, poet . . . former officer . . . actively promoted the composition of a counter-revolutionary proclamation." He was also accused of plotting to bring about a counter-revolutionary rising in Petrograd.[1] The sinister episode is a reminder of the dangers to which citizens of the new state were exposed even in an era of relative tolerance. This remains true even though the oppressions of the OGPU — successor to the Cheka — were at first on a smaller scale than had been customary during the Civil War.

The immediate effect of Gumilyov's execution on his former wife, Anna Akhmatova, was to intensify the sombre tone dominant in the small spate of lyrics with which she briefly resumed creative work in late 1921. In one of these she speaks as a Cassandra rehearsing old memories.

> I have called ruin on my dear ones;
> They have fallen one by one.
> It was my word, alas,
> Foredoomed those graves.
> As ravens, wheeling, sniff
> Hot, fresh blood —
> So my love, exulting,
> Has sent forth wild songs.

Another particularly haunting lyric begins

> Fear, fingering objects in the dark,
> Directs moonbeam to axe.
> Sinister rap beyond wall.
> Rats? Ghost? Burglar?

The poet is so distressed by her mysterious fears that she would prefer any terror which she could see and understand.

> Better glint of rifle
> Barrels sighted at my breast.
>
> Better I should, on village green,
> Lie me down on rough scaffold
> And bleed, to gleeful shrieks and groans,
> All my red blood out.

Another lyric of the period also depicts an execution, and was presumably suggested by that of Gumilyov."You shall not be among the living, / You shall not rise from the snow. . . . So dearly does it love heart's blood, / Does Russia's earth."[2] Akhmatova's lyrics often echo the language of folk poetry, as has been noted, and she went out of her way to evoke such resonances when writing a moving verse obituary of Aleksandr Blok, who had died only a few days before Gumilyov's execution. She also weaves in the idiom of the Russian Church.

> Day of Smolensk Madonna.
> Blue incense uncoils over grass.
> Requiem's chant wells forth —
> Bright, no longer sombre.
> And red-cheeked widows bring
> Boys and girls to graveyard
> To see fathers' graves.
> And graveyard is nightingales' grove,
> Hushed in sun's shining.
> We have borne to the Smolensk Intercessor,
> We have borne to the Holy Mother
> In our arms in silver coffin,
> Our sun set in anguish —
> Pure, swan-like Aleksandr.[3]

The biblical motif is sustained in the three poems on prominent Old Testament women which form a small self-contained enclave within Akhmatova's work of the period. These heroines are Rachel, wife of Jacob; Michal, who loved David; and Lot's wife. Akhmatova portrays the last-mentioned as she follows her husband into exile, tormented by the temptation to look back

> At darling Sodom's red towers,
> The square where she sang, the yard where she span;
> At empty windows of tall house
> Where she bore her dear husband children.

After describing the celebrated conversion into a pillar of salt, the poem ends as follows.

> Yet never shall my heart forget her
> Who gave her life for one last glance.

Many years later Tsvetayeva was to maintain that the final couplet of "Lot's Wife" spoils the poem, and that "feeble endings tailing off and leading nowhere" are frequent in Akhmatova's work as a whole.[4]

Akhmatova remained as resolutely opposed to emigration at the end of the Civil War as she had been at the beginning. Expressing her pity or contempt for exile, as now experienced by many hundreds of thousands of Russians in the aftermath of Red victory, she reaffirms the stoicism with which she was always to meet her many tribulations. She also claims that her native country possesses a similar capacity for surviving the most extreme ordeals.

> I'm not with those who left our land
> For foes to rend.
> To their crude fawning I am deaf.
> My songs they shall not have.
>
> Yet always do I pity outcasts —
> As prisoners, as the sick.
> Dark is thy path, O Wanderer,
> Alien corn has wormwood tang.
>
> But here, where holocaust's crass fumes
> Ravage what's left of youth,
> No single blow
> Has made us quail.
>
> We know the final reckoning
> Shall vindicate each hour.
> We are the ones that weep the least,
> The haughtiest, the simplest.[5]

Though Akhmatova's vogue, both as a woman and as a poet, had been sustained throughout the Civil War, the political atmosphere of peacetime made her seem more and more obsolete. She was repeatedly contrasted with Mayakovsky — that poet of modernity rampant, machinery militant, revolution triumphant, and Bolshevism exultant — while her lyrics increasingly incurred censure, as did those of the other three poets, for sounding discordant notes in an era of boundless hopes and expectations. Here (their enemies argued) was a heroic people engaged in building a new society, in which no voice, however exquisitely modulated, deserved a hearing if it expressed personal and private concerns. Not that any of the four poets was exclusively narcissistic, for all were paying increasing attention to the world around them while focusing less on their individual egos. Such is the common evolution of maturing poets, even without any revolution to concentrate their thoughts. But it was not enough, in this rapidly evolving society, for authors merely to devote greater attention to the external scene; they were also required to extol the new way of life along certain increasingly prescribed lines.

This atmosphere helps to explain why Akhmatova suspended the writing of new verse in 1922, and was to preserve a creative silence, broken only by a few isolated lyrics, for some thirteen years. Her output consequently falls into two distinct periods: before 1923, and from 1936 onwards. Mandelstam, Pasternak, and Tsvetayeva were also to reduce or suspend the writing of lyrics by the mid-twenties, though none of them was to preserve as long a silence as Akhmatova.

Ironically enough, Akhmatova's silent years were heralded by a lyric, "To the Many," in which she claims that she no longer speaks for herself alone but for her contemporaries as a whole.

> I am your voice, your breath's glow;
> I — your mirrored face.

Despite this claim (dated September 1922) to represent the multitude, the poem ends by obliquely announcing the suspension of creativity which was to follow it.

> I now would be — forgotten.[6]

The news of Gumilyov's death reached Mandelstam in Tiflis, for by the summer of 1921 he was again wandering the southern marches of the former Russian Empire. But he was no longer alone. Leaving Petrograd and his collapsed love affair with Olga Arbenina early in the year, he had proceeded to Kiev and rejoined his former love, Nadezhda Khazina. Together they travelled the newly Bolshevized south: the same general area — including the Ukraine, the southwest of European Russia and the Caucasus — that the poet had so hazardously toured in 1918–20, when the region had been under White or independent control, and when he had been in danger of execution as a supposed Bolshevik agent. The young lovers registered their marriage in the course of these journeys, and they were never again to be long separated until the poet was arrested for the last time in 1938.

Mandelstam's bride was a woman of rare strength and resilience, but she delightedly submitted — according to her own account — to the despotic demands of her husband. The hypersensitive Osip had not previously revealed potentialities so tyrannical; but here he was, treating her like some prey that he had captured and dragged to his kennel. He isolated her, adapting her to his ways in small things as well as great: he would think nothing of snatching a lighted cigarette from her lips and annexing it as his own. Their union was marked from the start by a carefree spirit paradoxically combined with awareness that both were doomed to eventual persecution or death inflicted by the new society of which they were now witnessing the birth pangs.

Even as early as 1922 Mandelstam was already expressing his concern at having involved his wife in the fate of a doomed poet. In one lyric he reverts to antique Greek inspiration, comparing his bride to Europa and himself to the Bull: the guise in which Zeus abducts that hapless but eventually triumphant heroine and carries her off on his back over the sea.

> Pink foam of weariness at soft lips,
> Ragingly cleaves green billows Bull:
> Snorting, hating the paddling, uxorious,
> Unused to backbone's load and great toil.
>
> Out swoops occasional dolphin's wheeling leap,
> Out periodical bristling sea urchin pops.
> Hold on, Europa, clasp your tender arms.
> Where can be found more desirable yoke for neck?
>
> Grievingly hearkens Europa to powerful splash.
> Ponderous ocean around her boils and spouts.
> Visibly dreading waters' oily gleam,
> Gladly she'd slither off those matted bluffs.
>
> Ah, dearer far to her is rowlocks' creak,
> Broadly extending boat-deck, drove of sheep.

Dearer is glittering fish-flash beyond high poop.
Oarlessly sweeping her onward, paddler swims.[7]

One of Mandelstam's most sensitive interpreters has said that this poem
cannot be rated among his highest artistic achievements,[8] but this is
surely too harsh a verdict.

From the seas and mountains of the south the Bull bore Europa
back in the spring of 1922 to Moscow, where they secured lodgings
in Herzen House — the large apartment block assigned wholesale to
writers in accordance with the new society's policy of concentrating
members of each profession in close proximity to each other. But the
Mandelstams lost these quarters in the following summer through an
unfortunate practical joke, and were compelled to stay with one of Osip
Emilyevich's brothers, or to accept other unsatisfactory temporary ar-
rangements. Throughout their life together they were never able to
make a stable home.

By 1923 the relaxations of the first peacetime years were yielding
to a harsher atmosphere as the new society braced itself to pioneer a
glorious new era in human relations. Writers now became increasingly
polarized into "us" (pro-régime) and "them" (anti-régime), as Mandel-
stam's widow has explained. To become one of "them" was all too easy.
There was no need to publish material ideologically abhorrent to Bol-
shevism: it was enough merely to ignore such vital issues as industriali-
zation, agricultural output, and workers' morale — and thus gain the
reputation of being "out of tune with the epoch." Few authors of lyric
poetry — so highly personal, often, in its themes and inspiration —
could have escaped censure and persecution in such a context.

With Gumilyov out of the way, Mandelstam and Akhmatova be-
came the first surviving Russian writers of note to fall foul of the new
dispensation. Their disgrace became distinctly apparent from 1923 on-
wards.

Mandelstam's famous lyric "The Age" demonstrates how far he
was from endorsing the political enthusiasms of his era, as fostered by
official propaganda. That the shedding of blood may be a necessary
condition for constructing a new society — as the breaking of eggs for
constructing an omelette — is a familiar politicians' thesis. In his first
stanza Mandelstam seems to accept it, but only tentatively. His Age is
a wounded beast, an object of pity rather than fear, and he asks who is
to diagnose its ills and cure its broken backbone.

My Age, my beast, who shall contrive
To look into thy pupils?

> Who with his blood shall glue
> Two centuries' vertebrae together?
> Blood the builder gushes
> From living creatures' throats.
> None but a parasite shall tremble
> On new era's brink.

In the middle of the poem Mandelstam answers his own search for a potential healer of his Age by implying that only the creative artist can achieve this feat of surgery. The poet's flute is a symbol for his own art.

> To snatch the Age from durance,
> To start new world —
> Joints of nodular days
> Must be bonded by flute.

In his penultimate stanza he invokes the invigorating atmosphere of spring, but continues in a pessimistic vein unlikely to restore his status as an officially accepted poet in an age of self-conscious optimism.

> And buds shall yet swell,
> Sputtering greenery shoot.
> But your spinal column's smashed,
> My lovely, wretched Age!
> And with senseless grin
> You look back, cruel and weak,
> Like beast once supple
> At own paws' prints.[9]

Mandelstam's unease is further reflected in his other, increasingly rare, poems of the period. One begins with a couplet dissociating its author from the current assumption that writers had the obligation to reflect the burning issues of the day by cultivating "contemporary" themes.

> No. Never was I anyone's contemporary. No one's.
> Such honour is too great for me.[10]

In "First of January 1924" Mandelstam directly refers to the silencing of his Muse even as it is in process of being imposed.

> I know life's puff weakens daily.
> Soon they'll curtail

My simple song of earthen sufferings;
Seal lips with lead.

Again addressing his Age, which he now describes as expiring, the poet
fears "That only he shall understand thee,/Who wears the helpless smile
of one/Who has mislaid himself." To write poetry under these condi-
tions is "To collect herbs for alien tribe by night."[11]

It was now, even as Mandelstam was poised to suspend poetic
creativity, that he wrote "Horseshoe Finder" — a triumphant evocation
of art's capacity to survive disaster throughout the ages. He described
it as a Pindaric fragment; and it is indeed Pindaric in its élan and
preoccupation with horses. But the metre is un-Pindarically free; and
this — combined with the avoidance of rhyme — makes the poem
exceptional in Mandelstam's work. It also happens to be his longest
poem.

The thesis is art's capacity to survive catastrophe, as the long-
abandoned Horseshoe preserves for its Finder the essence of the living
creature to which it was once attached. At the end of the poem Mandel-
stam changes the image by likening the transmission of art throughout
the ages to the discovery of ancient buried coins.

Sound still vibrates, though sound's cause be gone.
Horse lies in dust, lathered; snorts.
But neck's sharp wrench
Still commemorates flurry of galloping hooves,
When they were not four,
But numberless as road's cobbles,
Renewed in foursomes
With fiery, mettlesome trotter's every thrust from ground.
Thus
Finder
Blows dust off Horseshoe,
Rubs it gleaming with wool;
Then
Hangs it on lintel.
Let it rest.
Never need it cut sparks from flint again.
Human lips, having no more to say,
Retain form of last word spoken.
Hand retains sense of weight
Though pitcher
  be half spilt
    while carried home.

What I now say is not said by me,
But dug from soil as fossilized wheat grains.
Some
      depict a lion on coins.
Others
      a head.
Sundry copper, gold, bronze flakes —
Equally honoured — lie in earth.
Trying to munch them, age has etched its tooth prints.
Time cuts me like coin.
I haven't got enough me left.[12]

This is one of the finest of the few lyrics — barely a score — that Mandelstam wrote between the end of the Civil War and his period of poetic silence from 1926 until 1930.

As his output of poetry declined, Mandelstam found himself drawn into journalism. One curiosity in his published work is an article on an obscure young Indochinese whom he interviewed at length, and who later became famous as the North Vietnamese leader Ho Chi Minh. More noteworthy, to students of Russian poetry, are the poet's short, incisive, impressionistic, scintillating, and occasionally brash excursions into literary criticism. In these Pasternak earns high praise for the harmony of his verses, and for pioneering a new poetic mode "without playing tricks." Mandelstam stresses the need to study his colleague's art seriously, also expressing the hope that Pasternak's work will not release a torrent of "lyrical inanities" such as all recent poets, from Blok onwards, have provoked from their critics and admirers.[13]

Mandelstam's admiration for Pasternak may be contrasted with his harsh comments on the other two poets. The "Madonna-like needlework" of Tsvetayeva's verses is said to augur ill for Moscow's literary future, while her lyrics on the theme of Russia are described as tasteless, historically inaccurate, pseudo-folksy, pseudo-Muscovite, and much inferior to the writings of Adalis, a long-forgotten poetess of the period; *her* voice — says Mandelstam — "occasionally attains masculine force and sincerity." Akhmatova is similarly dismissed, as a vulgarizer of the Symbolist poet Annensky, though she is credited with success in cultivating folk idiom such as "permits us to sense the Russian peasant woman in the twentieth-century Russian literary lady." Mandelstam's general verdict: "The worst thing about literary Moscow is its female poetry."[14]

The female poets of the period fare even worse in Trotsky's *Literature and Revolution*. Deriding the religious element in Akhmatova's

verse, the Bolshevik leader complains that her God is too gentlemanly
— a fashionable doctor with an excellent bedside manner, a specialist in
women's ailments. "How this personage, no longer young and bur-
dened with personal and often most troublesome errands from Akh-
matova, Tsvetayeva, and the rest, still contrives to cope with the fate of
the universe in his spare time — this baffles all comprehension."[15]

7

REBEL IN HEAD AND WOMB

THERE was a tendency for Russia's newly arisen poetesses to attract amused condescension, as is illustrated by comments of Mandelstam and Trotsky cited in the previous chapter. One grotesque episode of the period was a collective recital by lady versifiers staged in Moscow's Polytechnic Museum early in 1921 by the Symbolist poet Valery Bryusov. But his "Poetesses' Evening" did not proceed according to plan, and that was due to the participation of Marina Tsvetayeva, whom a Bryusov might patronize only at his peril, and whose attitude to the solemn occasion was, to put it mildly, sardonic. Besides, she believed that "assignability to the male or female gender is not one of the more significant criteria for assessing poetic worth." As for creativity in general, she maintained that "the Woman Question is out of place. But there are . . . one or two Woman Answers. . . . Sappho, Joan of Arc, St. Teresa."[1]

Tsvetayeva's truculence, antisuggestibility, persistence in championing lost causes, and casual willingness to risk arrest as a counter-revolutionary were fully demonstrated at the poetesses' recital of 1921. While the other participants dithered around at the beginning of the proceedings, decked in such finery as shattered Moscow could still provide, each coyly effacing herself and waiting for someone else to begin, Marina Ivanovna strode forward. She was grotesquely garbed in an old green dress cut like a cassock. Her slender waist was girt with a military belt as worn by officer cadets, and she had a brown leather officer's pouch slung over one shoulder. Peering shortsightedly at her notebook, she proceeded to declaim in a loud, clear voice a sequence of her own most militantly monarchist lyrics, including some of the pro-White and anti-Bolshevik poems that were later to be published in *Swan Encampment.* Yet she was greeted with deafening applause from an audience of Red Army men, Red Army cadets, and assorted Communist

Party members. Could these respectable citizens suddenly have become politically disaffected? According to Tsvetayeva they had simply failed to understand. (Besides, they always were required to applaud whenever they attended a public meeting.) In any case there was nothing obscure about these particular items. The point was, according to their author, that no one understands any poetry whatever when encountering it for the first time, and in recited form. Why, then, do audiences flock to poetry recitals — a practice more common in Russia than in many another country? Not because they are concerned with poetry's meaning, Tsvetayeva suggests, without offering any explanation beyond a single dry and surely indisputable comment: "Poetesses' Evenings have nothing to do with poetry anyway."

Tsvetayeva has explained that she had five distinct motives for reciting these particular works at the Poetesses' Evening. First, she wanted to show that there was at least one woman who could declaim a string of her own lyrics without ever using the first person singular, or making any reference to love. Secondly, she wanted to test her theory that all verse is always wholly unintelligible to all audiences. Even so, she hoped (thirdly and inconsistently) that she might yet establish communication with some isolated sensitive individual. Fourthly, she regarded it as a matter of honour to champion the White cause publicly in Red Moscow. Her fifth and final motive: "Let's see what happens."

Barely credible though it must seem, the fact is that Tsvetayeva stood up in public in this, the fourth year of the Soviet régime, to declaim such lines as "Hurrah! For the Tsar! Hurrah!" And she robustly affirmed her own independence in an age of growing submissiveness.

Placing hand on heart,
I'm no lady of quality,
But a rebel in head and womb.

So much for her boast that she had avoided the first person singular. Still, she never made a truer claim for herself, and the remark shows how ill-adapted she was for a "revolutionary" society in which (now that the revolution had been successfully accomplished) the need was for pliant conformists — and certainly not for rebels in head, womb, or anywhere else.

In the end Tsvetayeva's taboo-breaking recital was cut short by an "imperiously beseeching whisper" from the chair. Bryusov, if no one else, had taken in enough to appreciate the need to terminate a flow of words so stridently out of tune with his — if not with her — epoch. She had been typically brave and foolhardy, and perhaps more than a little lucky. One wonders, for example, whether the executed Gumilyov's "counter-revolutionary" activity included any sins more flagrantly offensive to the new public order.[2]

In the early 1920s Tsvetayeva not only remained the most prolific of the four poets, but she was also the one who most strenuously sought to probe the limits of her art by persistent experiment. Her work consequently became far more difficult, far less penetrable, than it had previously been. The transition may be monitored in the volume *Craft*, containing lyrics written between April 1921 and April 1922. It progresses from *The Pupil*, the cycle of easily intelligible verse with which the collection begins, to the obscure, incantational, and folkloristic *Alleyways*, with which it ends. This evolution was accompanied by continuing metrical experiment, enhancing the verses' dynamic impact, while the poet was also extending her vocabulary by intensified use of folk language, archaisms, and Biblical idiom. Through audacious ellipses she made her readers work harder, conveying a whole spread of meaning and emotions with economy that had earlier eluded her.

Though it is instructive to monitor the technical innovations in *Craft*, they are perhaps more significant as indications of future prowess than of current achievement, for the level of the lyrics is uneven. Among the least effective are the numerous addresses of homage that she continues to direct at individuals. For example, her new lyrics to the recently deceased Blok are inferior, with their sometimes injudicious use of religious imagery, to those that she had addressed several years earlier to the same poet in life. Similarly, though her professions of devotion to Prince Sergey Volkonsky (an elderly friend) contain some scintillating lines, they are for the most part insipid — not least where she anticipates the Prince's death by offering to commit suttee on his behalf.

> Oh, to be first with smile ecstatic
> To climb on to thy pyre.[3]

More robust, more in tune with the Tsvetayeva of the future, are her verses in praise of Mayakovsky, that flamboyant, rugged young poet of her own age.

> Singer of miracles in city squares,
> Proud plebeian — I hail you,
> Heavyweight, for choosing stone to work in,
> Unseduced by diamonds.[4]

Other objects of poetic homage included the poet's absent husband, Sergey, last heard of as an officer of the defeated White forces in Russia. While still a missing person so far as his wife knew, he figured prominently as the subject of two new cycles of verse. A third followed in July 1921, after she had learnt that he had survived the war and made his way into Western European emigration.

> Lark dropped me
> News from sky —
> You're over seas,
> Not over clouds.

Marina also tells Sergey that her thoughts have followed him to foreign cities, just as they had been with him throughout the battles on the Don; the clock that he has wound up in her breast has never rusted; she would rather face a firing squad than marry another. She refers to his dominion over her heart yet more hyperbolically.

> Know that in Red Russia
> There's still autocracy.[5]

From the absent Sergey the poet's thoughts easily turned to militant pro-White sentiments such as she had previously expressed in *Swan Encampment*. She even calls for a renewal of the Civil War in one of the lyrics addressed to her White officer husband.

> In vengeance' name
> Hold fast, my Winged One!
> Transition's hour has struck;
> Reckoning's yet shall. . . .
>
> Where, on steep
> Euxine's shore,
> Flight's hooves then thumped —
> Victory's yet shall.[6]

As much of this material indicates, Tsvetayeva was not always at her best when professing her devotion to defunct or lost individuals and causes. She could be more at home with invective, as was made clear on 9 February 1922, when she denounced the entire Russian Revolution, together with its pretensions to inaugurate a global upheaval, in a broadside directed at her country and what, to her, was its squalid folly of the last few years. She pillories herself and her fellow citizens as bears, as Tatars, as scabs and leprosy incarnate, as arsonists consumed by lice who have "humped universe's hatred on back."

> Russia's star
> Against all!
>
> Whither, patricides?
> Into what tomfoolery?
> Mind you don't come unstuck,
> O universal scourge![7]

In these early postwar poems Tsvetayeva further develops the theme of sexual renunciation. It is expressed in the sardonically entitled cycle *In Praise of Aphrodite,* in which the poet taunts the Love Goddess with her traditional trappings — her doves, her birth in the sea's foam.

> Frail froth, sea salt,
> All foam and pain —
> How long shalt thou be obeyed,
> Armless stone?

The poet herself is now immune from the lures of the Love Goddess. "Beating against my throne's calm, / Thou — foam-born — perish as foam."[8]

Allied to the theme of sexual renunciation is Tsvetayeva's growing conviction, as she approaches the end of her twenties, that her own youth is over. She has outgrown it; she looks back on it as a snake at its sloughed skin, also feeling like a swallow all too rapidly metamorphosed into a witch.

> Youth, farewell. . . .
> Let us stand in the breeze together.
> Dusky-complexioned, comfort thy sister. . . .
>
> I part from thee as from my lover.
> Torn from my breast's depth,
> My youth — go now to others.[9]

Love renounced also figures in a notable poem of some two hundred lines written in January 1921: *On Red Steed.* Its theme is the renunciation of everything in life — childhood, love, religion — for the sake of Art, but not of Art as incarnated in some kindly, beneficent, pipe-playing Muse such as Akhmatova was accustomed to invoke.

Tsvetayeva's genius is infinitely the more eruptive and savage: a mysterious armoured, winged, plumed Rider. Stern, violent, imperious, he intervenes on his red charger to rescue her from three fantastic nightmare predicaments vaguely redolent of folklore. First, her soul is ablaze like a house from which the Rider rescues a doll — but then commands her to break it, so that she may liberate herself from Love; it is known from other sources that dolls symbolized unreciprocated affection to the child Tsvetayeva.[10] Then the poet hides from a raging blizzard in a mysterious "hundred-cupolaed temple," and is about to consecrate herself to the crucified Saviour when up careers the Rider and restrains her through a hoof placed on her breast. Finally, he appears on a violent, dimly discerned battlefield to claim her as his own.

The poem's conclusion affirms its creator's unconditional dedication to an art too violently explosive to be inspired by so passive an emblem as a Muse.

> Not, not Muse; not kinship's
> Frail bonds; not thy fetters,
> Friendship. By no woman's fingers, by fell hand
> Is taut on me
> This knot. . . .
>
> Dumb witness
> Of live storms,
> I recline; observe
> Shadows,
>
> Until swept
> Into the blue
> On Red Steed by
> My Genius.[11]

In the spring of 1922, just as Tsvetayeva was preparing to leave Moscow and Russia for emigration, she received an unexpected visit from Osip and Nadezhda Mandelstam. The occasion was not a success, for though Marina Ivanovna immediately greeted her lover of 1916 with an ecstatic "Akh!" she barely acknowledged his wife, scarce deigning even to shake hands. She took Osip Emilyevich to see little Alya, leaving Nadezhda Yakovlevna to wait outside, on the grounds that the child "couldn't bear strangers." This cavalier behaviour turned Mandelstam "green with fury." Nor was Marina's rudeness mitigated by her domestic environment — "dust, dirt, and ruin," with a sort of "witch-like" element added: a grimy lamp, obviously uncleaned since the Revolution, spread no light but rather darkness visible. Mandelstam was so enraged by the discourtesy to his wife that he would only mouth a few monosyllables in "an ultra-Petersburg accent," instead of picking the quarrel that would have cleared the air. The visit was abruptly terminated.[12]

This was the last meeting of two of Russia's greatest twentieth-century poets, as caustically recorded nearly fifty years later by Nadezhda Mandelstam. But it is no less characteristic of that inspired memoirist, who can be generous as well as cantankerous, that she also pays admiring tribute to her husband's ex-mistress. In Nadezhda Mandelstam's eyes Tsvetayeva's genius was sufficient excuse for her minor eccentricities and discourtesies. She tells us that Tsvetayeva, whose hair was bobbed and who walked like a boy, made an impression of absolute naturalness combined with breathtaking capriciousness. Her voice reminded one of her verse. She could never have cultivated an Akhmatova's self-discipline. Reading her poems and letters, Nadezhda Yakovlevna later came to realize that Tsvetayeva "sought ecstasy and maximum emotive content everywhere and in all things. She craved love's raptures — but also those of being deserted and abandoned, of being a failure." In this attitude the memoirist discerned rare nobility of spirit, regretting only Marina Ivanovna's total indifference to anyone who could make no direct contribution to her emotional orgies.

Far from nursing any grievance against Tsvetayeva, Nadezhda Mandelstam has bracketed her and Akhmatova as "two authentic and brilliant women as far above myself as a star in the sky." Both Tsvetayeva and Akhmatova managed to squeeze the uttermost drop of joy and suffering from love, according to the same witness, who also says that their volcanic passions rendered them liable to intense gusts of jealousy; Akhmatova even claimed herself prepared to strangle a rival with her bare hands, believing any woman incapable of jealousy to be a total mediocrity.[13]

Few aspects of Tsvetayeva's creative evolution are more astonishing than the extent to which she took self-imposed exile in her stride. Far from cutting short her career as a working poet, her abandonment of Russia in May 1922 coincided with her emergence as a writer of the front rank. This first occurred through verse composed before her departure — part of the numerous Russian writings that had been unpublishable during the Civil War, and were now released to the presses in bulk. And so it came about that Tsvetayeva, who had not brought out a new book since 1913, suddenly emerged in 1922–23 with a very spate of new material, individual volumes being issued in Moscow or Berlin according to convenience, or even in both. They include items already discussed — *Mileposts* and *Craft,* the folk-epic *Tsar-Maiden,* the collected poems to Blok — as well as two other small collections, *Parting* and *Psyche.* This work, all written before the poet's emigration, at once focused attention on her and was much appreciated by the many Russian poets, critics, and editors whom she met in summer 1922 in Berlin cafés. Among those who praised her or helped to place her work were Balmont, Bely, and Ehrenburg. They were quick to acclaim her as a major talent, and she had not been long on foreign soil before she found herself rated the equal of Akhmatova, that reigning queen of Russian poetesses. Tsvetayeva was, however, soon to become a controversial figure among Russian émigrés. Some of them found it difficult to accept the succession of daring technical ingenuities cultivated — not in every instance successfully — by so original an artist. Others objected to her refusal to adopt the militant anti-Soviet posture now cultivated in many émigré circles.

Even as Tsvetayeva's pre-exile material was appearing in so many volumes, not to mention isolated items that were still being published in periodicals, she was continuing to maintain a high rate of poetic productivity stimulated rather than interrupted by so significant a change of life as the abandonment of her native country. She was not only more prolific than ever during her first few years of emigration, but she was also writing finer poetry than ever before. This applies particularly to the collection *After Russia,* and to the long elegies *Poem of the Hill* and *Poem of the End.* Tsvetayeva's Prague period also includes other major items, to be discussed later: the verse play *Ariadne* and two more folk epics, *The Swain* and *Rat-Catcher,* besides a number of prose articles. Few poets, Russian or non-Russian, have generated so spectacular a creative eruption over a mere four-year period.

The bulk of this material was written in Czechoslovakia, where Tsvetayeva — reunited at last with her husband, Sergey Efron — was to live until late 1925. The Efrons first set up house in a small village within easy reach of Prague, where the Czech government maintained a university for Russian émigrés. Here Efron enrolled as a student, along with many other former officers of the White Russian armies; he was awarded a scholarship, while Marina herself — in common with many other Russian émigrés — also received a small subsidy from the Czechs. Despite this financial support and Marina's sporadic income from émigré Russian journals, the Efrons suffered severe privations in their new homeland. Tsvetayeva seemed to spend nearly all her time shopping, cooking, cleaning, caring for her daughter Alya, and coping with the eccentricities of a recalcitrant stove. These obligations were so oppressive, especially the last-mentioned, that — as she wrote to Pasternak in November 1922 — her conditions of life were possibly worse than they had been in Moscow,[14] where she had been similarly engaged during the Civil War in circumstances desperate even by the standards of that grim period. Yet her literary creativity was even less impaired by the rigours of domesticity in the environs of Prague than it had been in the heart of Muscovy.

The Efrons' marriage had already proved its durability in pre-revolutionary years by surviving the frequent, intense "crushes" that the wife had conceived for so many other men, quite apart from those of her love affairs that had not remained on the purely cerebral plane. But these episodes had not seriously undermined her relationship with her adored Sergey, and mutual tolerance continued into her Czech period. During these years the poet was periodically separated from her husband, but also periodically reunited with him, and in February 1925 she bore his third child — a boy whom they named Georgy.

Meanwhile she had experienced — suffered rather — two particularly intense love affairs outside marriage. One of these characteristically reached an advanced stage of intensity before she had even met the young man in question — the literary critic Aleksandr Bakhrakh, with whom she conducted one of her many passionate correspondences. Investing him with an array of imagined qualities, she fell profoundly in love with the romantic image created by herself, only to be cruelly disappointed when he eventually turned out an unwilling target for feelings so excessive. This was a shock, but Tsvetayeva herself was now beginning to realize — it was by no means the first or last such episode in her life — that people were horrified by the emotions which they aroused in her.

She who had always expected — even demanded — that love should generate pain was plunged into still greater misery by a second, yet more passionate, brief encounter in late 1923 with another young Russian — a former White officer. She became his mistress, and was traumatized into a spasm of glorious creativity when the affair collapsed after a few months. According to a friend who knew both parties, the young man "was bowled over and terrified by the tidal wave of Marina's impetuosity, and fled from the storm into the quiet refuge of bourgeois domesticity and a respectable marriage."[15] The episode also provided the impulse for the two superb verse sequences *Poem of the Hill* and *Poem of the End,* both written in early 1924.

These laments for a past love have been rated by Nadezhda Mandelstam, and not by her alone, as the most powerful of all Tsvetayeva's works.[16] The hill of the earlier poem was a real hill in Prague, on which

she had been accustomed to meet her lover. This bare knoll, with its
military barracks, had once possessed the enchantments of paradise for
Marina and her lover. But their love is denied the prospect "Of family's
quiet charms, / Of fledglings' babble," and when love ends, its passing
is mourned by the hill itself as part of the transitoriness of the *rerum
natura.*

> Hill grieved, that what is today —
> Rome, the World — shall be but smoke.
> Hill grieved that we're both destined to others.
> (I little envy those others!)

The poem foresees the hill as infested with dwellings and peopled by
conformist bourgeois such as the poet — now Bohemian in two senses
of the word — utterly despised. But the complacent suburbanite of the
future will discover that the seemingly harmless hill is the crater of an
active volcano — to Tsvetayeva's delight, as she goes on to pronounce
a potent curse on smug flat-dwellers who will have the impertinence to
enjoy a happy love denied to her. Those ants shall know no content-
ment. May their daughters become whores and bear bastards. May their
sons waste their substance on Gipsies, and — direst imprecation of all
— end as poets! Developed in emigration, this vituperative, satirical vein
reveals a new, more robust Tsvetayeva.[17]

The longer *Poem of the End* traces the same lovers' parting. After
the young man has indicated to the poet that he wishes to end their
affair, they wander Prague together, revisiting all their familiar haunts
and postponing the moment of final separation. Strolling through the
city, they pass along the river embankment, turn in at a café, and go
through the Jewish quarter, where she recognizes the inhabitants as
fellow outcasts, rendered such by their race.

> In this most Christian world
> Poets are Yids.[18]

The narrative sections of the poem are taut, economical, elliptical, and
syntactically crisp, in accordance with Tsvetayeva's new manner, while
the no less laconic conversation between the two lovers punctuates
staccato reports on the townscape and the poet's emotional state. A high
degree of concentration is required from her reader, so intensely has she
developed the use of colloquialisms, archaisms, folk idioms, and creative
omissions. Other Russian poets had combined these elements, but has
any ever done so with such force? An example is the untranslatable line

which comes as near as three words can to expressing Tsvetayeva's fundamental conviction that love is above all a nonevent: a failure to hold and keep the beloved, or even a failure to meet him in the first place. Here, with typical élan, she has converted the preposition *mimo* ("by," "past") into a neuter noun.

> *Lyubovnik — sploshnoye mimo.* [19]

"A lover is the very essence of that which bypasses or comes to be bypassed"; a cruder translation might be "Love is missing out on everything."

At a time when the three Russia-based poets had all much reduced their output, the indomitable Tsvetayeva was not only writing the longer poems already discussed, and certain others to be examined below, but was also composing — first in Berlin and then in Prague — the lyrics of *After Russia*. It is surely the finest collection of new verse ever to be published as a single volume by any of the four poets, and consists of over a hundred and fifty short lyrics written between 1922 and 1925. The themes are strong — death, love, God, jealousy, the nature of poetry, the nature of nature. But the poet's technique is more than equal to them: daring, flexible, revelling more than ever in hyperbole, rich in surprises and tantalizing mysteries. Tsvetayeva herself makes this point while arguing two favourite contentions of poets: that they represent a special dimension in unpredictability, and that they are nature's outcasts. It is in the devastating three-lyric cycle *Poets* that she asserts "Poet's path" to be "comets' path" and claims his eclipses as "unscheduled in the almanac." As for the Poet's isolation from the human community, is he not

> One of the extras, the redundant ones,
> Unrecorded on your retinas,
> Unentered in your catalogues,
> Whose home is refuse dump?

What can the Poet, "blind stepson" that he is, achieve in a world where all others come equipped with eyes and fathers; where tears are ascribed to having caught a cold in the nose; where inspiration is confined as in a thermos flask? What, in sum, is the Poet to do

> With all that weightlessness
> In dumbbells' land. . . .
>
> With all that boundlessness
> In limits' bourns? [20]

Reverting to a favourite theme, death, Tsvetayeva cultivates a heavy incantational style in the most narcotic of her poems, which begins as follows.

> Blindly oozing Lethe's gulp,
> Discharged is thy debt — merged
> With Lethe, scarce animate
> In willows' silver-streaming burble.[21]

If *After Russia* has a principal theme it is neither death nor poets, but love that extrapolates the peculiar brand of hyper-frustration characteristic of the poet. She can surprise by the quietness of her tone, as in the short poem that calls love (without using the word) "Pain familiar as palm to eyes, / As own child's name / To lips." But her normal mode is of course tempestuously emotional, as in the well-known lyric "An Attempt at Jealousy," in which she rebukes a former lover who has had the impudence to desert her for some "ordinary" woman. "How is life with simulacrum, / For you who've trodden Sinai . . . ? / After Carrara marble, / How's life with crumbling plaster?"

> Be honest: are you happy?
> No? In trough's shallownesses
> How fare you, darling? Worse?
> As I do, with another?[22]

In her Czech period Tsvetayeva took over Mandelstam's role as Russian poetry's most impressive transmuter of ancient Greek themes. Besides writing the verse play *Ariadne* and its successor, *Phaedra,* she was also invoking those two heroines, together with Orpheus, Euridice, Achilles, and other figures from Hellenic mythology, in some of the finest lyrics of *After Russia*. They include the portrait of Helen of Troy looking down from the city's parapets at a world ruined by her beauty. Conscious that "By my nakedness four Arabies are desultrified, / Five seas depearled," Helen

> Marvels at swarm
> Of royal heirs unhoused,
> At lineages' founders swooping into fray. . . .

> At ditch
> Crammed with royal heirs;
> At fivescore genealogies' defiliation.[23]

If it is objected that "desultrified," "depearled," and "defiliation" are found in none of the dictionaries, the reply must be that this is also true of Tsvetayeva's freshly coined *obezznoyeno, obezzhemchuzheno,* and *obessynovlennost.*

Similar hyperbole is found in the passionate plaint put into the mouth of Phaedra, who has fallen in love with her stepson Hippolytus, as already celebrated by other poets from Euripides to Mandelstam. Translation unfortunately tends to reduce it to ranting.

> Hippolytus! Hippolytus! Pain!
> Burning. Blazing cheeks.
> What cruel horror lurks
> In Hippolytus' name . . . ?
>
> I'm scorched by Hippolytus.
> I swear by, rave about, Hippolytus.

Phaedra's mind is enflamed, her arms want to leave her shoulders, her teeth threaten to grind themselves to gravel, her nostrils and lips seem choked with volcanic dust. "Hippolytus, Hippolytus! Give me to drink. . . . / Here is lava, not flagstones, / Underfoot."[24]

In this and other Sappho-outsapphoing poems Tsvetayeva champions the love-crazed Phaedra against a stepson who is the complacent incarnation of male chastity. That the same poet could also praise female antisensuality, proclaiming herself immune from the lures of Aphrodite, may also be remembered. The two angles of vision are far apart, but when did the poet ever lay claim to self-consistency, being as mobile, as gloriously *varium et mutabile,* as any Verdi or Virgil could conceive? "Disbonded links between / Cause and effect" — they were (to revert once more to the cycle *Poets*) her glue. She it was who "Shuffled cards, / Outwitting weights and calculations." Whose, if not Marina Ivanovna's, were the comets' trails, the "bearded loops," the total eclipses and other astrobatics that have all gone "unscheduled in the almanacs"?[25]

The passionate rejection of male antisensuality by this sporadic apostle of female sexual renunciation also figures in some remarkable poems of *After Russia* in which Shakespeare's Hamlet is denounced as a despicable virgin and misogynist compounding the sin of failing to lust for Ophelia, like any decent, self-respecting lover, with that of incestuously and officiously interfering in his queenly mother's sex life. The Danish prince should note that virgins cannot be judges of passion.

Mixture of chalk
And corruption — bandy slanders with your bones,
Prince Hamlet! To arbitrate blood inflamed
Is undreamt of in your philosophy.

This robust onslaught on the spineless Dane surely deserves to be as well known as Pasternak's campaign to enhance the same Shakespearian figure's status as *the* symbolic hero of the modern age.[26] But though the two poets might differ over the significance of Hamlet, Pasternak himself is in a sense the chief hero of *After Russia,* for a dozen of the finest lyrics in the book were written with him in mind. Between the two poets there was little more than a nodding acquaintance, based on a few casual meetings in Moscow, where he had remained while she was living in Prague. Still, such obstacles as distance, inaccessibility, and the lack of remembered intimacy could only fuel the infatuations of Tsvetayeva, whose love thrived on absence and frustration.

In her poetic world true lovers must always be apart; it is perhaps even better if they have never met in the first place, and better still if one of them is, or both are, already dead. In any case it is their fate to "cross" *(razminutsya)* like letters in the post. Having barely met Pasternak in Moscow before her departure from Russia, Tsvetayeva had heard him give a single poetry recital, at which he kept forgetting his lines. Only when she read *My Sister Life* shortly after arriving in Berlin in mid-1922 did she begin bombarding him with a passion expressed exclusively through the pen and initially fired by a letter from him to her. His high opinion of her poetry was many times expressed in the course of his life. But she was the more militantly enthusiastic of the two, and so even more compliments are found flowing in the opposite direction. They include the ecstatic essay *Cloudburst of Light,* mentioned above, which so lavishly praises the lyrics of *My Sister Life.*

The lively correspondence between the two poets soon reached the point of familiarity at which they were calling each other "thou" — a breakthrough in intimacy which would hardly call for comment were it not that Tsvetayeva, her husband, and their children all addressed each other by the polite "you," for whatever eccentric reason. Though Pasternak's letters to Tsvetayeva are not available (they are believed to be buried in her daughter's archive in Russia), copious missives from her to him have been published. These include the obscure but tantalizing passage in which, conscious of her own irresistible drive towards frustration in love, she claims: "I could not live with you, Boris . . . not through lack of understanding, but through excess thereof. . . . Meeting you, I'd meet myself, all my sharp points turned against me." Should she ever encounter him again she would be cured of loving him in a second — just as she would were she to meet a Goethe or a Heine. She goes on to draw a distinction between "Psyche" (spiritual love) and "Eve" (sexual love). She herself is all Psyche, and has renounced men in their sexual capacity. Rarely has anyone fallen in love with her, and no one has ever shot himself on her account. "I don't understand the flesh . . . don't recognize that it has any rights." She also claims to lack sexual attractiveness; but though evidence to the contrary could be adduced, it is also true that harangues such as those in her letters to Pasternak would quickly rob the most seductive woman of appeal. Be that as it may, this particular letter forms a valuable commentary on the love poems of *After Russia,* in which Psyche rampant often seems to reach a pitch of frenzy denied even to the most Eve-like of Eves — as in the second of Tsvetayeva's two short poems on Phaedra and Hippolytus.

> Quench my soul! (Not without lips' touch
> Can our soul be quenched!) To kiss lips
> Is to kiss Psyche, lips' fluttering guest.
> Quench my soul: that is, quench my lips.[27]

The lyrics addressed to Pasternak inevitably revive the key theme of separation from the beloved.

> I shall await thee — fingers twined into wisp,
> As lover awaits Empress —
> Patiently as rhyme's awaited,
> Patiently as hands are gnawed. . . .
>
> I shall remain for thee
> A treasury of random similes, gleaned
>
> From sands and rubble, overheard
> In breezes and on railroad sleepers.[28]

In other lyrics Tsvetayeva invokes both Homer and Germanic legend for unconsummated loves comparably earthshaking to the great nonaffair of Marina and Boris. Such are her examples based on the *Iliad.* Would a poet endowed with eyesight (unlike Homer) have failed to mate Achilles and Helen, "Achaea's prime hero, / Sparta's most luscious woman"? After a passing glance at the problems of Siegfried and Brünnhilde, Achilles is also rebuked for slaughtering another suitably heroic bride, the Amazon queen Penthesilea, in battle.

They missed each other: Thetis' son
And Ares' daughter — Achilles

And Penthesilea. . . .

What though he now have but one
Urge — to snatch her from shades as wife!
Like is not destined to like.
Thus we too miss each other.[29]

A further link between the two poets is provided by Tsvetayeva's
long narrative folk-poem *The Swain*, which appeared in Prague in 1924
and is dedicated to Boris Pasternak. Like *Tsar-Maiden* before it, *The
Swain* is adapted from one of the traditional Russian folk tales in Afana-
syev's collection. It reflects yet another facet in Tsvetayeva's creatively
frenzied philosophy of love. The poem describes how a Vampire courts
a village girl, Marusya, who becomes so infatuated with her sinister
"swain" that she does nothing to stop him from fatally exercising his
special skill at the expense of her brother, of her mother, and finally of
herself. Vampirized by her lover, she magically turns into a flower, but
then — no less magically — resumes her original guise and weds a local
squire. At this point the poet replaces Afanasyev's conventional happy
ending with a twist all her own: *her* Marusya spurns her eligible earthly
husband in order to be reunited with the Vampire, and she ascends into
the heavens with that demon-lover in a pillar of fire. Similarly, the poet
had described herself as swept off into the sky by the Rider in *On Red
Steed*. Whether or not *The Swain* can be read as a comparable tribute
to the all-conquering demands of creative art, it is at least clear that its
author wished to celebrate — as in many lyrics of *After Russia* —
the destructive and all-consuming power of love. As she herself com-
mented, "Reading my Afanasyev, I wondered why Marusya, who
feared the Vampire, so stubbornly refused to admit what she had seen,
though she knew that to name him would be to save herself." The
answer was that she preferred slavery in love to freedom without love.
Marusya refrained from naming the Vampire because she loved him,
"which was why . . . she lost her mother, her brother, and her own life,
one after the other."[30]

8

TIME'S GREAT DISLOCATION

To turn from Tsvetayeva to her three colleagues, and from Prague to Moscow, is to be reminded that Lenin died near his capital city on 21 January 1924. The passing of the great revolutionary was a historical landmark, and was followed by the renaming of Petrograd as Leningrad in his honour. But it must also be remembered that Lenin had been largely incapacitated by illness during his last two years of life, and that his death was more important as a symbol than for any practical impact on political developments. Would-be successors had jockeyed for power round his sickbed, and they continued to do so round his embalmed corpse, with Stalin's star in the ascendant and Trotsky's in decline.

Though Stalin's chief concern was with political developments as they could be manipulated from his controlling position as Secretary General of the Soviet Union's Communist Party, literary affairs were not outside his sphere of interest. This became evident in the winter following Lenin's death, when Pasternak and two other leading poets — Mayakovsky and Yesenin — were summoned by the Secretary General to discuss the prospects for translating poetry from his native Georgian into Russian. During this, their only meeting, Stalin impressed Pasternak as the "most terrifying" person that he had ever set eyes on — a crab-like, disproportionately broad dwarf with a yellow, pock-marked face and a bristling moustache.[1] To what extent Pasternak's translations of the 1930s from Georgian poetry into Russian may have been stimulated by this encounter with Georgia's most famous son is hard to say. But it is clear that Stalin's personality fascinated the poet, whose later attempts to conduct a long-distance dialogue with the leader will be described in due course.

Whatever fruitful inspiration Pasternak may have derived from exposure to Stalin's personality, it did not extend to the other two leading poets whom the Secretary General interviewed at the same time. Yesenin and Mayakovsky were both to commit suicide within a few years: a vivid comment on the extent to which rising Stalinism was becoming unpropitious to the arts.

For Pasternak the middle and late 1920s marked a change of emphasis, both in his personal life and in his literary evolution. Confined to the Soviet Union by restrictions now imposed on foreign travel, he settled down to a period of domesticity in his native Moscow, having recently married. As *Doctor Zhivago* almost too amply testifies, he prized stability and family life more than the average run of poets, but he had unfortunately picked the wrong country and the wrong century. He also turned out to have selected the wrong wife in Yevgeniya Lurye, for their marriage was to end in divorce after a few years. Pasternak has left no memoir-writing widow with detailed recollections going back to his late twenties, as Mandelstam did; nor — despite his own valuable autobiographical sketches — has he commented extensively on his adult private life in his writings, as Akhmatova and Tsvetayeva have. And so the inner history of his first marriage remains obscure.

After fathering a son and a book of lyric poems *(Themes and Variations)* in 1923, Pasternak continued to produce a trickle of lyrics during the remaining years of the decade, and was far from cultivating the eloquent silence of Akhmatova and Mandelstam. More significant than Pasternak's new lyrics, however, are his excursions into a new poetic genre, the long quasi-narrative poem of between three hundred and twelve hundred lines. He published four of these between 1924 and 1930: *Lofty Malady, The Year Nineteen Hundred and Five, Lieutenant Shmidt,* and *Spektorsky.*

These works reveal him as the only one of the poets ever to make any serious, sustained attempt to place his art at the disposal of the country's new political dispensation, and to write in conformity with its aims. Pasternak himself called his latest development a transition "from lyrical thinking to epic," believing that the latter genre was appropriate to the age in which he lived.[2] This is a modest restatement of a common thesis of the period — that the heroic spirit of revolutionary society could not be expressed in the personal, self-obsessed statements of any lyric poet, but required large forms: spectacular architecture, panoramic films, monumental novels, epic poetry. It was this widely promoted contention that had helped to silence Akhmatova and Mandelstam, while diverting Pasternak to the long poem. Not that any of his four long poems of the 1920s evolved as a grandiose revolutionary epic such as critics were calling for on all sides. Those masterpieces either remained unwritten, or fell short of the high hopes invested in them; the most successful is perhaps Mayakovsky's *Vladimir Ilyich Lenin.*

Lofty Malady is the first, the shortest, the most philosophically intense, and the most puzzling of Pasternak's four long poems. Its beginning, invoking the Trojan War as the inspiration of epic poetry, is indeed heroic in conjuring up the spectre of some Soviet-style *Iliad*. The poem also ends in the heroic manner with a eulogy of Lenin, whom Pasternak had seen at the Ninth Congress of Soviets in 1921, and for whom he had conceived an extravagant admiration. He conveys this in a few forceful lines, while never sinking into the jargon of hagiographical cliché. Pasternak's Lenin

> Was like rapier's lunge.
> In follow-up to own words
> He hewed own line, made jacket bulge,
> Stuck boot-toes out.
> His words might be of fuel oil,
> But his frame's twist
> Breathed stark Being's soaring
> That split husks' oafish crush. . . .
> He governed ideas' flow —
> His only way to govern Russia.[3]

Pasternak's enthusiasm for Lenin is confirmed by the autobiographical jottings in which he speaks of the Bolshevik leader's "inflammatory speeches, striking directness, insistency, and drive. Unprecedentedly bold in his attitude to the eruption of popular revolt. . . . With the ardour of genius he unhesitatingly assumed responsibility for bloodshed and destruction such as the world had never seen before." Pasternak himself seems to have approved of these activities wholeheartedly, to judge from the fervour of his language. And yet, despite his avid sentiments, and despite the stirring lines to Lenin contained in *Lofty Malady*, the poet contrives to end that poem on a distinct downbeat, and with an ominous reference to the persecutions that were to follow the Soviet leader's death.

> Genius comes portending bounties,
> And avenges his parting with oppression.[4]

Sandwiched between its epical Trojan beginning and its near-epical, Lenin-dominated end, the bulk of *Lofty Malady* is far from reflecting the demands of the revolutionary epoch. It is, rather, a lament on the uselessness of the poet's craft as Pasternak had hitherto practised it, and on the sad fate of the social class to which he himself belonged — the prewar Russian intelligentsia. Both are doomed. And lyric po-

etry, the Lofty Malady of the title, has become alien and futile in a world
that has

> Flounced off from books
> To pikes and bayonet.

The poet accepts that he must "leave the stage" along with his own
doomed milieu, since the old-style intellectual is now only good for

> Printing and painting posters
> About the joys of his own downfall.[5]

Pasternak celebrates his own eclipse in this poem. Signifying his submis-
sion to the new society, while proclaiming that he himself, and his art
as previously practised, are now redundant, he has to that extent written
a revolutionary work. But his affirmation is conveyed with a weariness
of spirit equally remote from the period's propaganda clichés ("blazing
eyes," "full speed ahead") and from the life-affirming, sometimes jaunty
tone of the author's own previous lyrical writing. For this reason *Lofty
Malady* could not conceivably gain acceptance from the architects of
literary policy as one of those ecstatic hymns to revolutionary society
that verse was now required to supply at whatever cost to poetry. Nor
is *Lofty Malady* a masterpiece in its own right: though it contains
sequences of impressive and disturbing lines, it makes an awkwardly
fragmented and blurred impact as a whole.

Far more successful as a revolutionary poem than the deviously
apologetic *Lofty Malady* is *The Year Nineteen Hundred and Five.* But it
is hardly the epic that the author himself called it, though he also called
it "epic fragments."[6] Nor is it a narrative poem, since it is far from
offering a chronicle of 1905 — the year of Russia's first, unsuccessful
revolution. Pasternak flashes revolutionary snapshots intelligible only to
those acquainted with the historical background. The scenes include
Bloody Sunday — the massacre that occurred in St. Petersburg on 9
January 1905, when the Tsar's troops gunned down several hundred
demonstrating workers; the mutiny of the battleship *Potyomkin,* as also
recorded in Eisenstein's film; peasants burning manor houses; workers'
revolts in industrial Poland; the December rising in the working-class
district of Presnya in Pasternak's native Moscow.

As examples of the poet's new manner these lightning glimpses are
impressive. No less so are the verses at the beginning, in which he looks
back to the decades of Russian revolutionary activity preceding 1905.
He apostrophizes the Spirit of Revolution as follows.

Joan of Arc from Siberian bondage,
Jailbird turned leader — you're the sort
Who dived into life's well
Too fast to plan a run-up.

Socialist maid, from gloaming
Striking light as from piled steels;
Sobbing, basilisk-visaged —
You illumined, chilled us.[7]

The first of the poem's six cantos displays a Pasternak more blood-thirsty than he appears elsewhere in his works, as he lavishes praise on the revolutionary assassins who blew the Emperor Alexander II to pieces with a homemade grenade in St. Petersburg on 1 March 1881, led by the pioneer lady terrorist Sofya Perovskaya. The young women who constructed dynamite bombs in secret laboratories were, according to Pasternak, "Our mothers, / Or mothers' friends." He further invokes Dostoyevsky, who had also been a revolutionary of sorts in the 1840s. In these passages the poet expresses a greater sympathy for Russia's revolutionary past than will be found in his other writings. All in all, *The Year Nineteen Hundred and Five* was far more acceptable to Soviet literary policy makers than *Lofty Malady*.[8]

Referring to the symbolic freezing mist out of which fires so fateful were to blaze forth, the poet compares the writhing of revolution's smoke plumes to the famous Greek statue of the contorted, snake-entwined Laocoön. The passage is among his most memorable, and was to be invoked by Akhmatova in her celebrated poem on Pasternak of 1936. It was also to be quoted (in 1928) as containing the "most perfect" of all the poet's lines by the critic Vladimir Weidlé — at that time a harsh judge of Pasternak's verse.

Like Laocoön
Shall smoke
In bitter frost,
Stripped
Like athlete,
Clasp and throw clouds.
Dwindling day
Shall float
On iron runners
Of telegraph meshes
Fanning from attic.[9]

In the second canto the poet invokes childhood memories of his own: his apprenticeship to music; the patronage of the composer Skriabin; his school examinations; the revolutionary demonstrations in the streets of Moscow that marked "the bursting of the joints of the oaths sworn to the Dynasty." In this section he also updates his approval of revolutionary terrorism by mentioning, with evident satisfaction, the assassination (in 1905) of the Grand Duke Sergey Aleksandrovich — official Visitor to the Moscow institute at which the poet's father was a professor.[10]

Pasternak's next essay in the genre, *Lieutenant Shmidt,* zooms in from the 1905 Revolution as a whole to concentrate on a single spectacular episode, the naval mutiny that occurred at Sevastopol in October and November. Pyotr Petrovich Shmidt, who belonged to no revolutionary or other political party, was a junior officer commanding a torpedo boat. He assumed leadership of the insurgents in the port and of a dozen vessels of the Black Sea fleet, hoisting his signal on the cruiser *Ochakov:* "I command the Fleet. SHMIDT." He was not to do so for long: the mutiny was suppressed, and Shmidt and two other leaders were executed by firing squad the following year.

In making these events the subject for a series of sketches, Pasternak maintains the allusive approach of *The Year Nineteen Hundred and Five.* Never systematically narrating the course of events, he again speaks as if they are matters of common knowledge. This was to ask a great deal, even of contemporary Russian readers: they might well take the familiar episodes described in the earlier poem in their stride, but they were unlikely to carry in their heads the detailed background to such a local occurrence as the Sevastopol mutiny. Still, obscure though some of the references remain, Pasternak's general purport is clear throughout. Once again, as in *Lofty Malady,* he confronts the conflict between private life and public duty — a conflict that was of course his own as well as his hero's.

Shmidt has fallen in love with a mysterious young woman whom he had first come across at a Kiev race meeting, but he sacrifices his hopes of happiness with her so that he may respond to the call of the revolutionary people. The point is well brought out in Pasternak's version of Shmidt's speech at his trial, where the transcript of the actual court-martial proceedings is closely paraphrased, yet transmuted into poetry. The lines anticipate Pasternak's own role of thirty years later, when he was to challenge the Khrushchevite "establishment" by allowing *Doctor Zhivago* to be published in the West. Like his hero Shmidt, Pasternak was a private person rather than a public posturer — one whose instincts made him shun the limelight, but who was yet compelled by his sense of duty to court the very publicity that he so disliked. This, the theme of the celebrated "Hamlet" (which begins the sequence of lyrics appended to *Doctor Zhivago*), is also the burden of Shmidt's speech to the judges. In their extreme simplicity, too, the lines foreshadow Pasternak's later development.

> "How vain, in years of chaos,
> To seek a happy issue.
> Some punish and repent,
> Some end on Golgotha.
>
> "Like you I am a part
> Of time's great dislocation,
> And I'll receive your sentence
> Without anger or reproach.
>
> "Surely you will not flinch
> When brushing me aside.
> Martyrs to dogma — after all,
> You're the times' victims too.
>
> "For thirty years I've cherished
> Love for my native land.
> Your clemency I neither
> Count on, nor yet count lost.
>
> "In those days — you have witnessed them,
> You remember how they were —
> I was lifted from the throng
> By elemental surge.
>
> "Not rising with my country,
> I would have suffered more.
> The path I have trodden
> I do not now regret.
>
> "I know this stake by which
> I stand shall be the frontier
> Of two historic epochs.
> Glad am I to be chosen."[11]

Lieutenant Shmidt is dedicated to Marina Tsvetayeva, and includes in its original version a fourteen-line acrostic verse dedication of which the initial letters spell out her name. But though Tsvetayeva had long admired Pasternak and his work beyond idolatry, she judged this particular poem severely. Her remarks, contained in a long letter to the author, are valuable for the light shed both on the unfortunate lieutenant and on herself. Tsvetayeva castigates Pasternak for creating no true revolutionary hero, but yet another Russian *intelligent* ("intellectual") of the type associated with well-meaning dithering and the wearing of a pince-nez. Shmidt is "no whit a sailor, and so much the *intelligent,* so much the Chekhov at sea, that all his years in the service haven't knocked the *intelligentsky* jargon out of him. Your Shmidt is a student, not a sailor, a fey undergraduate from the late 1890s." There was too little of Pasternak himself in the poem, and what there was seemed eclipsed by the "tiny" figure of Shmidt. But the Shmidt-free sections of the poem, including "the elements," she thought splendid.[12] The same reproach was often made by Pasternak's admirers, including Akhmatova: he could describe *things,* especially meteorological and other natural phenomena, with verve and originality, but human figures were either ill-realized or absent from his canvas altogether.

Pasternak took Tsvetayeva's criticisms seriously enough to remove lengthy passages from the poem when it was reissued in later editions, but he could not meet the brunt of her attack without liquidating the work entirely. It is one more essay on the clash between the Individual and Society. The intellectual approach of which Tsvetayeva complains — and on which dissenting opinions are possible — is an essential ingredient in what the poet had to say.

Spektorsky, the longest and the last to be completed of Pasternak's four quasi-revolutionary studies of the 1920s, differs from its predecessors in being a work of fiction; he himself has called it a "novel in verse."[13] In it he still maintains the allusive method of his poems set in 1905. In other words, he does not *tell* his story; he offers only a series of glosses based on the unspoken assumption that its contents must already be familiar to the reader. But since this is a work of fiction, there are no historical studies or archives to explain the more recondite allusions. And so nothing but patient detective work applied to the text will serve to chart the fortunes of Sergey Spektorsky and his relations with other, no more clearly visualized, figures. They include two women who reproach the hero for being yet another dithering intellectual; his pistol-toting ex-mistress Olga; his sister, who criticizes him for being "cut off from his generation" and wants to know what political "camp" he belongs to. There is a third female figure too — Mariya Ilyina, who can be vaguely identified with Pasternak's assiduous correspondent Marina Tsvetayeva. As the versifying daughter of a Moscow professor, and as one poised on the verge of emigration, Ilyina is at least in those respects a portrait of the expatriate poet.

Spektorsky is far less of a revolutionary poem than *The Year Nine-*

teen Hundred and Five, or even than *Lieutenant Shmidt.* Like *Lofty Malady* before it, the "novel in verse" lacks fervour. The scenes set in early revolutionary Moscow purvey a dismal picture of that city, which seems to face total collapse rather than a glorious future. Spektorsky himself is yet another depressed and doomed intellectual, like his predecessor Shmidt — and also like his creator, as he elusively characterizes himself in this poem and in the earlier *Lofty Malady.* No attempt is made to portray Spektorsky in the round; like everyone else in the poem he remains a shadowy figure to whom Pasternak does not introduce the reader. As he writes at one point,

> We can't even mention personalities,
> So let's expunge them here and now.[14]

The remark occurs in the context of the riotous skiing party, dated Christmas 1912, which is vividly described in the second canto, with its bustle, laughter, and snow-girt woodland dacha. The virtues of this, and of *Spektorsky* as a whole, are those of rapid glimpses into a dimly discerned scene, and the poem is certainly no novel in verse in any conventional sense.

Pasternak's hesitancies of the late 1920s are strikingly illustrated in a work of prose fiction, *A Tale,* which was not only written and published during the years when *Spektorsky* was taking shape, but also has many points in common with that poem. The two works have the same hero, Sergey Spektorsky, whose prose incarnation can be more closely identified than its poetic counterpart with the author himself. As a young tutor working in the Urals, the Spektorsky of *A Tale* fuses two features of his creator's wartime experiences. Moreover, this prose Spektorsky is, like Pasternak, a poet simultaneously obsessed with the mysteries of artistic creation and the sufferings of the female sex, serving in both these key preoccupations as a prototype of the eponymous hero of *Doctor Zhivago.* That novel of the future is also foreshadowed in another short story of the 1920s, *Aerial Paths.* Its hero, Polivanov, anticipates Antipov-Strelnikov in the later work by renouncing personal emotions in favour of political dogma, as communicated to the hero along the "aerial paths" of his office telephone. *Aerial Paths* was published in 1925 in a collection that also included *The Childhood of Lyuvers.* This too contains fragmentary anticipations of the long novel which Pasternak had already been planning for years (he was talking of it back in 1918, according to Tsvetayeva),[15] and which was eventually to emerge as *Doctor Zhivago.*

Pasternak's prose works of the late 1920s further include the autobiographical study published in 1929, *Safe-Conduct.* The title alludes to the mysterious salutary force — akin to a document guaranteeing un-molested passage through enemy lines — that had three times saved him as a young man from pursuing a career alien to his true destiny: musical composition, professional philosophy, the writing of verse excessively influenced by the poetic personality of Mayakovsky. Couched in the allusive, quirky manner of Pasternak's youth and early middle age, *Safe-Conduct* was to be translated — so to speak — into more straight-forward Russian by the author himself nearly twenty years later. This second description of his life, *Autobiographical Sketch,* was originally written as an introduction to a volume of its author's verse scheduled (abortively, as it turned out) for publication in the USSR in 1957. *Safe-Conduct* is dedicated to Rilke, whom Pasternak had met in child-hood and whose aesthetic beliefs — in the artist's need to be impersonal, in art's capacity to transform nature, in nature's craving to be preserved in the artist's utterance — had influenced Pasternak's own conception of the poet's task.[16]

In *Safe-Conduct* Pasternak touches on his philosophy of love in order to propound an attitude more positive than that of Akhmatova and Tsvetayeva, with their emphasis on the darker aspects of Aphrodite and Eros. Discussing "sex education," Pasternak claims that it and all discus-sions of sex (including the very word) are intolerably vulgar; that they can only render confusion worse confounded in the minds of the young; but that this is a positive advantage, however paradoxical, since it gives passion a suitably formidable obstacle to surmount. Lust is infinitely the noblest thing in life — or, as Pasternak puts it, "The impulse to concep-tion is the purest element in the Universe. And such is this purity, many times triumphant throughout the ages, that it alone would suffice to impart a contrasting whiff of limitless smuttiness to everything other than itself."[17]

Despite efforts expended on prose works and long poems, the Pasternak of the middle and late 1920s was still writing occasional lyrics. Two of them are particularly worth noting, since they are addressed to Tsvetayeva and Akhmatova.

Whereas Tsvetayeva's dozen poems to Pasternak in *After Russia* concentrate on the emotions that he aroused in her, his single lyric dedicated to her (dated 1928) hardly seems to have her in mind at all, for the theme is the poet in general, together with his indifference to his environment. He does not care "what makes the mist damp"; is indifferent to "whose conversation, floating from nowhere" he may chance to hear; recks nothing of "what style of clothes is decreed" in his own age, since he belongs to the future. It is for the poet that his own age will be remembered.

Wreathing into many channels,
Like smoke he'll drift
From fateful epoch's fissures
Into some black dead end.

He'll burst, smoking, from crevasses
Of destinies squashed pancake-flat.
And his grandchildren will say, as of peat:
"So-and-so's epoch's burning."[18]

Pasternak's lyric to Akhmatova makes a more specific attempt to characterize its addressee, in whom he discerns a certain "pristine" or "primordial" quality akin to "chatter of wet roofs" and the "eclogues of muffled paving blocks." Her verse reminds him of a mysterious town where a dressmaker sits working over a lamp for some exacting customer. The dressmaker goes for a walk in what, from its canals and other details, becomes recognizable as Akhmatova's native Leningrad at the season of round-the-clock daylight. Here she is seen peering from a bridge into that

Solution of most fearful potency —
Nocturnal vistas under white night's eye.

Of Akhmatova's gaze Pasternak writes

From your first books,
With their firm grains of unflinching prose,
It has in all of them, like spark's conductor,
Caused events to throb into life.[19]

The comparison with prose is a compliment to the plain, matter-of-fact — in a word, Acmeist — style of Akhmatova's youth.

Akhmatova responded to Pasternak's ode to her in a lyric which picks up his allusion to a chemical solution in its second line.

If moon's eeriness is splashed abroad
The whole town's put in venomous solution.

Peering through a green haze, she seems to discern cypresses in their "permanently petrified dance" over the grave of a dead lover. In an

elegy of the following year she again invokes a city which can only be
Leningrad, as contemplated in a wistful mood pierced by the joyful
memory of past love.[20]

These few lines of Akhmatova's were written during the thirteen-
year period (1923–35) during which she came close to suspending the
output of verse entirely. This is not surprising, for she knew that publi-
cation was now denied her, rightly or wrongly attributing the ban to
a secret Communist Party resolution of 1925.[21]

It is true that a banned poet may yet continue to write "for the
drawer," as Russians express it; but if Akhmatova indeed did so during
these years, most of the product has vanished. Such lyrics as survive are
melancholy and brief, but a few stimulating fragments from a projected
longer poem of the same period, *The Russian Trianon*, have recently
come to light. In later years Akhmatova was to deny that she had ever
abandoned poetry, and she was also to express acute resentment at any
reference on the part of foreign critics to her "period of silence" —
just as she acutely resented so many other fancied affronts in her dig-
nified, aristocratic style. But she was also known to admit in private that
she had "written no verse" during the thirteen years that she spent
living with the art historian Nikolay Punin in the House of the Fountain
in Leningrad.[22]

It was probably in 1926 that Akhmatova left Shileyko for Punin,
but the new union was to prove no more harmonious than its predeces-
sors. That she and Punin never formally registered their marriage mat-
tered not at all in the permissive atmosphere of the 1920s. A more serious
inconvenience was imposed by the housing shortage of the period
— that of having to share Punin's small flat with his discarded former
wife, a medical doctor and another Anna, who was persuaded to move
into a separate room. The Punins' small daughter, Irina, also belonged
to the ménage, and the arrangement was to last into the late 1930s. But
the poet wearied of it early on, and would probably have moved out had
a suitable opportunity presented itself. And so her suspension of
creativity can be attributed to domestic pressures within the House of
the Fountain as well as to those applied outside it in an age when the
expression of personal feelings in lyric poetry had begun to seem like
a form of high treason.

While living at Tsarskoye Selo and afflicted by tuberculosis, in
spring 1925, Akhmatova had first become closely acquainted with an-
other sufferer — Mandelstam's wife, Nadezhda. Thus began the firm
literary and personal triple alliance between Akhmatova and the Man-
delstams — between two of the era's finest poets and its premier literary
memoirist.

How close Osip Emilyevich felt to Anna Andreyevna is shown in his letter to her of 25 August 1928 — approximately the seventh anniversary (the precise date is disputed) of the execution of Nikolay Gumilyov, her first husband. Mandelstam, once so close an ally of both Gumilyovs in helping to found the Acmeist movement, now tells Akhmatova that she and Nikolay are the only two people with whom he can conduct an imaginary conversation: he has never ceased "talking" to Gumilyov in this way, and he never will.[23] As for relations between Akhmatova and Nadezhda Mandelstam, far from being rivals for influence over Nadezhda's husband, they became firm friends — exacting, touchy, and imperious though each could be in her dealings with others. The friendship long outlasted Mandelstam's death, and ended only with Akhmatova's in 1966.

In 1925 Mandelstam embarked on a brief, passionate love affair with one Olga Vaksel. It was the only profound extramarital infatuation that he contracted during his life with Nadezhda Yakovlevna, and at one point it even seemed likely to lead to divorce. Mandelstam addressed a delicious poem to his new love, referring to "The land beyond eyelashes, / Where thou shalt be my wife." But he cut off the affair in characteristically peremptory style soon afterwards, on suddenly realizing that he risked losing Nadezhda for ever.[24]

After his ode to Olga, Mandelstam wrote a few more lyrics in 1925, but then suspended the creation of original verse for five years, having incurred publication restrictions comparable to those suffered by Akhmatova. The ban was neither formal nor absolute, but fell with especial severity on original works in verse, and on publication in the press of Moscow and Leningrad. Prose articles, translations, and so on might still appear, provincial publication being relatively easy to achieve. The poet derived desultory earnings from such sources in this period of acute poverty, ill-health, and homelessness. Often separated from his wife, whose tubercular condition obliged her to spend much of her time in the south, he himself began to suffer from heart trouble as he continued the struggle for existence under conditions ever more oppressive, living largely in Moscow, Leningrad, and Tsarskoye Selo. But in spite of all these obstacles he was somehow able to publish small editions of no fewer than three books — largely reissues of earlier work — in the year 1928.

Still quixotic in temperament, still horrified by the idea of capital punishment — in an age when alleged saboteurs and industrial wreckers were being shot on all sides — the poet contrived to save the lives of five bank officials under sentence of death by sending an impassioned appeal and his latest volume of verse to his patron Bukharin. It was a noble and impressive feat, but did little to halt the avalanche of persecutions for economic "crimes."

During this period the poet became involved in an ugly literary scandal that festered around one of his translating activities. In 1928 he had completed a commission to revise for the press two existing Russian versions of the cumbrously entitled French novel *La Légende de Thyl Ulenspiegel et de Lamme Goedzak* by Charles de Coster. But when this work appeared, Mandelstam was quoted on the title page as the sole translator. And so, through no fault of his own, he appeared to have plagiarized the two translations that he had merely revised. He was the first to point out the error, and also offered to make financial amends; but one of the earlier translators, an A. G. Gornfeld, chose to make the most of the unintended injury by seeking legal redress. The result was a prolonged, squalid public quarrel that lasted until 1930. This absurd affair offered endless opportunity for ill-intentioned busybodies to make the poet's life a misery, and he was subjected to repeated harassment and interrogation by judicial and literary organs. His fiery temperament made him an easy butt for such persecution, which — believing it inspired by anti-Semitism — he and his wife took to calling their "Dreyfus Affair."

Surprisingly enough, this scandal was eventually instrumental in raising the poet's morale, and even in clearing his mind so effectively that he was able to resume writing original verse in late 1930. The background to his change of heart has been filled in by his widow. She explains that he had become more and more alienated from Soviet society in the 1920s, while yet wishing to give the new dispensation the benefit of the doubt. During this phase he had been inhibited by the suspicion that it must be he personally, and not the new political dispensation, that was at fault. Hence his repeated allusions to himself, in verse of the early 1920s, as "the ailing son of the Age." By the end of the decade, however, the ramifications of the Gornfeld affair had shown that it was the age that ailed. The poet himself was perfectly healthy.[25]

Exasperated by the Gornfeld affair, and especially by the extent to which the literary fraternity as a whole was now toadying to political authority, Mandelstam vented his indignation in a short, vitriolic essay, *Fourth Prose*. It was not published until 1966, and then only in the West. The reasons for this are nowhere clearer than in the passage in which Gornfeld, the Soviet literary world as a whole, and finally the smallpox-disfigured Stalin are all dismissed with loathing and contempt. Dividing world literature into that officially permitted and that written without

permission, Mandelstam calls the former "trash," and the latter "pur-
loined air." As for the authors of material officially sanctioned in ad-
vance, "I want to spit in their faces and beat their heads with a stick."
The poet would also have liked to sit them all down at table in Herzen
House, the writers' apartment block in Moscow, while placing before
each a glass of undrinkable tea "and an analysis of Gornfeld's urine."
Such writers have "sold themselves and succeeding generations to the
Pockmarked Devil."[26]

9

LOVING AND LOPPING

In 1925 Tsvetayeva transferred her residence to Paris, now the main Russian émigré cultural centre. Her original intention had been to pay a temporary visit to the French capital, where she had been invited to give a poetry recital. It was so successful that she decided not to return to Prague, and was to spend her next fourteen years in the suburbs of Paris. For a time the local Russians flocked to hear her recite, acclaiming her as their country's leading modern poet. But her years in France were to mark a decline in her reputation: many of her fellow expatriates found her work obscure and overingenious. Only a few enlightened spirits perceived that the splendour of the poetry outweighed these defects.

Tsvetayeva's unpopularity in France was increased by her enthusiasm for certain home-based poets, particularly Mayakovsky and Pasternak. She did not hesitate to say that better poetry was being written in the Soviet Union than outside it, and she also seems to have believed that her own writings could be better appreciated by Soviet than by expatriate readers. These were purely literary judgements, but they were taken as political pronouncements by those Russian émigrés who so little understood the poet as to think her "pro-Soviet" simply because she admired Mayakovsky. That poetry was everything to her, and politics less than nothing, was not easy to discern in the atmosphere of the Russian emigration in France.

Tsvetayeva was still sporadically united with, and separated from, her husband Sergey, as she struggled to maintain a family home in a succession of suburban Parisian lodgings, where they lived in squalor and poverty. Earning only a pittance from her writings and no longer subsidized by the Czechs, the poet continued to slave away at the housekeeping chores that she detested.

With the move to Paris Tsvetayeva's output of lyrics sharply declined, and so no further new volume of her short poems was to be published in her lifetime. She was now concentrating more and more on longer poems. Three of these straddled the move from Czechoslovakia to France: even while adjusting to the change of domicile she was asserting her status as a citizen of the world by writing her verse dramas on classical Greek themes, and also a further folk epic.

For the last-mentioned item she abandoned Afanasyev's traditional Russian tales — previously exploited in *Tsar-Maiden, The Swain,* and *Alleyways* — in order to explore a well-known medieval German legend in *Rat-Catcher.* This, the finest of her folk poems, retells the episode best known to English readers from Robert Browning's *The Pied Piper of Hamelin.*

Tsvetayeva's playful, pungent, metrically dynamic, elliptically ingenious version of this cautionary tale is notable as her only major work of political and social satire. Her barbs first transfix the smug burghers of medieval Hamelin, where everyone is cut to a single boring pattern. At night Hamelin's husbands dutifully dream of their wives while those wives in turn dutifully dream of their husbands. Equally on cue,

> Baby dreams of nipple;
> Plump-cheeked beauty
> Of Dad's sock,
> Darned by her.

Complacent Hamelin's symbol is the buttoned-up button; its citizens are the very antipodes of "Beggars, geniuses, rhymesters, Schumanns, musicians, / Convicts." Deriding the buttoned-up principle, Tsvetayeva calls on her own Muse to

> Flee buttons' void,
> Flee docked verities!
> No button will stop
> Revolution. Let them burst —
>
> All. If thou art demons' kin,
> Bard, unbutton utterly.[1]

As Tsvetayeva warms to her rats it soon becomes clear that this is not one more antibourgeois satire, but a denunciation of other brands of conformism as well. Thriving in the city's barns, the regimented rodents evolve into a symbol of the Bolshevized and collectivized Russian masses, throwing up their own bureaucracy on the Soviet model, with comically entitled officials and institutions such as Chief Fornication Officer *(glavblud)* and People's Commissariat for Infernal Affairs *(narkomchort).* These revolutionary rodents are no less odious than the reactionary burghers whom they are eating out of house and home.

As the swarming rats threaten to take over the town, the Burgomaster offers to marry his daughter to the newly arrived Piper if he will only rid Hamelin of the plague. Tsvetayeva's Piper represents the Artist — a creature generally despised, but immeasurably superior to all politicians, as well as to the dragooned masses, both human and rodent.

In one magnificent passage the seductive, green-clad flautist lures the swarming rats in procession to the magic land of Hindustan. There is some hesitation: while certain rats boast that they will conquer India and build a new world, others raise objections.

> "I have some uneaten cheese."

> "You can't spit higher than your own nose."[2]

When the deluded cortège approaches the stinking town pond, mistaking it for exotic tropical waters complete with crocodiles, one senior rodent begins, as it were, to smell a rat. What his deceived fellows take for pagodas and Rajah's palaces surrounded by turbaned Brahmins, cobras, and dervishes, the Old Rat recognizes for what they really are: the barns and sheds of Hamelin's unprepossessing environs.

> *Palm tree?* Windmill. *Bamboo?* Road barrier.
> *Condor?* Kite. *Maize?* Peas.
> We're only four miles
> From Hamelin.

The Wise Old Rat goes on to denounce the Piper as an enemy agent, but his protests are vain, for the rat collective is duly drowned in the town pond.[3]

In the next scene the Town Council cheats the Piper, foisting a wretched papier-mâché flute case on him in place of the promised Burgomaster's daughter. The poet imparts a high satirical gloss to the objections raised against the Pied Artist by the embattled philistines of Hamelin as she logs their denunciations of Art.

> Music? Bird's twitter.
> Joke. Child's play.
> Music? Roar in ears.
> Wedding entertainment.

But though Art may be mere entertainment, it can also be dangerous, as the Burgomaster himself warns.

Music — typhus!
Music — explosion!
Scythian in steppe!
Veins' stoppage . . . !

Direr than roar in ears
Are dreams with narrowed eyes.
Music is bank crash,
Is Furies' unleashing.

Music is also rebellion, flute players being lost souls and no fit sons-in-law for burgomasters. Musicians are all undischarged bankrupts, while artists in general are "Hierophants in wheels' mud, / Gods in brothels' fumes." Their proper role is a subordinate one.

To weep and watch that we may sleep,
To die that we may multiply.[4]

Rat-Catcher inspiringly champions the individual personality in an age when it was doubly menaced by bourgeois conformism and by Communist collectivism. Tsvetayeva drives this point home through her sarcastic picture of the Hamelinites as one big happy family.

No pronoun *I*.
No. None. All together. . . .

I means *All*.
Fine word, most profitable —
All. Clings like fur coat.[5]

At the end of the poem Hamelin's children are drowned according to schedule, the last word and sentence being "Bubbles." Yet there is a hint that the Piper has somehow rescued them by the magic of his art, conducting them into a world where each can be an individual, not a regimented burgher-rat.[6]

Tsvetayeva's two plays on ancient Greek themes span her move from Czechoslovakia to France, for *Ariadne* was written in 1923–24 and *Phaedra* in 1927; her original, unfulfilled, intention had been to add a third drama, thus completing a trilogy on the Wrath of Aphrodite as triply visited on the hero Theseus. Not directly based on Euripides or any other ancient source, the Russian poet's reworkings of classical myth derive from a nineteenth-century collection of Greek legends retold in German by one Gustav Schwab, who sounds more like a

Hamelin burgomaster than a suitable conduit for water from the Pierian
Spring. Yet Tsvetayeva has tapped this source for verse that need not
fear comparison even with that of Greek tragedy. *Ariadne* culminates
in the death of Theseus' father, Aegeus, by suicide, and *Phaedra* in the
death of his son Hippolytus through the familiar traffic disaster pro-
voked by Theseus' curse, implemented by Poseidon through the agency
of an enraged bull from the sea. Each play also echoes and supplements
the sonorous lyrics of *After Russia*, in which Ariadne, Phaedra, and
Hippolytus all figure memorably.

Tsvetayeva the dramatist continues to ventilate a favourite theme
of her maturity, the "by-passing" of love: its frustration, its nonachieve-
ment, its nonconsummation. In *Ariadne* renounced love attains its most
sublime moment with the scene on Naxos where Theseus is persuaded
to yield his sleeping bride to the God Bacchus: the God — as he elo-
quently explains — can confer immortality on her, which Theseus can-
not. In any case, Bacchus continues, the benefits, joys, and advantages
of carnal love have been grossly exaggerated: a contention frequently
advanced by Tsvetayeva in her lyrics. Ariadne is engaged in sleeping
off Theseus' lustful embraces even as the God speaks to the lover who
will soon (convinced by these arguments) abandon her forever, thus in
turn triggering the wrath of Aphrodite, Goddess of Love. Here is no
loving, only lopping, Bacchus tells Theseus, playing on the jingle *lyu-
byat/rubyat;* and by adding *gubyat* ("ruining") says, in effect: sex
wrecks. It is vein-ripping, a flexing of muscles, dull, crude, and clumsy.

> Bed is fetters, counterfeit fever
> Of blood. Maid, having known man,
> Sleeps — sleeps off your brazier's fumes. . . .
> Wilts, sleeps off
> Your caresses; is gentler than old nag
> Foundered in death. Lips' spasm mouths
> Your marriages' and remarriages'
> Vile futility.[7]

In *Phaedra* the theme of antisexuality is inevitably borne by the
aggressively celibate Hippolytus, who curses women as "all ringleted
serpents . . . all stranglers, all cats with mice." Claiming to be the son
of an eagle in the sky, and not of some "steatopygous woman," he adds:
"Misogyny . . . ! I have sucked thee in / With milk."[8] It is on the crest
of this diatribe that the Nurse, who plays a particularly baleful part in
Tsvetayeva's tragedy, hands the clinically chaste hero the letter in which
his stepmother, Phaedra, declares her love for him. His consequent

revulsion provokes, in conformity with legend, first Phaedra's suicide and then his own death through the bull sent by Poseidon in response to Theseus' curse.

As in the relevant lyrics of *After Russia,* so too in *Phaedra* the poet's sympathies are with the sex-crazed stepmother and against the virgin stepson. Once again Tsvetayeva-Psyche and Tsvetayeva-Eve have clashed or united to create dionysiac poetry of the first order. Here, as in so much of her work, virulent cerebral sensuality reigns supreme — a characteristic that might be dismissed as distasteful were it not for the poetry that it has inspired.

Tsvetayeva went on to write a further half dozen longer poems of up to several hundred lines in Paris in the late 1920s. They include *New Year Offering,* her elegy to the recently deceased Rilke, whom she had never met, but with whom she had corresponded (introduced to him by a letter from Pasternak), and who had himself dedicated a most impressive verse elegy to her. Tsvetayeva once remarked that of all those whom she had met in life, only Rilke and Pasternak had been equal to her in human and poetic strength. Now, in her obituary elegy to the German poet, she claims that his poetry has confused the very concepts of life and death, substituting for them some third, mysterious, element.[9] Two other long poems of the period — *Attempt at Constructing a Room* and *Poem of the Air* — evoke dream sequences, and flirt with an almost trans-sensical dislocation of reality — reminiscent of Futurism — whereby walls, ceilings, and floors can dissolve and float into each other. It was a far cry, now, from her early odes to Mummy and Dolly.

The most tangible of these elusive items is *Staircase Poem.* It evokes the squalid back stairs of a city apartment block, and represents the poet's most eloquent treatment of a theme that had already surfaced in her *After Russia* lyrics — urban poverty. Of this she was entitled to speak, having had more than her share of it. Her staircase is a waterfall leading to hell down a trail of cabbage leaves perfumed by cats and garlic in this abode of the scum of humanity, who include "poet, bomb-thrower, and Apache."

> Roofs thunder,
> With plenitude of patchings,
> Marx's sermon
> In Stravinsky's mode.[10]

Especially ill-used are the building's material objects, which Tsvetayeva personifies, attributing to them a human sense of indignation and outrage. *Things* relied on man, but man has betrayed them:

Tree — trusting brash
Axes' whirr, nagging saws —
Held out hand with apple.
Man lopped it.

Now that Things have decided to assert themselves, the spiral staircase
feels the urge to stretch out straight in the middle of the night. Enlight-
ened by Man's example,

Thing counters crowbar with crowbar.
Table has always asserted trunkhood.[11]

In this world of humiliating poverty it is possible to insure against
every conceivable calamity except possessing property. And there is
only one protection against that disaster: fire. Sharing Tsvetayeva's own
antimaterialist bias, her naked Things long to clothe themselves in flame
and be gloriously consumed, red like the biblical burning bush or an
elder tree in full fruit; reference is not to that gardener's pest the black-
fruited Common Elder, but to *Sambucus racemosa* — familiar to Scot-
land and Siberia and distinguished by its bright red berries. In the end
the pyromaniac Things have their wish granted, except that their
longed-for conflagration turns out to be an illusion or dream when
morning dawns as usual on a staircase still unconsumed by fire.[12] More
than a mere denunciation of materialism, this highly original poem can
even be read as an early conservationist's defence of the much-abused
"environment."

The long poem *Perekop* commemorates a key campaign of the
Russian Civil War. The area is the Isthmus of Perekop (which joins the
Crimea to the mainland), and the date is mid-1920 — when the White
armies in the south were rallying under the last of their warlords,
General Wrangel. His troops burst out of Perekop into the steppelands
north of the Crimea, inflicting a signal defeat on the Red forces; they
were to be routed in turn on the same isthmus at the end of the year
in the battle that spelt the end of White resistance in the war as a whole
and preceded the last major evacuation of Whites from the Crimea.

It is of course the earlier Battle of Perekop — the White victory
— that Tsvetayeva celebrates. In throbbing rhythms, to which she now
harnesses the idiom of the mess or barracks, she hymns events as if she
had been an eyewitness, her description being based in detail on the
diary kept at the time by her husband Sergey, who had been one of
Wrangel's officers. She begins with the Whites' privations during the
weeks preceding their breakthrough, describing how they lived as moles
or gophers in the ground. An officer, vainly foraging for food in a local

village, is presented with a sprig of lilac that he feeds to his starving horse — one of the details from Sergey Efron's diary. The psychology of desertion is explored, as is the impact of the Soviet-Polish war of the same year, which happened to coincide with Wrangel's last offensive. The White Supremo visits the front; a regimental chaplain blesses the troops before they go into action. Echoes of the medieval Russian *Lay of Igor's Raid* add historical and poetic depth, and the poet sadly looks forward to the future of the Whites as it appeared in 1920. So many are to perish in exile that not a cemetery will lack its Russian dead; for some Turkey will be their sickle, for others Serbia their gravestone cross.[13]

Though Tsvetayeva gave several recitals of *Perekop,* she was unable to find a publisher for the poem, which is not one of her finest, and it did not appear in print until long after her death. Perhaps her espousal of so lost a cause embarrassed those who had once defended it — a reminder that her unpopularity among émigrés owed much to the mutually exclusive political postures that she was mistakenly thought to have adopted. Unacceptably anti-Soviet to some, she was unacceptably pro-Soviet to others. It was the inevitable fate of so disturbing a poet — all of her a creative artist, none of her a political symbol or thinker. This remains true despite the frankly partisan *Perekop* and despite such verses as *Red Bullock* — also of 1928 — in which a child has a nightmare about being chased by a sort of Bolshevik Minotaur. Yet another poem on a politically sensitive subject — the assassination of the Russian Imperial family in July 1918 — appears to have been lost irretrievably.[14]

Part Three

TERROR AND BEYOND (1930–1966)

I have known faces slump,
Terror peep under eyelids . . . ,
The shiver of fear in a dry laugh.

ANNA AKHMATOVA, 1940

10

FROLICS AND PITFALLS

S E V E R E though conditions had been for poets and others in the USSR of the 1920s, they were to become harsher still with the triumphant advance of Stalinism in the following decade. The transition was signalized by the abrupt change in economic policy that occurred in 1928 when the relatively casual dispositions of NEP were superseded by aggressive industrialization under the First Five-Year Plan. By the end of the following year Stalin had become unchallenged dictator — in fact, though never in name — after persistently asserting himself over political rivals for many years. That he had at last attained supreme power was announced, in effect, to the USSR and the world by the extravagant celebration of his fiftieth birthday on 21 December 1929.

Once Stalin's power could no longer be disputed he proceeded to use it with a degree of brutality of which his earlier years had given few indications. A few days after attaining his half century he propounded the new policy of "liquidating the *kulaks* [rich peasants] as a class," the result of which was to intensify the collectivization of agriculture by violence, including the use of military and police formations. Peasant resistance was broken by intimidation, cunning, forcible dispossession, exile, consignment to concentration camps, and execution. One outcome of the campaign was the famine of 1932–33, which caused fatalities that have been estimated as exceeding 5 million.[1]

These events made surprisingly little immediate impact on the towns and on the urban professional class, since official propaganda concealed the horrors of collectivization, portraying it as a triumph of planning, and of wisdom simultaneously humane and superhuman. So unpalatable, moreover, was the harsh reality, and so great were the penalties for being seen to notice it, that there was every inducement for town dwellers to ignore the crisis, especially as they themselves were not yet being imprisoned and executed by their millions. Nor did the famine strike the towns as severely as the countryside. Poets went hungry, but they did not starve to death like villagers. And so they were tempted to avert their eyes and minds from the pathetic peasants who begged for bread in the streets of the less effectively policed cities.

The massacre of intellectuals and members of the professions was yet to come, and was not to reach its peak until the later years of the decade. But it is only by comparison with rural sufferings that urban intellectual life of the early 1930s may be described as serene, for conditions in the towns soon deteriorated to the point where the 1920s were being wistfully remembered as the Golden Age that they had never been.

In 1929 Russia's writers received a sharp warning of the perils to which they were soon to be exposed when the USSR's first major literary witch hunt was launched. Two leading authors of prose fiction, Pilnyak and Zamyatin, were singled out as targets for virulent abuse in the press and on public platforms. They were accused of writing ideologically unsatisfactory works, and were also held responsible for the publication of this material by the Russian press of Western Europe. The practice of pillorying carefully selected literary scapegoats — often in pairs, for whatever reason of administrative convenience — had begun. But neither of the two victims was arrested or physically molested at the time. Pilnyak recanted and rewrote some of his work to conform with official requirements, while Zamyatin remained unrepentant — and was eventually permitted, as a special concession by Stalin, to emigrate from the Soviet Union. Even so, the episode clearly served notice on the literary community that it was shortly to be regimented as never before.

It is a basic characteristic of the Kremlinite modus operandi that members of a given profession are manipulated in the first instance by members of the same profession, which meant that authors were now being chiefly disciplined by other authors. By the time of the Pilnyak-Zamyatin scandal such regimentation was largely channelled through a single literary organization, the Association of Russian Proletarian Writers (RAPP). It was on 14 April 1930 that a persecution campaign mounted by RAPP, frustrated love, and other aggravations combined to provoke the suicide of Vladimir Mayakovsky — at the time of his death the only living Russia-based poet of comparable stature to the subjects of the present study.

Mayakovsky's suicide was a political as well as a literary event, being more serious in its implications than the self-destruction of the wayward alcoholic Yesenin five years earlier. Mayakovsky had more closely identified himself with the Bolshevik cause than Yesenin; he had done so since long before the Revolution; he had written prolific verses of varying excellence celebrating the new dispensation's aims and achievements. But here he was parading what could only seem ideological disillusionment *à l'outrance,* and with even more than his usual flair for showmanship. As his suicide also emphasized, his temper and personality were out of tune with developing Stalinism, and this despite the enthusiastic support that he continued to offer the system until the last.

Mayakovsky might sincerely endorse Stalin's politics, but he could never acquire the habit that increasingly distinguished the true servant of the Secretary General from the false: that of expressing oneself exclusively in such officially sanctified clichés as "full speed ahead," "ready to sacrifice our lives," "freedom-loving peoples," "in the name of mankind," "all progressive humanity." Mayakovsky might adopt these locutions on occasion, but never employed them as his basic medium of expression; he could not have done so without denying the poet in him. And since true poetry is the opposite of cliché, it is not surprising that potential poets laureate were hard to find in a state that was becoming ever more formulaic in style.

Not only did Mayakovsky's anticonformist bias make him unpopular with the period's literary bureaucrats, as did his immense talent, but he had also lost his knack of inspiring audiences with declamations of his poems. This was forced on his attention at a public recital of his poetry that he gave, only five days before his death, to an assembly consisting largely of students. They heckled the former darling of the avant-garde and scandalizer of the bourgeoisie, jeering at him for writing in language unintelligible to the masses, whose champion he had long claimed himself. Attempting to overwhelm the hecklers by declaiming more and more poems, Mayakovsky failed to establish any rapport with his audience, which continued to display open hostility.[2] It was a grim experience for so sensitive a public performer, and the fiasco must have contributed to his decision to take his own life a few days later.

Though Mayakovsky was alien to the poets considered here, both in his politics and in his creative technique, he was yet greatly respected by them all. They considered him a major poet, and their individual reactions to his death are significant.

Pasternak was the first of them to write memorial verses to a man whose talent he continued to admire even while deploring the strident political poetry of the other's later career. In "Poet's Death" Pasternak emphasizes the impact that the dynamic Mayakovsky had made on all his contemporaries. Even in the sleep of death he was still violently mobile.

Cheek pressed to pillow, you slept —
Slept at legs' and ankles' full tilt,
Repeatedly ripping headlong
Into newborn myths' ranks.
You sliced in all the more saliently
Through reaching them in one bound.
Your shot was Etna
To foothills' cravens.[3]

Tsvetayeva was the second of the four poets to obituarize Mayakovsky in verse. News of his suicide reached her in Parisian exile, where she was outraged to find other Russian expatriates intemperately denouncing the dead poet as a versifying puppet of the Soviet government who had never been a great artist. It was not so much that she rejected Mayakovsky's pro-Bolshevik views as that she considered them irrelevant to his achievements as a poet. In adopting this attitude she generously ignored the many adverse comments that Mayakovsky himself had made in public on her verse. Undeterred by personal resentment, she was disgusted by the eagerness with which other expatriate Russians hastened to denigrate so fine an artist on the occasion of his death, and so she fired off a volley of seven remarkable obituary lyrics dedicated to his memory.

Tsvetayeva's cycle *To Mayakovsky* begins by expressing her respect and admiration for the dead poet, but she feels sufficiently intimate with him to adopt a slangy tone, and even to deride his suicide as wildly inconsistent with his record as premier prophet of the workers' revolution. His self-slaughter was more Shah-like than Mayakovskian.

You lived as great grandson,
Died as great grandad.

In other words, the suicide had chosen to finish himself off in the style of a member of the effete pre-Revolutionary generation — and this despite his repeated claims to have pioneered the glorious future. He should be ashamed to carry on like a member of the former upper classes, says Tsvetayeva. Was he a Soviet Werther, or some spoilt officer cadet of Tsarist times shooting himself out of boredom at a performance of *Tosca?* "It ain't proletarian, mate," sneers the poet, adding that Mayakovsky had behaved like a "typical gent."[4]

There is something eerie about this robust badinage directed at a poet-suicide of the recent past by another poet whose own self-inflicted death was to follow in the not-so-distant future. Still more chilling is the resonance of Tsvetayeva's verses when they conjure up the ghost of Sergey Yesenin, the first major Russian poet to commit suicide during the Soviet period — by hanging himself in 1925. *That* act had been promptly denounced in the striking verses "To Sergey Yesenin," penned by a Mayakovsky who was, at the time, so far from contemplating any repetition of the deed in his own person that he ended his ode to his dead colleague with the following self-righteous aphorism.

Dying's easy in this life;
Building life's a great deal harder.[5]

In the penultimate section of her Mayakovsky cycle the future suicide Tsvetayeva latches on to this wry reprimand by devising a conversation between Yesenin and Mayakovsky as she imagines it taking place in the hereafter. Does any other literature contain such a phantom exchange — and in comic dialogue! — between two poets, each dead by his own hand, as concocted by a third who was eventually to follow suit?

Referring to Mayakovsky's celebrated suicide note, in which he complains that his "love boat" has been shipwrecked, Tsvetayeva's Yesenin asks his colleague if he really did do himself in "for a bit of skirt." Mayakovsky fires back a well-merited retort at his dipsomaniac colleague: "For vodka's worse. Still sloshed, eh, frowsty-face?" The amazing sequence ends with the two unruly deceased poets compounding their bantering quarrel as they reject the idea of implementing a second, joint, suicide in the hereafter: it occurs to them that they cannot, now, lay *hands* on themselves, for they no longer possess those appendages. Handless though they may be, they are left plotting to bomb the afterworld to smithereens.[6]

Tsvetayeva ends her obituary sequence in a more serious vein, with a brief prayer for the militantly atheistic and blasphemous Mayakovsky — who had once offered to act as a pimp for God, or to carve the Deity up with a knife. Her final line is: "Rest in peace, O Lord, the soul of this Thine enemy." By substituting the surprise word "enemy" for the familiar "servant" of the Orthodox liturgy, she has concluded her deliciously sardonic verses to Mayakovsky on a note poignantly Mayakovskyesque.[7]

Though Mayakovsky's suicide occurred during Akhmatova's thirteen-year poetic silence, she eventually commemorated him in a lyric written ten years after his death. Reminding the dead poet of his "stormy dawning," she also recalled his flair for making

Each thing you touched seem different from before.
All your destructive efforts brought destruction;
Each throbbing sentence was a guilty verdict.
Lonely and often discontented, restless,
You kept on telling fate to get a move on.[8]

Mandelstam did not commemorate Mayakovsky in verse, but was the first to defend the other's memory, and in a context ludicrously unpoetical. News of the suicide reached Osip Emilyevich when he was on his way to Armenia, and chanced to be staying at a state guest house at Sukhumi on the Caucasian Black Sea coast. The other residents included writers, but also Communist Party officials, one of whom happened to be Nikolay Ivanovich Yezhov. This junior functionary was destined to become notorious in 1936–38 as the head of Stalin's political police, and was also to be the person ultimately responsible to Stalin for Mandelstam's arrest and death in 1938 — shortly before he himself was liquidated at Stalin's behest as part of a sequence of events typical of the period.

When the news of Mayakovsky's suicide reached the Sukhumi guest house Yezhov was more innocently employed — he was making merry with his cronies and dancing his favourite dance, the *gopak.* Observing this from the garden, Mandelstam was disgusted. Was this the way to behave on the day when a great Russian poet had died? And so Mandelstam sent his wife into the house to request Yezhov to comport himself in more cultured style. The future organizer of mass liquidation was good enough to comply by desisting from his *danse macabre.*[9]

Mandelstam comes nearest of the four poets to dominating Russian verse of the 1930s, for he eclipses Akhmatova's, Pasternak's, and Tsvetayeva's scanty contributions of the period with the sequence of superb lyrics contained in his two Moscow Notebooks and three Voronezh Notebooks. Those works place him in the foremost ranks of the world's poets active at the time, but the scale of his achievement has become evident only belatedly. Not until the late 1960s, and in the United States, were his verses of the 1930s published comprehensively enough to be judged as a whole. In his own country his writings became strictly taboo under the Stalin dictatorship, but have been cautiously revived, semi-tolerated, and selectively published in more recent years.

Mandelstam will also claim our attention because the abominable circumstances of his decline and fall were so closely linked to his creative vocation, his premature death being the direct outcome of continuing politico-literary indiscretions such as have been logged already. They included glaring failures by omission — his obstinate refusal to extol the glorious present and future of the Stalinist state, his neglect of the idiom of officially sanctified cliché. There were also to be gross errors of commission, including the denunciations of Stalin and Stalinism in his verse. But above all Mandelstam offended by deploying so remarkable a degree of artistic originality. To write superbly — here, surely, was the most heinous political crime among the many that he committed; for writers were now being increasingly regimented by other writers, and there is nothing that your author-turned-functionary so fears and persecutes as the authentic accents of creative genius.

How did Mandelstam recover his voice after falling silent as a poet in 1925? One fount of inspiration was his visit of 1930 to Soviet Armenia, where he spent precisely two hundred days, according to a lyric written after his return. He was in the south from April till October. It was not in Armenia, but on the first stage of the return journey and in the Georgian capital Tiflis that he began to write poetry again after a five-year interval.[10] The chief subject of his first new verses was Armenia itself, to which a score of loosely interconnected lyrics are devoted — a sequence that was followed shortly afterwards by the delightful prose memoir *Journey to Armenia.*

Since Mandelstam had now been out of favour with authority for several years, and had been finding it more and more difficult to place his work, it is astonishing that a dozen of the Armenian poems, and also *Journey to Armenia,* were published in Soviet journals within a year or two of being written. After the verse had appeared, in *Novy mir* (Moscow) of March 1931, *Journey to Armenia* became Mandelstam's last work to receive publication in the Soviet Union for over thirty years when it was brought out by the Leningrad journal *Zvezda* in May 1933.

No connoisseur of Mandelstam's mind would have expected his Armenian writings, verse or prose, to paint a panoramic picture of the country. His method was characteristically impressionistic and vivid. The capital, Erivan, and its ancient religious centre, Echmiadzin, are pictured as dominated by the huge bulk of Mount Ararat, which has "drunk up all their air," yet can suddenly reduce itself to "a hiker's tent." The mountain can also be charmed by a pipe or ocarina, and lured towards the poet, who will lick the snow off its summit. At lower elevations colours are spattered about in profusion as if an imaginary lion, endowed with the ability to sketch, had clutched half a dozen crayons in his paw: yellow, mustard, "hoarse" ochre, red-lead, and the contrasting azure of the sky. Clay dominates the scene: "clays congealed

like black blood." The local women saunter past like lionesses, bestow-
ing their beauty on beholders. The Armenian children too are affection-
ately compared to animals, being called "little beasts."[11]

The Armenian verse and the Armenian prose both extol a people
with a long, eventful history. "What more instructive and enjoyable
than plunging into the company of a completely different race which
evokes your respect, sympathy, and pride as an outsider?" The poet is
enchanted by the Armenian language, prickly as a wild cat, yet at the
same time seductive, as is its script.

> How I love your macabre speech,
> Your young tombs —
> Their letters like blacksmiths' tongs,
> Each word a clamp.[12]

Far from finding Armenia's culture and speech alien, Mandelstam
regarded the country as a cradle of European and Christian civilization,
of which his writings elsewhere eulogize the Judaic, Greek, and Italian
origins. It was not on racial or religious grounds that he prized his own
Jewish ancestry, but because it made him a Mediterranean man and a
cultural European — which in turn made him kin to the Caucasus. That
the Armenians and Georgians had been converted to Christianity in the
third and fourth centuries, some six hundred years before the Russians,
he was well aware. Hence his reference to certain Armenian ecclesiasti-
cal ruins as "unpolluted by Byzantium" — which certainly could not be
said of Russia's. Fascinated by Armenia's "octagonally shouldered, bull-
like" early Christian monuments, he evokes their impact with brutal
relish. "Eyes' teeth crunch and crumble on first view of Armenia's
churches." So steeped in ancient lore was the region that Mandelstam
called it "a bookish land . . . a bookful of vibrant clays . . . a hollow book
from which the first men learnt their lessons." Far from belonging
culturally to the East, this little country "on the world's edge" has
"Turned away in shame and grief / From Orient's bearded cities."[13]
For Mandelstam, one is tempted to add, better fifty years of Colchis than
a cycle of Cathay.

In Ararat's shadow the poet delightedly cultivated the learned men
— elderly philologians, local historians, chemists, and antiquaries —
who figure in *Journey to Armenia*. In this brilliant, discursive study he
is always ready to drop matters Caucasian for French Impressionist
painting, Linnaeus's zoological writings, the evolutionary theories of
Lamarck, the nature of cognition, Persian poetry, and the structure of
fish's eyes. As these topics indicate, *Journey to Armenia* is rich in echoes

of Mandelstam's poetry, as are so many of his other prose works. Neither body of writing can be adequately appreciated without the other.

Mandelstam's work is remarkable for what it omits as well as for what it contains. *Journey to Armenia* is written as if he were touring those exotic regions on his own, whereas he was in fact accompanied by his wife. That there was no place in his travel jottings for someone so close to him will surprise no one who remembers that the poet's memoir of his childhood, *Buzz of Time*, omits his two brothers and tells us precious little of his parents. Both as a poet and as a prose writer he had his gaze turned outwards, away from himself and from those nearest to him. But Nadezhda Yakovlevna is momentarily glimpsed in the seven-line lyric with which her husband broke his long poetic silence. Here he teasingly alludes to her "large mouth," while reflecting wistfully on the attractions of the carefree life that was never to be his.

> Starling-like I might have chirped my days away. . . .
> But I can't. Obviously. No question of it.[14]

Here is another effectively understated prophecy of impending trouble.

No less striking than the neglect of Mandelstam's wife is the failure of the poet's Armenian writings to respond to the political and social realities of Soviet rule as it surrounded him during his tour. Far from eulogizing Armenia's *achievements* under the First Five-Year Plan, or the collectivization drive which exactly coincided with his visit, he barely mentions these themes at all. But he was of course well aware that insipid dithyrambs to Soviet actuality were now being increasingly extracted from the country's imaginative writers by literary officials, themselves often failed authors, who were in turn implementing policy laid down on high. Mandelstam's very expedition to the Caucasus had presumably been sanctioned on the understanding that he too would contribute something of the sort. Were not his more malleable contemporaries spawning novels of the "full-speed-ahead" variety on all sides? Such were, for example, Valentin Katayev's *Time, Forward* and Marietta Shaginyan's *Hydrocentral*. That Mandelstam had nothing similar to offer is no surprise, for he was as temperamentally incapable of writing political advertising copy as of composing a novel. But he was equally far from attempting to portray the stark realities of the scene around him. His Armenia is an idyllically happy land that seems to exist in charmed segregation from the rest of the world — an isolated utopia with its churches, beautiful women, plentiful roses, ochreous clays, and historical traditions. The country does not seem to be part of the modern world at all, least of all its Soviet component.

And yet a few perfunctory hints at political reality break in from time to time. The prose memoir briefly alludes to a local guest house as the former home of evicted *kulaks;* it also mentions with sympathy a former schoolteacher who has been expelled from a collective farm, and an itinerant carpenter who has refused to join a trade union. More disturbing and significant are the implications of the lyric "Phaeton Driver." It recalls a journey by horse-drawn carriage through a remote Armenian town, Shusha, where Turks had massacred the inhabitants just before the annexation, by Moscow in 1921, of what is now Soviet Armenia. Mandelstam is thrown into panic by the ghost settlement, with its "forty thousand dead windows visible on all sides." Is this an oblique hint at the sufferings inflicted on the local citizenry through collectivization? Could the malign and mysterious Driver of the poem conceivably be equated with Stalin himself? There is an allusion to the man's disfigured face, which he keeps covered, and he is described as "baked as a raisin" — from which the image of the pockmarked Secretary General naturally arises. This same Driver emits a "throaty scream" (a possible reference to Stalin's guttural Georgian accent) as he lashes his horses along their sinister, jolting journey to an unknown destination, while the "dark blue pestilence" of a lowering sky ominously hovers over the proceedings.[15] Was this, in Mandelstam's mind, the dangerous, nightmare route along which the pockmarked Leader was conducting the USSR? Poetry may legitimately raise such questions without necessarily offering answers.

In 1931 Pasternak followed in Mandelstam's footsteps by visiting the Caucasus. He did not penetrate as far as Armenia, but toured the northern areas and Georgia — travels which inspired over a dozen fine lyrics contained in *Second Birth,* his fourth volume of collected poems, published in 1932.

Pasternak's Caucasian verse differs from Mandelstam's in offering more sustained passages of nature description. They are characteristically daring in their imagery and creatively quirky in a different mode from that of Mandelstam's artistic lion and his urge to lick Mount Ararat like an ice-cream cone. One of Pasternak's most stirring passages breathes life into two major rivers of the area, the Kura and the Aragvi, and into its ruined castles.

> We clamber round the Caucasus,
> And in that gasping fabric
> Kura stalks, like gas attack,

Mountain-hemmed Aragvi.
And into August's marble vault,
Like docked heads' gullets,
Decapitated castles' silhouettes
Throw up their Adam's apples.[16]

While Mandelstam's scenery is alive with bulls, horses, lions, birds, and human beings, Pasternak's is a less animated Caucasus; it is memorable for forests and precipices, and is contemplated from a greater distance. Mandelstam takes his readers through the streets, and even inside the bakeries, of Erivan, whereas Pasternak looks down on *his* Caucasian capital, Tiflis, from the faraway mountains, evoking the city — no less strikingly — as "flickeringly writhing in the depths, like sword hilt's niello-work."[17]

Pasternak's Caucasus is all cliffs, tombs, glaciers. He casually mentions on one occasion that there were "four of us" in his party, but typically fails to identify his companions or describe them in any way. In one lyric he takes farewell of these or other mysterious figures as they disappear from view down a beach "into foam's chimes." The only other humans in his Caucasian landscape are long dead. Like Mandelstam, he conjures up the historical past, referring to Russia's nineteenth-century conquest of the Caucasus, whereby the area was invaded by "hordes, hordes, hordes of serfs, old sweats, exiles." He refuses to glorify war, but mentions the love that the Russian incursor felt for the vanquished land — a love not reciprocated (it must be noted in passing) by all the local inhabitants. Pasternak is less concerned with these than Mandelstam, who so often harks back to Armenia's ancient traditions; and Pasternak's occasional glimpses of pre–nineteenth-century Caucasian affairs — of the conqueror Tamerlane and the mythical Prometheus — are all perfunctory.[18]

Pasternak's lyrics reflect the external scene less intimately than Mandelstam's, and are more intimate — if somewhat oracular — in their revelations of the poet's own mentality and of his emotional life. "Waves" shows him deep in contemplation of his past and future: a new departure for one whose lyrics had hitherto concentrated on capturing the present moment. His surf has been baked by the tide "like waffles," and is also compared to cattle driven out to pasture by the sky.

Curling, furling
At misery's full tilt,
Towards me rush my own deeds —
Crests of my past experience.[19]

What these "deeds" and "experiences" were the poet does not specify, but his personal life offers some clues. He was now estranged from his first wife, whom he had married in 1922, and was accompanied on his southern travels by Zinaida Nikolayevna Neygauz, who was soon to become his second wife. This new love affair was the "second birth" of his title. The scenic thrills provided by the mountains were also rejuvenating, as were the spectacular prospects opened up — Pasternak believed — by Stalin's ambitious economic innovations.

Pasternak's lyrics are now harping on the future in a spirit favourable to the ruling ideology. Eupeptic as ever, happy in his new love, none too critical of economic and political actualities, he sonorously belabours the future tense, beginning several of the poems with "These things shall be," and comes closer than any of the other three poets to satisfying the demands made on literature by authority. He thus improves on his own earlier record as the hesitantly revolutionary author of the four long poems of the 1920s. There are even passages in *Second Birth* suggesting that he might yet have become the bard of Stalinism triumphant, as when he claims to discern "our General Plan" towering ahead of him through the mists like a huge Caucasian crag.[20]

Pasternak rated an improvement in women's status as one of the major benefits conferred by the Russian Revolution. Women had always been ill-used by men in his view, and he was determined to leap to their defence. The posture may seem incongruous when one remembers the three principal ladies of this narrative, whose force of character exceeded even that of Pasternak himself. Still, not every woman is an Anna Andreyevna, a Marina Ivanovna, or a Nadezhda Yakovlevna, and it was their more vulnerable sisters whom he had in mind when addressing Stalin's Russia as follows.

> Land where women never more
> Shall cry like cuckoos in Putivl.

The reference is to the lamentations of Yaroslav's daughter from the ramparts of Putivl as recorded in the Russian medieval epic *The Lay of Igor's Raid,* and Pasternak indicates that now, more than seven hundred years later, the need for these agonized ululations has been removed by the new and equal status at last accorded to the female sex. He goes on to mention the two women closest to himself, his ex-wife and his future wife. In his Socialist utopia "Both breathe side by side, / and lust's hooks creak not."[21] It sounds a depressing prospect.

Current political developments are also enthusiastically acclaimed in some of the non-Caucasian poems of *Second Birth*. There is an ecstatic address to the First of May as the harbinger of a dazzling future. There is also the most outspoken of all Pasternak's acts of obeisance to the New Woman liberated by revolution.

> And since, from infant years,
> I've bled for Woman's lot;
> Since Poet's steps are but the trace
> Of Her paths, and no more;
> Since only She can move me;
> And since we've set Her free —
> Glad am I to efface myself
> At Revolution's will.

In another lyric Pasternak invokes the First Five-Year Plan, and again introduces the two women. He and they are already living in the future, he says; no matter that they may face it as cripples run over by the New Man as he rushes ahead in "Project's Cart."[22]

Besides voicing enthusiasm for future prospects, Pasternak also expresses scepticism. The first lines of "To a Friend" assert a willingness to sacrifice personal interests to the Revolution because it is bringing happiness to the masses. He asks whether he is such a monster as to prefer the meaningless happiness of a hundred privileged persons to "the bliss of hundreds of thousands," while claiming that his own morale rises and falls along with the Five-Year Plan. And yet: "What am I to do about my chest cage? / What about stagnancy out-stagnated?" In other words, there are aspects of the new society — no doubt including the regimentation of the arts — with which Pasternak still cannot reconcile himself, for all his theoretical readiness to submit. He concludes that there is no place in such a society for the poet.

> In days of weighty counsel,
> When higher passion has free scope,
> No place should be reserved for poets;
> Their post is dangerous if filled.[23]

Pasternak's scepticism about the poet's role did not deter him from attempting to influence events, and it was now that he first sought to conduct a long-distance dialogue with Stalin, whom he had met briefly in person in the mid-1920s. His first attempt to reach the Secretary General was with the lyric "A Century and More," published in *Novy mir* of May 1932. Not naming Stalin, the poet reveals whom he is addressing by expressing a longing for "law and order": who else could restore those amenities but he who had put himself above the law and imposed disorders so flagrant? Pasternak also appeals for a halt to the executions that had become so prominent a feature of the period.

The poet could never have urged clemency on Stalin in public if he had not evolved an ingenious method of encoding his message. He begins by inviting his reader to look back "a century and more" to the year 1826, when an earlier Russian poet (Aleksandr Pushkin) had addressed to an earlier Russian despot (the Tsar-Emperor Nicholas I) a celebrated lyric entitled "Stanzas." In those verses Pushkin had, in turn, directed the nineteenth-century monarch's attention back a further "century and more" to an earlier Tsar-Emperor, Peter the Great. Pushkin had reminded Nicholas I that

> The beginning of Peter's glorious days
> Was darkened by mutinies and executions.

And yet, Pushkin maintains, the eighteenth-century sovereign had shown mercy to his enemies. That Pushkin's message to Nicholas — be merciful — was Pasternak's message to Stalin no discerning reader could fail to grasp, though Stalin is not, of course, mentioned by name.[24] This is not one of Pasternak's most impressive lyrics, but his concern for the public weal must be saluted, together with his courage and skill in directing this muffled harangue at the dreaded Secretary General. Whether the message was received or not is not known. In any case, it was not Stalin's (nor Nicholas I's) nature to heed such appeals, a lesson that Pasternak was slow to learn.

In November of the same year, 1932, Pasternak made his next attempt to establish an understanding with Stalin. The vehicle was a letter published in the press, and the occasion was unusual. On the seventh of the month Nadezhda Alliluyeva, Stalin's second wife, had committed suicide by shooting herself after a quarrel with her husband. The very existence of any wife of Stalin's had so far been kept secret; but her death — officially ascribed to peritonitis — was announced in the press, and evoked public expressions of condolence from various bodies, including one representing writers. Their letter appeared in *Literaturnaya gazeta* above thirty-three signatures, and was couched in the accepted formulaic style: "devoted all her strength . . . cause of liberation . . . millions of oppressed humanity . . . ready to sacrifice our lives." All this was routine liturgical speech. It was in the postscript, signed by him alone, that Pasternak spoke — and with the evident intention of dissociating himself from the preceding text. His words struck an especially discordant note because of their style: plain, straightforward, jargon-free. He himself shared the feelings of the letter's signatories, Pasternak stated. On the day before the announcement of Alliluyeva's death he had chanced to think "deeply and intensively about Stalin, as a poet — for the first time"; then, when he had learnt of Stalin's bereavement, he had felt as deeply involved as if he had been present in person.[25]

Stalin's domestic life remains an enigma, and his wife's death is one of the few episodes of which anything at all is known. It seems clear that her suicide profoundly shocked him, and that it came at a low ebb in his political fortunes. One of his main initiatives of the period, collectivization, appeared to have failed, and he had not yet made it sufficiently unsafe for his subjects to say so. It may also be suspected that Alliluyeva's suicide helped to trigger his paranoiac fantasies, and so caused him to unleash the Great Terror of the late 1930s. The significance of Pasternak's postscript is as an assertion of individuality in an age of conformism. He would support Stalin — yes; but he would do so without employing Stalinist jargon. This course was dangerous, but it has been suggested that the poet's immunity from arrest may have been due to the personal relations that he established with the dictator through his unconventional postscript. As for the attendant risk, it is well defined by Nadezhda Mandelstam. She remarks that it became a normal security precaution during the fully developed Terror to exterminate not only those who rejected the official ideology — which the Pasternak of the early 1930s did not — but *above all those who rejected its phraseology.*[26] This crucial thought is here italicized, since it seems so important to the understanding of the Soviet Union as a whole, and not only of its Stalinist phase.

In seeking communion with the Secretary General, Pasternak was taking a grave risk. But then, writing almost anything for publication — be it a letter to the press or a poem — was hazardous under present conditions. Poetry had always been a high-risk profession in Russia, and Pasternak knew this as well as anyone else. What is poetry, indeed, but a protracted and elaborate form of suicide? He makes the point himself in one of his best-known lyrics of the period, contrasting his carefree youthful attitude to his calling with his present awareness of the hazards to which artistic creativity had exposed him.

> Ah, had I known the way of it
> When launching my career —
> That verse is deadly, murderous
> Haemorrhage gushing from throat!

All frolics with such pitfalls
I would have turned down flat.

Equating himself — as later in his famous lyric "Hamlet" — with an actor who accepts his duty to play a part that will end with his death, Pasternak continues as follows.

Like Rome, old age from actor
Demands no make-believe,
No feat of elocution,
But — literally — death.[27]

During the 1920s Pasternak was gradually changing his style of writing. The exuberant, ingenious young poet of *My Sister Life* and *Themes and Variations*, whose verse comprehends so much magnificent obscurity, by no means disappeared. But now, alongside such familiar material, a new and more straightforward approach was also to be found — an anticipation of his later technique, as it was to evolve from the 1940s and into the period of *Doctor Zhivago*.

The interest of the collection *Second Birth* derives partly from the combination of these two modes — their alternation within the same lyric, rather than their fusion. In one famous passage the claims and credentials of the new method are defined in lines that themselves partly exemplify it — but with a curl of paradox at the end to warn the reader that Simple Pasternak and Complex Pasternak are still, fundamentally, the same unique poet.

In great poets' usage
Are traits so artless;
To savour them
Is to be struck dumb.

To be sure of kinship with nature,
To feel at home with the future,
Is to end by adopting the heresy
Of devastating simplicity.

That simplicity we must conceal
Or pay the penalty;
For though it's what man really needs,
He grasps the complex better.[28]

Pasternak's new, hard-won simplicity is also exemplified in poems addressed to his new love and future wife, Zinaida Nikolayevna. In one of them the poet imagines himself alone in his flat in winter, watching the snow fall outside his window and brooding guiltily over his estrangement from his former wife, when her successor suddenly appears on the scene.

> Unawaited, across door's curtain,
> Flits intrusion's quiver;
> Steps will measure silence;
> You'll enter like my Future —
>
> Vision at door
> In artless white,
> Cut straight from the material
> They use to fashion snowflakes.[29]

The ethereally enchanting Zinaida was not long to retain her capacity for spurring Pasternak to poetry, though she was to preserve until his death her status as the disapproving but efficient mistress of his household. She was also to suffer, justly or unjustly, from the hostility of contemporaries. Akhmatova once said that she disliked *Second Birth* because of Zinaida's presence, and also because Pasternak cuts the figure of a "distraught suitor" in the verses in which she appears.[30] Maligned by Akhmatova, tartly dismissed in Nadezhda Mandelstam's memoirs, Pasternak's second wife receives fractionally more sympathy in the reminiscences of Olga Ivinskaya, who was later to supplant Zinaida Pasternak in the poet's affections, just as Zinaida herself had once replaced his first wife.

To consider Pasternak's evolution from 1932 onwards is to be struck by yet another contrast between the impact of the exotic south on him and on Mandelstam. Whereas the latter's Caucasian expedition helped to restore his creativity after a six-year period of silence, exposure to the southern mountains heralded an opposite reaction on Pasternak's part. From 1933 to 1940 he wrote little original verse.

It was not the scenic marvels of Daghestan, Mleti, the Georgian Military Highway, and Tiflis that struck the poet dumb, so much as his increasing awareness that the society around him failed to match the economic and feminist utopia of his poetic reveries. But the newly silent Pasternak by no means fell into immediate disfavour with authority, for though he was not writing new poetry, no fewer than seven collections of his previously published verses were brought out in the four years 1932–35. This is an index of his continued acceptability to authority, by contrast with Akhmatova and Mandelstam, neither of whom had any volume of verse published or republished in the 1930s.

11

HARDER TO BREATHE

AFTER returning from the Caucasus, Mandelstam continued on the collision course with authority that was to culminate in his death eight years later. From the passive crime of his Armenian writings — failing to praise Stalinism — he graduated to active misdemeanour. His later verses abound in forebodings of doom, and even include forthright denunciations of Stalin.

Was he consciously inviting trouble? According to his widow, "He imperiously steered his life towards the disaster that lay in ambush." One night in the early 1930s he woke her to explain that he was now writing each of his lyrics as if expecting to die the next day. But he was not seeking martyrdom. Nor was he immune from the general "narcosis" of his era, for there were moments when he "wondered if he was blind to be the odd man out and to ignore what was obvious to everyone else."[1] He was no Solzhenitsyn engaging the embattled post-Stalin state in single combat; nor would so heroic a duel have been a practical possibility in the 1930s, even for a Solzhenitsyn. Mandelstam's was the special courage of the frightened man who is tempted to adopt the servile postures that might save him, but is temperamentally precluded from doing so.

His verse pursued its dangerously nonconformist progress after he and his wife had gone to Leningrad in November 1930, hoping to make a home there. By the end of January he had written four magnificent poems about this, his native city, conveying the awareness of past and future calamities that it aroused in him. He also fed in the local colour scheme, a combination of yellow and black reminiscent of Russia's past, for they were the colours of the Imperial Russian flag.

Now you're back — quick, gulp
Leningrad's river lamps' cod-liver oil.

Quick now — recognize the December day:
Egg yolk mixed with baleful tar.

The poet's address book contains the telephone numbers of the dead. The bell of his flat, "torn out, flesh and all," slams into his forehead, and his door chain seems to fetter him as he spends all night awaiting certain "dear guests." This sardonic pointer to his fear of a night raid by the OGPU might have been designed to bring about that very horror: a journalist acquaintance who read the poem remarked that such verses could be expected to provoke a visit from "a trio in uniform."[2]

Mandelstam reverts to his youth in another Leningrad poem, pointing out that he had never belonged to the imperial capital's social élite of aristocrats and guards officers. No lover of oysters or Gipsy dancing girls, he had abandoned the city during the Civil War and gone south to the Black Sea and its Nereids, "sensing future beheadings and fleeing the bellow of turbulent happenings." In a third lyric Mandelstam imagines himself sitting in a Leningrad kitchen with his wife, surrounded by the sweet smell of white paraffin, a sharp knife, a loaf of bread, and a primus stove that he invites her to "pump up tight." Or else she is to weave a string bag so that they can take their few possessions to the railway station, "to stop anyone tracking us down" — again a hint at the poet's fear of arrest. In his fourth Leningrad poem he prays for strength to survive the night, since "Petersburg life is coffined sleep"; these desperate lines he never showed to his wife, who learnt of them only after his death.[3]

The Mandelstams' hopes of settling in Leningrad were dashed after Nikolay Tikhonov — an influential local poet turned literary functionary and arbitrator of humbler authors' living conditions — had proclaimed his determination to run his deviant colleague out of town. "Mandelstam shall not live in Leningrad because we won't give him a room."[4]

Thwarted in their attempt to take root on Neva's banks, the poet and his wife reluctantly re-established themselves in the capital. They were "forcibly brought back to Buddhist Moscow," according to a lyric of the period;[5] by "Buddhist" Mandelstam understood "stagnant, oriental, Stalinized." In Moscow they once again secured quarters in Herzen House, and lived there from summer 1931 until autumn 1933. The accommodation was sordid; but their hardships were slightly alleviated by a small official pension, and by access to the special shops where food unavailable to the general public could be bought. During three years in the capital Mandelstam was to compose two magnificent collections: his Moscow Notebooks, containing over ninety lyrics or lyrical fragments.

To judge from verses of the First Moscow Notebook, written in 1931, Mandelstam's fears were not allayed by residence in the capital. This is particularly evident in "Wolf," in which he speaks of having sacrificed his birthright, joy, and honour for future generations' sake. His own age — which he had once addressed as a wounded, yet by no means hateful beast — has now become powerful and menacing: "The Wolfhound Age springs on my back." He longs to escape, even at the cost of Siberian imprisonment, this being the first among several lyrics in which he sees himself in a concentration camp; he sarcastically compares Siberia's bleak steppes to a warm fur coat, and asks to be thrust into it "like cap into sleeve." In the last stanza he defies the Age by denying its ability to harm him, its superior.

> Lead me into the night where flows the Yenisey,
> Pine brushes star;
> For I am no wolf by blood,
> And my equal alone shall slay me.[6]

"Wolf" is the key poem in a cycle that further develops kindred themes: doom, defiance, isolation. One especially sombre vision has the poet awaking one morning in a prison camp with a choking sensation — a reference to the asthma from which he now suffered, and to his continuing heart trouble. Yet he is "deadly eager to live" as he sits up in his bunk and hears a fellow convict sing a rough camp song while a streak of dawn appears above the prison.[7]

A lighter touch is cultivated in other items from the same cycle. "I Drink to Military Asters" is a toast to the amenities of Western Europe, from which the poet has long been cut off; the "asters" probably represent officers' epaulettes. It is to them, and not to record-breaking tractor drivers or jolly milkmaids, that he boldly raises his glass, as also

> To Savoy pines' music, to petrol in Champs Elysées,
> To roses in Rolls-Royce cabin, to Parisian paintings' oils,
> To Biscay's waves, to jug of Alpine cream,
> To haughty English blondes, to distant colonies' quinine.[8]

Mandelstam continues to express defiance in lyrics following the "Wolf" cycle, invoking the city of Moscow more frequently, and occasionally favouring an ebullient manner reminiscent of Pasternak. The longish poem "Today We Can Take a Transfer" begins with a spray of quasi-Pasternakian kakophony by comparing the Kremlin to a nest of pistachio-hued dovecotes and the city as a whole to the inside of a grand piano, while also proposing to send the bell tower of Ivan the Great abroad "to complete its education." But the poet is soon contemplating his own alienation, that repeated theme of the period.

I shall not march in step with Youth
Into demarcated stadiums. . . .
Even as flimsy ghost I shall not enter
Their quaint crystal palaces.

Every day I find it harder to breathe.[9]

The Second Moscow Notebook, on which the poet began work in May 1932, finds him neglecting his own fate for other topics — especially the creative arts. He offers a striking portait of a French Impressionist painter, probably Monet or Pissarro, who depicts

Lilacs' deep trance,
Laying pigment's vibrant rungs,
Scab-like, on canvas.[10]

But it was naturally Mandelstam's own art that received most emphasis. He affirmed his enthusiasm for Germany's romantic poetry and cultural traditions in "To the German Language." But it was on Italian literature that his main attention was fixed: it was now that he first seriously learnt Italian and devoted himself to Dante. The long essay *Conversation About Dante*, unpublished in his lifetime, offers an electrifying, characteristically impressionistic interpretation of the author of the *Divina Commedia*, whom Mandelstam so rightly regarded as the poet of poets. He also translated four sonnets by Petrarch and wrote the lyric "Ariosto," of which two versions exist. There is also the curious, whimsically superstitious lyric "Do Not Tempt Alien Dialects, but Try to Forget Them," in which he expresses the fear that he may one day suffer for his interest in foreign writers. Perhaps Ariosto and Tasso are no more than "blue-brained monsters with scales of wet eyes"?

What if, to punish your pride, O incorrigible phonomaniac,
You get a vinegar sponge for your treacherous lips?

This moment of disloyalty to Italian poetry was exceptional in one who prized both Russian and Western European culture, considering them complementary to each other. The alliance between East and West proposed in the first version of "Ariosto" was more characteristic of his dominant attitude.

In broad, fraternal azure blend
Let's mingle your sky's blue and our sea's black.[11]

As this proposed union suggests, Mandelstam's tributes to foreign poetry are balanced by those to Russian. There is the requiem cycle dedicated to his older contemporary Andrey Bely, and there is the cycle playfully celebrating poets of the past — Tyutchev, Batyushkov, Derzhavin, and others. There is also the sequence of eleven eight-line verses in which Mandelstam abandons individual writers and studies poetic inspiration in general. He believed that poets could somehow seize on phantom word combinations that floated on the air around them, and he associated artistic creativity with the dynamic tension of sprung forces generated by spherical, crescent-shaped, or arc-like forms. They included architectural vaults, and the wind-filled sails that helped him to fish the following delectable proposition out of the ether.

I love fabric's look
When — after two, three,
Four gusts —
Comes rectifying sigh.

And I feel so well, so gravid
When looms the instant,
And suddenly arched tension
Throbs in my mutterings.[12]

Mandelstam was not only permitted to publish a few poems in Soviet journals as late as 1932, but he was also — despite the semi-disgrace to which he had long been consigned — still in demand for poetry recitals both in Moscow and Leningrad. One such reading of his work took place in November 1932 on the premises of *Literaturnaya gazeta* in Moscow, and led to the publication by that periodical of three poems that had so far circulated only in manuscript or orally.

Early in the following year the poet gave another, more memorable recital to a packed auditorium in Leningrad, where his hearers included enthusiasts for his work, but also political activists eager to embarrass him. "Certain malcontents" were scuttling about the hall, whispering ironically, frowning, shrugging their shoulders. Then one of them handed up a note inviting him to give his opinion of contemporary Soviet poetry. This intervention was at once recognizable as a gross political provocation. The poet would either have to praise conformist versifiers of his own generation, and in terms that the audience would

recognize as deliberately mendacious, or else he would have to compro-
mise himself by expressing the sincere sentiments that would be sure to
get him into trouble. How, in particular, could he avoid the dangers
presented by the liturgical word "contemporary," which expressed all
that officialdom regarded as most forward-looking and praiseworthy?
The creative arts were required to cultivate contemporaneity: to march
with the times, or (in the cant of a later age) to be "relevant to society."
Mandelstam had long ago responded to this parrot cry in the triumphant
first line of a celebrated lyric.

No. Never was I anyone's contemporary. No one's.[13]

Now this hypersensitized term had arisen to plague him yet again. At
first he blenched and searched for words, aware that he was undergoing
a form of police interrogation in public. But then he stepped forward,
threw his head back, and hurled his own challenge at the anonymous
questioner.

"What do you expect from me? What answer . . . ? I am Akh-
matova's contemporary!"

A storm of applause showed the audience's appreciation of the
poet's skill in turning the sinister word against his would-be discomfit-
ers. That he delivered his well-found retort "with flashing eyes" no
student of Russian literary memoirs will need to be told. What is cer-
tainly more significant is that some members of the public still dared,
even as late as 1933, to applaud both the disgraced Akhmatova and her
disgraced champion.[14]

Mandelstam and his wife toured the Crimea in the summer of the
same year. They revisited Koktebel, his former haunt, and it was now
that he became friendly with the poet Andrey Bely, of whose death he
was to learn in the following January. It has been suggested that Man-
delstam conceived his obituary cycle on Bely as the requiem for
himself that — he was now convinced — no one else would ever
write.[15]

The Mandelstams' travels showed them something of the sufferings
imposed by the collectivization of agriculture in terms of deportation,
execution, and famine. Even the most self-centred traveller could not
fail to notice that the peasants of the south had been dying of starvation
in droves; and anyone observing their distress was bound to be less
impressed by the tourist attractions of the Crimea than by the dearth of
amenities for sustaining life of any sort. In a lyric that he cannot have
expected to see published, the poet compares local conditions as he saw
them in 1933 with those of the Civil War and of the last White resistance

under General Wrangel. The poem's title, "Stary Krym," refers to a small spa in the southeastern Crimea.

> Cold spring weather. Starving Stary Krym —
> Shamefaced, as in Wrangel's time.
> Sheepdogs in yards. Patches on rags.
> The same grey smoke with the bite in it.

Mandelstam goes on to invoke the "dread ghosts of the Ukraine and the Kuban" (the areas most exposed to famine and repression), together with almond blossoms and horizons visible afar. He describes these horizons as "absent-minded" in his bowdlerized final version; but in an earlier variant he had employed the more macabre epithet "executed by shooting." *Vsyo tak zhe khorosha rasstrelyannaya dal* ("Lovely as ever are those bullet-riddled vistas").[16] With or without this variant "Stary Krym" expresses the mood of protest that had previously been reflected in Mandelstam's Leningrad poems, in the "Wolf" cycle, and (on one interpretation) in "Phaeton Driver."

On his collision course with authority Mandelstam was now approaching the point of no return. It was marked by an authoritative article in *Pravda* of 30 August 1933 denouncing *Journey to Armenia*. The complaint was, all too predictably, that the poet had ignored Soviet Armenia's "achievements" — always a key word in official jargon. This accusation was true; he had said nothing whatever about them, either in his lyrics or his prose. And yet it was still not too late, according to his widow, for him to have averted or postponed his fate, had he only been willing to recant and vilify his work in response to the *Pravda* article.[17]

Mandelstam did not recant, but only became more irreconcilable after moving from Herzen House in the autumn to less uncomfortable quarters in another Muscovite writers' residential block, in Furmanov Alley. The move chanced to provoke his exasperation with Pasternak, who was still favourably disposed towards the Stalinist dispensation. Pasternak had visited the Mandelstams in their new quarters, and had congratulated his colleague on being tolerably well housed. "With a flat like this you can write poetry." Mandelstam was outraged, but politeness compelled him to wait for the other to leave before giving vent to his feelings. As his widow has explained, he regarded comfort — of which there was, incidentally, precious little in the new flat — as utterly irrelevant to creativity. "It was his deep conviction that nothing could stop an artist doing what he must do." And so he was always to remain "a nomad and a wanderer" in an era when other authors were busily accumulating such rewards of subservience to authority as mahogany furniture, American refrigerators, cars, chauffeurs, attractive new actress-wives, town apartments, and dachas. Such were the status symbols that writers acceptable to authority have been accused of amassing later in the decade out of greed or self-importance; and though Pasternak too might collect some of them in passing, he was by nature the very reverse of acquisitive or status-obsessed. But the Mandelstam of 1933 was in no mood to draw such fine distinctions. He himself was not averse to creature comforts, but he was neither able nor willing to pay for them by doing what he was told; and he believed — wrongly — that Pasternak was. One possible cause of the misunderstanding was a striking difference in their working methods. Pasternak considered a desk and appropriate surroundings indispensable to creativity, but Mandelstam simply generated verses in his head while walking about wherever he might happen to be.[18]

This clash of temperament, aggravated by Pasternak's well-meaning congratulations on the new apartment, helped to inspire Mandelstam's vitriolic lyric of November 1933, "The Flat Is Quiet As Paper." Barely moved in, he already wants to move out and make way for some conformist writer of the sort that the place was intended to accommodate.

> Some embellisher,
> Some comber of collectivized flax,
> Some blood-and-ink merchant,
> Should be staked thus.
>
> Some honest traitor,
> Boiled out of the purges like salt,
> Some family man
> Should swat these moths.

Listening to his radiators gurgling, watching his squat, frog-like telephone, the poet can think only of pulling on his boots and stamping out of the place.[19]

This was not his first poem to take issue with Pasternak. An earlier lyric, "It Is Night," voices indignation at certain lines in which the other poet appears to congratulate himself on possessing, through his poetry, a "voucher" entitling him to privileges and creature comforts. Both Pasternak's poem and Mandelstam's counter-poem are obscurely phrased, and Mandelstam had probably failed to understand the passage that annoyed him. Nor must his anti-Pasternak lyrics lead us to imagine the two at daggers drawn. The widow Mandelstam's memoirs favour that impression at times, since she is characteristically tart in dismissing Pasternak as anything but a close friend. "We never visited Pasternak and he seldom called on us — an arrangement that suited us completely." But Nadezhda Yakovlevna's references to Pasternak are not all uncharitable, and she herself has wisely stressed the error of attempting to allot praise and blame between two artists and individuals so different from each other.[20]

Life in Furmanov Alley soon began to justify Mandelstam's intimations of calamity. According to his widow, the winter of 1933–34 was the most terrible time of her whole life, even though it was spent in the nearest equivalent to a home that she and her husband were ever to occupy. Through the thin wall could be heard the ukulele played by Semyon Kirsanov, a writer who believed that it was poetry's function to boost industrial production. There were the smells of authors' meals, and of authorial bug-killer, drifting through the ventilation system. There was no money; there was nothing to eat; there were masses of visitors, half of them spies sent by the authorities. Death was now inevitable, and might come rapidly or slowly. As an active man Mandelstam gave his preference to the former, his widow tells us.[21]

It was now that he composed his most notorious and biographically significant lyric, the "Poem on Stalin." The Secretary General is not named, but who could fail to recognize the cockroach-whiskered, gleamingly booted "Kremlinite Highlander" (a reference to the dictator's origins in mountainous Georgia) with fat, greasy, worm-like fingers, whose words are like heavy weights? Surrounded by a rabble of whistling, miaowing, snivelling, servile half-men,

> Only he blabbers, points finger,
>
> Forges command on command, like horseshoes
> To hurl at groin, forehead, brow, eye.
>
> Each execution is a treat
> To the broad-chested Caucasian.

There was also a variant version calling the Kremlinite Highlander an "assassin and peasant slaughterer."[22]

The poem was composed in November 1933 — composed rather than written, since to have committed it to paper would have been an even grosser indiscretion than conceiving it in the first place. But the author was sufficiently rash to recite or whisper the offending material to eighteen or nineteen people in all, including Akhmatova and Pasternak.[23] The decision to communicate the Stalin verses to others was recklessly inconsiderate: merely to be present while lines so sensitive were recited was to become vulnerable. Should it later transpire that the listener had failed to inform the authorities of so signal a breach of taboo, he would himself incur repression for "lack of vigilance," along with everyone else who might turn out to have heard the poem and failed to denounce the reciter. For these reasons Pasternak was understandably horrified when Mandelstam confided the Stalin poem to him one evening in April 1934, after accosting him on the Tver Boulevard in Moscow. "I didn't hear this and you didn't tell me it" was the sensible reply. Unabashed, Mandelstam went on to explain that he had composed the poem out of "hatred of Fascism in all its forms."[24]

When the text came to the authorities' notice it created such a stir that the very OGPU head, Yagoda, eventually turned out capable of quoting it by heart in conversation with Mandelstam's political protector Bukharin. A copy, in the "assassin and peasant slaughterer" version, also turned out to be in the possession of Mandelstam's interrogator after his arrest.[25] But did Stalin himself ever see or hear the poem? It is barely conceivable that anyone would dare to recite such words to him in person or submit them for his scrutiny, and yet the main actors in the drama have all spoken as if his knowledge of the text should be presumed. It most certainly cannot be disproved.

To Nadezhda Mandelstam's winter tribulations in Furmanov Alley must be added her husband's infatuation with a young actress, Mariya Sergeyevna Petrovykh. It was an involvement less serious than the passion for Olga Vaksel that had nearly broken up his marriage nine years earlier. Akhmatova has testified that his love for the bewitching Petrovykh was "tempestuous"; but then, everything about Mandelstam was tempestuous. Akhmatova also adds that the attraction was short-lived and unreciprocated. A longer, more astringent account has been given by the poet's widow, who dismisses Petrovykh as a "man hunter . . . trying out her powers on another woman's husband." Nadezhda Mandelstam remembers the drama's climax as a stormy scene: she had raised violent objection to the association, crowning her protests with the "classic" gesture of smashing a plate. Her husband had responded by brusquely terminating the affair with scant consideration for the susceptibilities of his "Mistress of guilty glances, / Proprietress of narrow shoulders," as he addresses the seductive Mariya Sergeyevna in his verse. His behaviour had been typically wild and unpredictable, his widow records, adding a pungent comment: "I have always marvelled at the weirdness of male psychology in the awesome business of love and sex."[26]

The love affair inspired Mandelstam's superb lyric to Petrovykh, written in February 1934. Akhmatova has called it "the best love lyric of the twentieth century." It is also one of the very few love poems that Mandelstam ever wrote. Though there is no lack of verses alluding to women whom he admired — Tsvetayeva, Akhmatova, Arbenina, Vaksel, and his wife are among them — those allusions tend to veer off into other themes: the rape of Europa, the siege of Troy, Russian seventeenth-century history, and the St. Petersburg theatre. Such extraneous topics "Mistress of Guilty Glances" scrupulously avoids in favour of playful eroticism. This is yet another of Mandelstam's lyrics which seems to swim in a roomful of water, the poet himself and Petrovykh's other admirers being compared to goldfish in a bowl.

> Fish move — fins aglow,
> Gills puffed out. Come now,
> Feed their silent mouths' ohs
> With flesh's quasi-bread.

The intriguingly phrased and surely irresistible "proposition" continues with the poet distinguishing himself from the red-and-gold fish by his

> Frail riblets in warm body;
> Futile, wet eyeball-gleam.

He goes on to compare his seductress to a crescent-lipped Turkish girl; asserts his intention of gulping down her dark words; even claims that he is going to get "sewn up in a sack" with her.[27]

In early 1934 yet another grotesque episode contributed to the clouds gathering round the lovelorn Mandelstam. During a visit to Leningrad the poet sought out one of the régime's most successful and prosperous writers, Aleksey Tolstoy, as he was conversing with colleagues in a Leningrad publishing office. Mandelstam made to shake Tolstoy's hand, but suddenly slapped his face, saying: "I have punished the executioner who ordered the beating of my wife." He was referring to a scandal of two years earlier, when the Mandelstams had been living in Herzen House in Moscow, and when their fellow tenants had included Sergey Borodin, who was later to achieve fame with his historical novel *Dmitry Donskoy*. Borodin had been recruited by the authorities to compromise the Mandelstams, and had taken to calling on the poet and his wife uninvited while seeking to involve them in such hazards as scrounging silk stockings from foreigners. Then some fracas had developed, and Borodin had struck Nadezhda Yakovlevna. Attempts by the incensed husband to prosecute the offender in the regular courts were blocked by the authorities, and the case eventually came up for arbitration by a so-called Comrade's Court of writers, with Aleksey Tolstoy as chairman. The tribunal found both sides equally to blame, and called the contretemps "a survival from the bourgeois system."[28] It was this preposterous verdict that prompted Mandelstam to strike Tolstoy's face — a rash gesture certain to aggravate the poet's troubles. Besides antagonizing an influential author and future top literary functionary, the episode made the eccentric Mandelstam more conspicuous than ever in an age when even to wear aberrant headgear was to risk arrest and liquidation as a deviant element.

The Moscow-based Mandelstams and the Leningrad-based Akhmatova kept in close touch during the early 1930s, exchanging occasional visits between the two metropolises. Mandelstam and Akhmatova seemed rejuvenated whenever they met — laughing, joking, and interrupting each other, while mocking the dangers and absurdities of the new society against which they felt united, together with Mandelstam's wife, in a spiritual Triple Alliance.[29]

Though Akhmatova wrote little verse in these years, a single lyric of 1933 shows that she had not lost her cunning. The poem has a theme — blood — that was becoming ever more topical, and it ends with futile attempts by two notorious blood-letters, Pontius Pilate and Lady Macbeth, to disincarnadine themselves.

Wild honey smells of open air,
Dust of sun's ray,
Girl's mouth of violets —
And gold of nothing.
Mignonette smells of water,
Love of apples.
But — one lesson we shall not forget —
Blood smells of blood alone.

And in vain did Rome's Viceroy
Wash his hands before the whole people
To mob's malign yells;
And Scotland's Queen
In vain from narrow palms
Rinsed crimson spurts
In stifling gloom of royal palace.[30]

On the night of 13–14 May 1934 Akhmatova had just arrived from Leningrad to stay with the Mandelstams at their Furmanov Alley address when she became a witness of Osip Emilyevich's first arrest by Stalin's security forces. Her eyewitness account of the event supplements that of the poet's widow.[31]

The warrant, signed by the OGPU chief Yagoda in person, was executed by a small posse of plainclothesmen. Kirsanov could still be heard playing his ukulele next door as the intruders embarked on a laborious all-night search for incriminating manuscripts. They discovered among other items the text of "Wolf"; but of course no copy of the "Poem on Stalin" was found. The search also failed to unearth a considerable archive carefully distributed in a variety of hiding places — pillows, saucepans, shoes — and after the OGPU men had gone some of these precious documents were spirited away to friends for safekeeping.[32]

While Mandelstam languished under interrogation in the Lubyanka's dungeons in central Moscow, Akhmatova and Pasternak were trying to rescue him by appealing to influential colleagues of Stalin. Akhmatova contrived to penetrate the Kremlin, where she interceded with Avel Yenukidze, a veteran ally of the Secretary General and a fellow Georgian; he received the poetess courteously, came straight to the point by asking whether "certain verses" were involved in the case, and seemed disposed to help. Meanwhile Pasternak was consulting Bukharin, long the Mandelstams' protector, at the offices of the newspaper *Izvestiya*, where he was now chief editor. Nadezhda Mandelstam too was received by Bukharin soon afterwards. When he delicately enquired if her husband might have written something ill-advised "in the heat of the moment," she replied that he had not done so. She was later ashamed to have misled Bukharin so deliberately, but has pointed out that the lie was indispensable if she was not to forfeit the support of one whose intervention earned her husband an extra four years of life.[33] Fortunately for their peace of mind, Mandelstam's friends could not know that Yenukidze and Bukharin themselves faced imminent disgrace and, within a few years, annihilation at Stalin's orders.

Meanwhile the poet awaited his fate in the Lubyanka. He was not violently ill-treated in that notorious OGPU headquarters — not, at least, by comparison with the methods to be adopted from 1937 onwards, when physical torture was the norm. But he was deliberately deprived of sleep and given oversalted foods as routine methods of undermining his resistance. It was in fear of worse ordeals, including summary execution, that he had secreted a Gillette razor blade in a specially cobbled hiding place in the sole of his shoe; how desperate he became in prison is evident from the fact that he cut both wrists in an unsuccessful suicide attempt.[34]

Mandelstam's fate still hung in the balance when Stalin suddenly made it the subject for an unheralded telephone call to Pasternak. The voice of the deus ex machina might have reduced anyone else to stuttering imbecility, but it made no difference to Pasternak, who possessed the rare gift of treating all men as equals. He accordingly burbled away, as was his custom at the beginning of any telephone conversation, about the difficulty of talking through the din made by children in the corridor of the communally shared flat where he was living. Then Stalin, who offhandedly called Pasternak "thou," managed to raise the Mandelstam case. From what he said Pasternak inferred that his own and others' attempts to intercede on the prisoner's behalf had met with some success. Stalin told Pasternak that the case was being reviewed, and that Mandelstam would be "all right." He also reproached Pasternak for failing to help his "friend" Mandelstam, either by approaching Stalin himself, or through the writers' professional organizations. Pasternak replied, only too accurately, that the writers' associations had not concerned themselves with protecting their own members for at least seven years, and then began analysing the implications of the word "friendship" as applied to his relations with Mandelstam. Stalin cut this short to ask whether Mandelstam was a genius — a question that Pasternak had the presence of mind to evade. Had he replied affirmatively, the Secretary General would no doubt have given orders for Mandelstam's immediate execution, deeply convinced as he was that the Soviet Union did not need more than one genius at a time.

Pasternak went on to say that he wanted to meet Stalin personally "for a chat." When asked what he wanted to talk about he replied in characteristic style: "Life and death." But Stalin, who was never one to bother his head over such trifles, brusquely hung up, after which attempts by the poet to have himself reconnected by the Kremlin switchboard were unavailing. On making further enquiry he was told by some minion that there was no objection to his speaking to anyone about his telephone conversation with Stalin, and so he went round Moscow recounting it to all and sundry. A whole folklore grew up around the matter, and there are wild discrepancies in different versions. The above is a collation of those given by Pasternak himself at various times to Olga Ivinskaya, to Akhmatova, and to Mandelstam's widow, who all considered that he had acquitted himself creditably in a difficult situation.[35]

As for Pasternak's wish to commune with the dictator about life and death, Nadezhda Mandelstam thinks the poet extremely lucky that no such conversation was ever permitted to take place. She ascribes his wish to meet Stalin to "a pathological interest in the Kremlin's hermit," further pointing out that the Pasternak of 1934 saw Stalin as the very incarnation of Time, History, and the Future. "He simply wanted a close look at this living, breathing prodigy."[36]

Influenced or not by Pasternak's comments over the telephone, Stalin decided to treat Mandelstam leniently. He was not sent, as originally intended, to forced labour on a canal construction site — under conditions that would surely have killed him — but received a term of three years' exile to the small town of Cherdyn in the Urals. Nadezhda Mandelstam was permitted to accompany her husband into exile, and was eager to do so, even though she would have been free to remain in Moscow. Osip Emilyevich needed her support more than ever now, for he was suffering from hallucinations aggravated by his prison experiences. His abiding obsession — by no means fanciful in the context — was that he would be shot, beheaded, or otherwise casually executed en route to his place of exile.[37]

12

DOOM'S BLACK WHISPER

AFTER Mandelstam had been sentenced, he and his wife were taken in charge by three armed and uniformed OGPU men. Prisoner, wife, and escort left Moscow by an eastbound train for Sverdlovsk, where they changed to a narrow-gauge line and chugged northwest through the forests to Solikamsk. Then they transferred to a steamer, and proceeded north up the River Kama. Mandelstam mentions some aspects of the journey in poems of the following year. The jetties are the Kama's "oaken knees"; endless fir trees stand "beard to beard"; so dense are the trees of the taiga that they have turned his eye into "coniferous meat." He alludes to the steamboat cabin where he and his wife were under orders to keep their curtains tightly drawn, lest military security be endangered through observations of the outside world made by such malignant enemies of the people. But the NCO in charge, the kindly Oska, was ready to bend the rules to help his prisoners as they steamed through the taiga, or sat waiting in stations and harbours. Guarded by OGPU men, they attracted no overt attention from the milling peasants, who prudently looked the other way.[1]

In another of his 1935 poems Mandelstam whimsically refers to his escort as "three splendid blokes from OGPU's iron gates." The Mandelstams had Pushkin's works with them, and were delighted to see how much Oska enjoyed reading *Gipsies* to his two subordinates, as is described in two comic lines.

> To save Pushkin's fine wares being bandied around among scroungers
> A tribe of pistol-packing uniformed Pushkinists brushes up its literacy.[2]

The "scroungers" are the poet and his wife, or educated readers in general.

The journey of over a thousand miles from Moscow to Cherdyn occupied five days and nights. Not having slept since leaving the capital, the poet and his wife reached their destination exhausted, and in no mood to appreciate the small town's fading archaic charm. It had been Russia's gateway to Siberia in the late sixteenth century, marking the start of the Cherdyn Route that led to the Far East.

Consignment to Cherdyn was the nearest thing possible to being sent to Siberia while still remaining within European Russia. Here was a backwoods town and minor administrative centre where political exiles had the last claim on such aids to survival as were available. Attractive though the historical associations might seem, it was unlikely that the ailing poet would survive a near-Siberian winter in such a place.

Mandelstam was still showing symptoms of mental disorder, and was admitted to the local hospital. But he was free to leave the premises at will; indeed, he was obliged to do so in order to report to the security authorities every three days. His obsessive delusions included the notion that Anna Akhmatova had recently been executed somewhere in the area; he scoured nearby gullies for her corpse. Nor had his fears for his own life subsided: he once chanced to see a *muzhik* carrying an axe, and concluded that he himself was scheduled for beheading in the style of Peter the Great's age. He also believed that his execution had been fixed for the precise hour of six o'clock in the evening on some day unknown, and his wife could relieve his apprehensions only by secretly moving the hands of their clock as the dread hour approached.[3]

One day horror leapt from apprehension to reality. Osip Emilyevich was standing with his wife by an open window of his ward, which was on the hospital's second floor, when he abruptly launched himself into space. Nadezhda Yakovlevna clutched at him, but was taken by surprise, and was left holding an empty jacket. Though the poet had fallen from a considerable height his attempted suicide failed, resulting only in a dislocated right shoulder. He alludes to this, his second attempt to kill himself, in a poem of the following year. A luminous half line — "One leap and I am sane" — suggests that the experience proved more therapeutic than such psychiatric treatment as Cherdyn could offer.[4]

After some distraught weeks in this remote outpost the Mandelstams received another favour wrested from Muscovite authority. The poet was told that permission had been obtained for him to leave the backwoods for a less uncongenial place of exile nearer to the hub of events. He was conceded some freedom of choice — but no time for deliberation — and picked on Voronezh, the large city in the south of central Russia, because the name happened to be on the tip of his tongue as the home of a biologist friend.[5]

Voronezh had its advantages as a place of exile, being a city of three hundred thousand inhabitants and an important provincial centre. It was a mere three hundred miles from Moscow, and so Nadezhda Mandelstam was able to visit the capital when resources permitted. She was thus able to retrieve copies of her husband's poems that had been secretly lodged there with friends. They became the nucleus of the two Moscow Notebooks, which were first written down in systematic form under the author's direction in Voronezh. To these and to the three Voronezh Notebooks that followed the Mandelstams would humorously allude, in the jargon of textual scholars, as "V" or "the Vatican Codex"; so far as they were concerned printing might never have been invented. The joke emphasized the irony of operating under "pre-Gutenberg" conditions in what was stridently advertised as the world's most modern and progressive country.[6]

Voronezh's advantages included its historical associations. It had been fortified in the late sixteenth century as a stronghold against Tatars raiding Muscovy's southern marches. Here also — a century later, near the confluence of the rivers Voronezh and Don — Peter the Great had built a fleet to launch against the Turks at Azov. Mandelstam relished such links with the past, but they were small consolation to him and his wife, depressed as they were by the stricken city's lugubrious atmosphere, by the acute food shortage, by the spectacle of peasants begging in the street. They had barely arrived when Nadezhda Yakovlevna contracted typhus; but she survived treatment in the local hospital, and eventually resumed the care of the sick husband so dependent on her. Then winter struck, and Voronezh was transformed into a cheerless ice-field. The poet would trudge the frozen streets at night — muttering half-formed verses, asking little more from life than tea and cigarettes.

Such comforts were not easily obtained, since he was desperately short of funds. His small State pension had been withdrawn; translating commissions had dried up; it was hard to obtain work locally owing to a well-founded fear of reprisals against employers of "hostile elements." Even so he obtained an ill-paid sinecure as the local theatre's literary adviser, and was also commissioned to write a radio script on Goethe's youth. But such earnings did little to relieve financial difficulties that were further aggravated by the desperate housing shortage. During their three Voronezh years the Mandelstams were to inhabit five different lodgings — all exorbitantly expensive, all varying from unsatisfactory to intolerable. Food was so scarce and expensive that they would have starved but for the charity of friends.

During three years of exile Mandelstam left Voronezh Province only once — in winter 1935–36, after he had received permission to be treated at a mental sanatorium in Tambov. The excursion did little for his mental or physical health.

Shortly after returning from Tambov, Mandelstam was visited at Voronezh by Anna Akhmatova, who was now writing poetry again after virtually abandoning it for thirteen years. She celebrated her expedition to the south with a lyric of March 1936 describing the city of Mandelstam's exile as encased in ice, its trees, walls, and snow all seeming glazed.

> I pass cautiously over crystals,
> So tentative is decorated sledges' course.

Akhmatova invokes two historical associations — the Battle of Kulikovo Field, fought in 1380 not far from Voronezh, and Peter the Great, whose bronze statue stood in the town's main street — and eloquently sums up her host's ordeal.

> In poet-outlaw's room
> His fear and Muse stand guard by turns
> While night draws nigh,
> That knows no dawn.[7]

As Akhmatova's poem emphasizes, Mandelstam knew himself doomed, knew that it was only a matter of time before he was exterminated through execution or the camps. The prospect aroused mixed feelings: of resignation and defiance, of depression and manic optimism. These moods are reflected in the First Voronezh Notebook — a collection of two dozen lyrics written in spring and summer 1935, his first original work since the previous February.

The poet commemorates the region's celebrated Black Earth — thick, sticky, oily, of legendary fertility.

> In early ploughing's days, black — almost blue. . . .
> How fondly gluey wafer cleaves to blade.

Silent, yet alive with fruitful potential, the Black Earth resembles the poet himself. Sometimes he feels full of energy. "I must live, though I've died twice" — a reference to his two suicide attempts. At other times, though death seems imminent, he feels stirring within him the poetry that will outlast its creator.

> What though I lie in earth, lips mumbling?
> That which I say shall every schoolboy con.[8]

In this optimistic mood Mandelstam still hoped to see some of his latest writings in print, and was even submitting certain items to metropolitan editors who could not dream of publishing them under present conditions. Verses now written with an eye to publication included "Stanzas," in which he sought to conciliate authority, only to prove psychologically incapable of carrying through the attempt. For example, he pictures himself as joyfully re-entering the community, "like a smallholder joining a Collective Farm," but this feeble attempt to mimic official propaganda conveys an image of eagerness so spectacularly unconvincing that it sounds sarcastic. No one was going to print such lines, least of all from a disgraced poet. Mandelstam is no more convincing when he states that he "must live, breathing and self-Bolshevizing." Once more equating the fertile soil with his own poetry, he writes that "the earth rings in my voice after the choking" (his arrest, Cherdyn). It is in "Stanzas" too that he speaks of his attempted suicide, by jumping out of the hospital window at Cherdyn, as having restored his reason. He also praises the exploits of Soviet aviators, and refers obliquely to Hitler — who had now been in power in Germany for over a year — as a combination of headsman and shipwreck-provoking Lorelei. In another poem of the collection Mandelstam tells his country to "Measure and retailor me." He says elsewhere that his native land has cauterized him — burnt him, as with a lens in the sun's rays.[9]

He reveals a more truculent mood at other times, as in the memorable quatrain taunting the authorities with their inability to quell his Muse. They may have cut him off from the seas and stopped him running or flying, but their "brilliant calculations" have achieved nothing: "My moving lips you could not cancel." In another defiant lyric he attacks the pretensions of the planned society, comparing its bombastic claims — fatal to so many conscripted implementers — with the futile, dangerous beating of breakers on a beach.[10]

Though the First Voronezh Notebook contains much truly exuberant — and some unconvincingly exuberant — material, it begins and ends with the major theme of impending doom. The poet foresees his wife's martyrdom in the first lyric, imagining the day when her shoulders will "bleed, whipped, and burn in frost"; when she will walk barefoot on glass and bloody sand; when he will "burn for her like black candle, and not dare to pray." He concealed these verses from her because he believed in poetry's prophetic power and wished to spare her; she learnt of them only after his death.[11]

The final lyric of the First Voronezh Notebook is among the gloomiest, but is surely the finest of all. The poet is suffering from an unidentifiable malaise, and evokes childhood memories of a life that had begun "In tub with slurred, wet susurration." Then the boy Mandel-stam's dawning consciousness is invaded by a threat from the sky, perennial source of death and poetry in his work.

> Squinting through coloured glass, I painfully discern
> Sky's menacing club, Earth's reddish pate. . . .
>
> Whiff of pitch — and is it putrid blubber?
>
> No, it's not migraine, it's sexless space's chill,
> Ripped lint's whistle, carbolic ukulele's racket.

The last line evokes disagreeable memories of the flat in Furmanov Alley and of a Moscow hospital where his wife had once been treated.[12]

It is with these disturbing intimations of individual and mass suffering that the First Voronezh Notebook begins and ends.

A crucial change in Kremlinite literary politics had begun when the Party decree of 23 April 1932 summarily dissolved all surviving literary associations after their many years of intriguing against each other. They were to be replaced by a single newly constituted organ, the Writers' Union of the USSR, which was to embrace all the country's authors. The most powerful of the bodies now liquidated was the un-popular RAPP, which had long bullied the writing fraternity as a whole, and so the latest move was at first interpreted — mistakenly — as a sign that the regimentation of the arts was to be relaxed.

The statutes of the Writers' Union were hammered out over two years, a new aesthetic doctrine — Socialist Realism — being declared mandatory for all members. It required writers and other artists to present "a truthful, historically concrete depiction of reality in its re-volutionary development." The formula possessed the merit of porten-tousness, and also of extreme flexibility, as guaranteed by authority's habit of arbitrating, defining, and redefining "truth" and "reality" at will.

The new doctrine had no influence at all on the theories and practice of the four poets, beyond becoming one more background irritation along with so many others.

The First Writers' Congress met in Moscow in August–September 1934 to adopt the doctrine of Socialist Realism and to launch the new union with due solemnity. Its sessions, swollen by fraternal delegations of workers and distinguished foreigners, were held in the Hall of

Columns of the House of Unions, shortly to become the stage for another Stalinist pageant — the show trials of the Terror period.

Pasternak was the only one of the four poets to attend the First Writers' Congress. He still was, or seemed, sufficiently well disposed to the new society to be publicly acclaimed during the proceedings by a leading political figure, though one already in decline: Nikolay Bukharin, Mandelstam's old patron. Bukharin called Pasternak "an outstanding master of verse in our time, who has threaded a string of lyrical pearls on his art and given us profound, sincere revolutionary works."[13] The profound, sincere revolutionary works included *The Year Nineteen Hundred and Five* and *Lieutenant Shmidt*, and the tribute suggests that Pasternak was being tentatively groomed as the brightest star in the constellation of officially approved bards. He was, after all, the only major poet prepared to offer political support — however eccentrically phrased — to the system.

Reports of Pasternak's attitude to the Congress reflect his own hesitancies. One chronicler has him disappointed and dispirited; another has him radiating a frozen smile of ecstasy from the platform. When, by a piece of typical stage management, a workers' delegation from the construction sites of the Moscow metro appeared on the scene, Pasternak chanced to notice a young female navvy carrying some heavy tool, possibly a pickaxe. He jumped up and gallantly made to relieve her of the burden, which, in the course of a prolonged tussle, the burly young woman obstinately refused to yield. Later, in his address to the Congress, Pasternak referred to this episode, and to the — no doubt embarrassed — amusement that it had caused. He explained that the pickaxe bearer had been "at that instant in some momentary sense my sister, and I wanted to help her as someone near and dear to me whom I had long known." Was his buffoonery intended to mock the solemnly ludicrous occasion? It seems unlikely. This was surely Pasternak the devoted feminist seeking to act out some of the sentiments of *Second Birth*, in which he had said how glad he would be to efface himself entirely in view of the rights secured for women by the Revolution. But he was far from effacing himself through the episode of the pickaxe. It only drew attention to him.[14]

Pasternak voiced loyalist sentiment in his short address to the Congress, while continuing to avoid the liturgical jargon increasingly adopted by others. His speech was cumbrously inarticulate even by his own standards — a reflection, perhaps, of his divided loyalties. As for material uncongenial to authority, his peroration is full of it. He warns writers not to sacrifice their personalities for the sake of status. "Given the enormous cordiality in which the people and the state envelop us, the risk of becoming a literary bigwig is too great." He also expresses the hope that "riches, which destroy a man, may pass us by," yet welcomes the possibility that one or two of those present may become modestly prosperous in a material sense.[15] Here was the tolerance, if not outright approval, of creature comforts that had so infuriated the Mandelstams, inspiring Osip Emilyevich's vituperative lyric "The Flat Is Quiet As Paper."

Pasternak's remarks on literary bigwigs show how keenly attuned he was to the potentialities of the Writers' Union, which was fast becoming a haven for the pliant and creatively impotent — now more than ever the recipients of preferential housing, as also of shopping, medical, and holiday amenities beyond the average citizen's reach. The age of the literary tycoon, of the writer turned functionary, was well under way, and though Pasternak was never to become one, he took a small step in that direction by accepting election to the board of the Writers' Union. As for riches passing him by, though he was never to become one of the new literature's rouble multimillionaires, he was always to retain greater access to the material perquisites of authorship than any of the other three poets.

Pasternak detested the fuss made of him at the Congress. Despite the harlequinade of the pickaxe episode, he loathed being in the public eye. Here was the dislike of fame that he expressed again and again during his life. Though he was to attract public attention — and to do so deliberately out of an overpowering sense of duty — his dislike of publicity made it as uncongenial to him as to the Lieutenant Shmidt and the Hamlet of his poems. In a letter of 1935 he mentions the distress that the Writers' Congress had caused him by deliberately inflating and artificially exaggerating his reputation without his consent. Nothing was more repugnant to him than being made a celebrity by the press.[16]

Attempts to groom Pasternak as an unofficial poet laureate soon lapsed, fortunately for his peace of mind. He was unfitted for that role by his spontaneous, childlike temperament, by the originality of his language, by the freshness of his mind, by his inability to simulate, by the unpredictability of his behaviour, by the political decline of his sponsor Bukharin. In any case another, far more suitable, poet laureate was available in Mayakovsky, whose enthusiasm for Bolshevism had notoriously transcended that of mere Bolsheviks. Mayakovsky also possessed the advantage of being dead, which meant that convenient sentiments and attitudes could be attributed to him without risk of public repudiation. And so Stalin promoted him to the position of premier bard in 1935. "Mayakovsky has been and remains the best and most talented poet of our Soviet epoch," the Leader decreed, and he added a sinister rider: "Indifference to his memory and words is a crime." After this "They began introducing Mayakovsky compulsorily, like potatoes under Catherine the Great," according to Pasternak. "This was his second death, the one that wasn't his fault." Mayakovsky's posthumous promotion delighted Pasternak, saving him "from the inflation of my significance, to which I began to be subjected in the mid-1930s during the Writers' Congress." He even wrote a letter to Stalin thanking him for switching the limelight elsewhere.[17]

How ill-fitted Pasternak was to become Stalin's poet laureate is illustrated by his reaction to a rural tour that he undertook in order to inspect the new Collective Farms and write about them. Such assignments were a staple feature of the literary system, but Pasternak's journey yielded no creative harvest other than the corrosive comments on collectivization included in *Doctor Zhivago* a quarter of a century later. At the time he was so shattered by exposure to agricultural reality that he fell seriously ill. Collectivization was, he later recalled, "an inhuman, an unimaginable, a fearful misfortune . . . the mind boggled. I fell ill, couldn't sleep for a whole year."[18]

In the wake of this ordeal, in June 1935, the long arm of Stalin again reached out for Pasternak, as he was recovering from "psychasthenia" at a holiday home. An emissary from the Leader suddenly descended on the ailing poet, and commanded him to set off with all speed to the International Congress of Writers for the Defence of Culture which was in the process of convening in Paris under Communist sponsorship. It turned out that certain French authors had approached the Soviet ambassador to France, asking that Pasternak and Isaak Babel be tacked on to the USSR's delegation: an indication of their international prestige and value as cultural assets.

Pasternak did not dare to refuse, and set off for Paris, where he was acclaimed before the congress as "one of the greatest poets of our time" by André Malraux. He himself made a brief speech describing poetry as "the celebrated peak, higher than all the Alps, that lies in the grass at our feet."[19] But his most memorable Parisian experiences took place outside the conference hall: his private encounters with Marina Tsvetayeva, long his assiduous correspondent.

After Tsvetayeva's chief outlet — the émigré Russian journal *Volya Rossii* — had lost its Czech government subsidy and was forced to close down, she found it increasingly difficult to achieve publication. Again and again she suffered the humiliation of having her work rejected or mutilated by editors whom she did not respect. And so the decline of the House of Efron continued. Her earnings dwindled, her husband's health was poor; they and their children, Ariadna and Georgy, moved from one squalid Parisian suburban lodging to another, plagued by the inability to pay their rent, living on what trifles the daughter earned by knitting bonnets. Once, when an émigré journalist asked for an interview, Tsvetayeva insisted on the meeting taking place at a Paris railway station, being unwilling for a stranger to witness her domestic squalor. This was far from her first taste of poverty, and she complained that she was still living in the same "puddle of soapy dishwater" that had been her life since 1917.[20]

There were few domestic satisfactions to relieve these hardships. Tsvetayeva and her husband still shared a home, and were never to abandon each other completely; but they had become partially estranged. One reason was political. Though Sergey Efron had once been active in the White cause, he was now a Red sympathizer eager to redeem his earlier ideological errors. When both her children turned out to share these leanings, their mother's sense of isolation was intensified.

This was less a clash between their pro-Soviet and her anti-Soviet views than between their politico-patriotic obsessions and her indifference to politics and to that sort of patriotism. She was so detached, so far from being either pro-Kremlinite or anti-Kremlinite, that she did not rule out the prospect of returning to Russia with her family. The dilemma — to go or not to go — is reflected in several lyrics of the period. They also echo the loneliness of one for whom there could never be a true home on earth — a point expressed in "Longing for Homeland" with such force that it almost contradicts the despair of her sentiments. She claims not to care where she lives; wherever it may be, she is inevitably bound to suffer a feeling of utter isolation while trudging back with her shopping bag to a house no more aware of being her home than is a hospital or barracks. Nor does she care whence she is to be "Extruded, inevitably, / Into myself, into my feelings' individuality."

> Kamchatka bear bereft of ice floe,
> Just *where* I won't fit in or even try to;
> Just *where* I'll be degraded I don't care.[21]

Though Tsvetayeva insists that there is no home for her on earth, she is violently partisan in her references to the competing claims of France and Russia. Her allusions to her homeland are affectionate, while her comments on Paris, and on exile in that city, are hostile or downright venomous. In *Verses to My Son* (1932) she calls the Soviet Union "his" country, commanding the seven-year-old boy to make his way there even though she herself can feel no urge to return. It is not for him to live on in Paris as a French bourgeois; is he to be the languid fiancé of some elderly, grey-haired American woman — a Gallic cock that has handed over its tail feathers as collateral to a bank? She cannot tell him what he will be, only what he will not.

> I, who all Russia
> Have pumped into you,
> As God's my witness swear:
> No outcast shall you be
>
> From your own land.[22]

In a vein yet more favourable to Moscow, Tsvetayeva wrote a spirited verse hymn to the daring, much-publicized exploits of the heroic aviators who rescued the crew of the ship *Chelyuskin*, trapped in Arctic ice on a voyage of exploration in 1934; the poem could have been printed in any USSR-published newspaper. In "Homeland" the USSR is "Faraway clime rendering proximity alien, / Singing to me: *Return home.*" Elsewhere the poet asks: "Russia, my Russia, / Why shine you so brightly?" With Russia she contrasts Paris, so boring, so ugly — even though she can almost reach out and touch the Eiffel Tower. And she derides the rich bourgeois of the French capital as cannibals in Paris fashions, embracing all modern urban civilization in her disapproval. This is the theme of "Ode to Pedestrians," in which she calls down a curse on the motorcar, and on

> Your Fords, your futile speed records,
> Your Rollses, your Royces.

She anathematizes advertisements, newspapers, and newspaper readers, hankering after solitude and communion with nature, as invoked in the poems "The Bush," "The Trees," "The Garden," and the glorious "Elderberry," with fruits suddenly ripening "redder than measles on my own body."[23]

Tsvetayeva wrote further obituary verses on deceased poets in the early 1930s. One was Maksimilian Voloshin, who died in 1932, and who had kept open house at his Koktebel villa during the First World War. Another was the young émigré poet Nikolay Gronsky, killed in a Paris metro accident in 1934. Tsvetayeva also contributed a striking six-poem cycle in memory of Aleksandr Pushkin. She firmly lays the blame for Pushkin's death — in 1837, in a duel fought at the age of thirty-seven — on "Tsar Nicholas the First, Bard-Slayer."[24] But though she puts the case with her usual cogency, and is neither the first nor the last to present it, her interpretation is questionable: did any Tsar or Tsarist bureaucrat ever seek Pushkin's ruin with half the zeal that the great poet himself committed to that cause?

Tsvetayeva's verse of the early 1930s claims attention through its new, arresting, hard-hitting, and rhetorical manner, which once again perplexed admirers of her earlier work. They had no sooner attuned themselves to one mode than the poet was betraying their expectations with fresh surprises. And yet, even as she was evolving a striking new poetic style, her overall output of poetry was on the decline. She was now concentrating increasingly on prose, and among her articles in émigré periodicals of the period are important critical studies, including a comparison of Pasternak and Mayakovsky. There are also the assorted memoirs of her youth — literary, personal, and mixed — containing valuable material on her early life. Writing predominantly about the past, she describes a day in her life at a boarding school in the Black Forest; a dream about the devil; a journey to her family's country cottage near Moscow. It was now, too, that she wrote so amusingly about the well-meaning efforts of her mother, a gifted pianist, to turn her into a musician. She also commemorated the achievement of her father, Professor Ivan Tsvetayev, in establishing the Museum of Fine Arts opened in Moscow in 1912.

The poet's prose deftly reconstructs a world seen through the eyes of a child who was never to lose a wholehearted commitment to emotional intensity. She writes of her capacity for love — one might say for vampirical infatuation — as lavished on relatives, poets, and friends of both sexes and all ages throughout her life. How uncomfortable it could be to attract affections so intemperate may be sensed more vividly in her over-effusive prose than in her superbly controlled verse.

Tsvetayeva's virtues as a prose writer outweigh her defects, as is particularly evident in the three literary memoirs of the early 1930s that link her to Mandelstam. There is the long, affectionate prose portrait of Voloshin with which she supplemented her obituary lyrics to Koktebel's most hospitable resident. There is the obituary memoir *(Captive Spirit)* of another older poet and endearing eccentric, Andrey Bely, whose death (in 1934) Mandelstam was simultaneously commemorating in poems written in Moscow. Finally, there is the article *History of a Dedication,* which provides evidence of Tsvetayeva-Mandelstam relations in 1915–16, the period of their brief assocation. It is not an intimate erotic chronicle, but a polemical broadside demolishing the inaccurate account of their relationship published by the émigré Russian memoirist and poet Georgy Ivanov in *Posledniye novosti.* But Tsvetayeva's riposte had to await posthumous publication, since the journal's editor refused to print it — a sign of her growing unpopularity with Russian exiles.[25]

Such were some of the writings that Tsvetayeva had behind her at the time of her meeting with Pasternak in June 1935.

After Pasternak had been paraded in Paris through Stalin's command to attend the International Congress of Writers for the Defence of Culture, he not surprisingly preferred to lurk in the corridors outside the conference hall, listening to Marina Tsvetayeva reciting her latest verses. She also invited him to her home in the suburbs, where he met her husband and children. All three were trying to persuade her to return to Russia, Pasternak later wrote. "It was partly homesickness, and sympathy for Communism and the Soviet Union, and partly that there was no room for Tsvetayeva in Paris, where she was perishing in a vacuum without readers."

When Tsvetayeva asked Pasternak whether she should return to Russia he replied evasively, and later bitterly regretted that he had not insisted on her remaining abroad.[26]

Akhmatova's Muse slowly regained consciousness in the late 1930s under the combined stimulus of domestic distress and political oppression. She was still living with Nikolay Punin, the art historian with whom she had long been united in a ménage complicated by the continued presence of his rejected wife. They grew accustomed to the arrangement, and it was to continue until 1938. By then Akhmatova and Punin had long become estranged. She had taken a firm decision to leave him as early as 1930, but had failed to find other accommodation; she had also lacked the moral strength to depart, as she later acknowledged. But for this admission one might have supposed Akhmatova's fortitude equal to any challenge, except perhaps to that of becoming a conventional housewife and mother. And yet she did her best to play such a role, so incompatible with her nature, in an ill-assorted household that also included two young people: Punin's daughter Irina, and (since 1928, when he was sixteen) Akhmatova's son Lyov Gumilyov.

In this domestic context Anna Andreyevna composed "My Last Toast," her only poem that can be assigned with confidence to 1934. It is a sharp denunciation of her spouse, and the word "treacherous" in the fifth line refers to his habit of favouring other women with his attentions.

> I drink to our wrecked home,
> To my baneful life,
> To loneliness in tandem.

To you too I drink —
To treacherous lips' lies;
To cold, dead eyes;
To the cruel, crude world;
To God's not having saved me.[27]

In the following year the cruel, crude world savagely invaded Akhmatova's domestic nightmare when Punin and Lyov Gumilyov were both arrested by the security forces. Akhmatova has described the occasion in verses that were later to be incorporated in the famous cycle *Requiem*. She pictures the arrest as it took place at dawn, with

Children weeping in dark room,
Candle guttering before icon-case.

More effective, probably, than these lines was the appeal that Akhmatova wrote to Stalin on behalf of her spouse and son. Both were released a fortnight later, but their martyrdom had only been postponed.[28]

Akhmatova was gradually rediscovering her poetic voice, and wrote two more poems in 1935. One is nostalgic, evoking the park at Tsarskoye Selo, where she had lived as a child. In the other she rebukes the authorities for punishing her refusal to mock her disgraced friends, also lamenting that "Without hangman and scaffold / Poets have no life on earth."[29]

Akhmatova's half dozen poems dated 1936 include further reprimands addressed to the unfortunate Punin. "From you I've hidden my heart, / Thrown it in Neva. / Tamed, wingless, / I live in your house. . . ." An eerie intimation of disaster follows.

Approaching cautiously,
Like water's gurgle,
Leans, fevered, to my ear
Doom's black whisper;
Mutters . . . :
"Yearning for refuge,
Know you where your refuge lies?"[30]

The reader must supply his own answer to this rhetorical question: imprisonment, death, or both.

The lyric "Dante" is a further reminder of Akhmatova's association with Mandelstam, for they both admired Italy's premier poet above all others, could now read him fluently, and would recite passages of the

Divina Commedia to each other. Akhmatova's lyric speaks of Dante's love-hatred of his native Florence (echoed by her own ambivalence towards Leningrad) as the city that he "Cursed from hell, / Couldn't forget in heaven."[31]

The links between Akhmatova, Mandelstam, and Pasternak were strengthened in the late 1930s. Akhmatova's visit to the Mandelstams at Voronezh, and the poem that she wrote in March 1936 commemorating her exiled colleague, have already been mentioned. Later in the same year Akhmatova and Pasternak jointly sent the Mandelstams a thousand roubles, which enabled them to enjoy a summer holiday at Zadonsk on the River Don north of Voronezh — perhaps the brightest interval in Osip Emilyevich's bleak last years. In 1936 Akhmatova also wrote a well-known ode to Pasternak, which begins by mentioning his habit of squinting at a sideways angle to the cosmos through his "horse's eye" — a reminder of Tsvetayeva's comparison of Pasternak to an Arab and his steed. Akhmatova then moves on to characteristic topics of Pasternak's verse.

> In mauve haze doze backyards,
> Platforms, timbers, leaves, clouds.
> Engine's whistle, melon rind's crunch,
> Timid hand in fragrant kid.

She ends by praising the man to whom she would often privately refer, with an old friend's licence, as to an idiot child — but whose childlike qualities she valued.

> For likening smoke to Laocoön,
> For hymning graveyard thistles,
> For filling earth with new throb
> Of stanzas echoing in new cosmos,
>
> He has been granted eternal childhood,
> Generosity, luminescent vision.
> All earth is the heritage
> That he has shared with all.[32]

The year in which Akhmatova wrote her tribute to Pasternak was a turning point for him, as for the Soviet Union as a whole: the country became markedly more Stalinized, the poet decidedly less so. Yet Pasternak began 1936 as — apparently — a would-be loyalist, resuming attempts to conduct a dialogue with Stalin, and also the publication of original verse, with two poems that appeared in *Izvestiya* on 1 January. One of these, "I Realized That Everything Is Alive," unconvincingly hymns the benefits allegedly conferred during three thousand years of history by Authority in the person of humanity's foremost leaders and prophets. Small things and great all form part of the same fructifying brew.

> Laughter near crofts,
> Hedgerow philosophy,
> Lenin, Stalin —
> And these verses.[33]

The other *Izvestiya* poem studies the complementary roles of the Artist and of Stalin, who is invoked (but not named) in terms more sycophantic than Pasternak is elsewhere known to have permitted himself. Stalin is "Less Man than Action: / Deed swollen to global bulk." Most extraordinary of all, in the context of the Leader's earthshaking activities since 1930, are the lines "While working these prodigious deeds / He left the scheme of things intact." Stalin has always remained a human being, says the poet; and when he shoots a hare in the woods the report of his gun exactly echoes any other man's. Pasternak goes on to imply that Stalin is himself a kind of poet in action, for the Other Poet in the following lines is himself.

> This Genius of Action
> So absorbs the Other Poet
> That he grows gravid as sponge.

In the last quatrain Pasternak employs a musical image to stress the Other Poet's humble function as a complement to the all-important Genius of Action. The Poet's "part in this two-voice fugue" is infinitesimal. But he "Believes in the mutual awareness / Of two ultra-extreme positions" — those of politics and poetry.[34] The lines illustrate Pasternak's persistence in trying to open communication between himself and Stalin.

Twenty years after writing his dithyrambs to Stalin, Pasternak annotated a typescript copy, calling them "a genuine attempt — one of my most intense, and my last in the period — to think the age's thoughts and live in tune with it."[35]

Despite homage offered to the Genius of Action in the *Izvestiya* poems, Pasternak was as far as ever from picking up the liturgical patter of Stalinism. This emerges clearly from his speech to the Third Plenum of the board of the Writers' Union at Minsk in February 1936. He denounced the "vulgar, high-falutin' fanfaronades" that had become a regular feature of speeches about literature, and called for a return to the straightforward style of Lyov Tolstoy, which he claimed to resemble that of Lenin. He also professed to accept the precepts of Socialist Realism, but protested against the current assumption that poetry should be judged by efficiency of performance and quantity of output, like a pump spewing out so many gallons of water an hour. And he hit back at critics who had rebuked him for not stumping the country giving recitals. Mayakovsky could carry off such performances, but they came ill from the versifying "music-hall heroes" and publicity seekers among Mayakovsky's epigones, who could never hope to repeat the master's triumphs. Forswearing public recitals — though he was not to abandon them entirely — Pasternak said that he preferred to meet his readers on the printed page, as Pushkin and Tyutchev had done. As for his own future writings, he promised never to repeat the era's commonplaces, for poetry's supreme function was to surprise. He went on to explain that he was now working his way towards a new style, of which his *Izvestiya* poems gave a foretaste, cumbrously cobbled though he admitted them to be. He further admitted that he was bound to write badly for a while, since he was making the transition from one poetic approach to another.[36] Hindsight enables us to correct this last observation: Pasternak was in fact engaged in proceeding from one phase of poetic silence to another.

Near the end of his speech Pasternak risked a sarcastic aside at the expense of the Stalin so recently hailed in the *Izvestiya* verses as a Genius of Action. "I do not recall any decree prohibiting genius in our legislation; otherwise some of our leaders would have been forced to ban themselves."[37]

It seems barely credible that the poet could deliver such a sally unpunished. Yet he was far from incurring any penalty, since he received through the Writers' Union the most bountiful material privilege available to an author of the period: his housing problems were solved by the assignment of two dwellings. One was a dacha — no mere cottage, but a substantial country house — in the authors' colony at Peredelkino, a few miles southwest of Moscow's outlying suburbs. The other was a flat in the new, lavishly appointed twelve-storey communal apartment house constructed specially for Moscow writers in Lavrushensky Street. Pasternak was to retain both these residences until his death, despite all his later troubles — in vivid contrast to the other three poets as they kept moving from one wretched communally shared flat or rented room to another, never being able to establish any permanent domicile. But there is no need to join Mandelstam's widow in the reproaches that she levels against Pasternak for enjoying easy living conditions denied to herself and her husband through their rejection of the era's political demands. These are not matters on which outsiders — themselves happily spared the pressures of that era — can decently indulge in censure; and even if they could, such censure would not be justified.

13

ALL CHANGE FOR FREEDOM CAMP

In autumn 1936 town dwellers and members of the professional classes began to be exposed to massive oppression on a scale rivalling that of the earlier collectivization campaign in the countryside. Vast numbers of managers, engineers, professors, and administrators, as well as officers of the armed forces and others, were either executed or removed to prison camps that few survived. Members of the Communist Party apparatus and of the security forces (now known as the NKVD) did not enjoy immunity, but were propelled into treating each other with especial harshness. The campaign also destroyed many creative and performing artists, the victims including a high proportion of Writers' Union members: at least six hundred of them were sent to concentration camps, according to one estimate.[1]

Stalin's motives for mounting the operation remain obscure. He may have felt that his system was too grotesque to survive unless the community could be rendered yet more subservient than it already was. There is also the ingenious theory propounded by Pasternak in *Doctor Zhivago* — that the new persecutions were a gigantic "cover-up" designed to camouflage the failure of collectivization. "I think collectivization was a mistake, a fiasco. . . . Concealing this meant that all forms of intimidation had to be used to stop people thinking for themselves, while forcing them to see what wasn't there and to assert the opposite of what stared them in the face."[2]

Though launched by a policy decision from on high, the new rigours proved alarmingly self-accelerating. Many an individual rushed to denounce neighbours and colleagues, thus securing sizeable privileges and avoiding dire penalties — but only to be denounced in turn by some custodian of integrity yet more vigilant. The chief motives were fear, gain, and self-importance, but not a few tackled the destruction of others with a relish suggesting that the activity was valued for its own sake, and that it must appeal to an element in the human spirit inadequately catered for in societies less progressive.

The intensified oppressions of 1936–38, sometimes called the Great Purge or Great Terror, were triggered by the show trial of the leading Bolsheviks Zinovyev and Kamenev in August 1936. This was quickly followed by the appointment of Nikolay Yezhov to be head of the NKVD — whence the colloquial term *Yezhovshchina* ("the Yezhov business"), by which the newly aggravated persecutions came to be known in Russia.

Two further show trials — of Pyatakov and others in 1937, of Bukharin and others in 1938 — helped to sustain the *Yezhovshchina*. Fifty-four defendants in all were sentenced at the three trials, mostly to execution, after pleading guilty to charges that included sabotage, terrorism, plotting the assassination of prominent Soviet leaders, seeking to restore the exiled Trotsky, and betraying the Soviet Union to the capitalist powers. The charges were false, the confessions having been extracted by torture, intimidation, and trickery applied by NKVD and judicial operatives themselves faced with liquidation should they fail to deliver their quota of self-incriminators. But the very baselessness of the accusations made them all the more effective as an instrument for cowing the citizenry at large, now intimidated into publicly affirming the justice of sentencing individuals to death for crimes that they had obviously — the obviousness was the point — not committed.

The show trials provided the rationale for oppressions that soon extended to many millions of victims, creating a self-generating terror. Since A's alleged failure to denounce B (for failing to denounce Zinovyev, for lack of vigilance, for sabotage, for Trotskyism, et cetera) could so easily lead to the denunciation by C of both A and B (for Trotskyism, for sabotage, for lack of vigilance, for failing to denounce Bukharin, et cetera), the chain A – B – C was theoretically extendable until it covered all the country's 170 million citizens. In this context the tradition, already well established, of execrating the victims of the show trials at elaborately staged public meetings and of signing collective letters applauding Stalinist justice became an important instrument of control, rendering recusants, backsliders, and those guilty of "facecrime" (inability to simulate an adequate degree of righteous indignation) liable to denunciation by associates who dared not remain silent.

One such letter, demanding the death penalty for Zinovyev, Kamenev, and their co-defendants, appeared in *Pravda* of 21 August 1936. It bore Boris Pasternak's signature with those of other writers — an indication that he was still a political supporter of Stalinism, or at least that he had not yet taken the hazardous decision to dissent. But this was to be his last act of obeisance. Later in the same year he refused to sign another of these officially inspired protest letters — a condemnation by the Writers' Union of a recently published book, *Retour de l'URSS*, in which the French author André Gide had expressed disillusionment with the Soviet Union. Pasternak offered the excuse that he had not read Gide's book. Nor had most of the signatories, and that only made Pasternak's action all the more outrageous.[3] The loyal citizen protests because he has been ordered to protest, not because he is familiar with the material that has purportedly provoked his spontaneous indignation.

The Gide episode began a long period of conflict between Pasternak and authority as embodied in the Writers' Union of the USSR, the organization's displeasure being voiced in denunciations of the poet delivered at a plenum of its board in early 1937. In that summer Pasternak compounded his sins by withholding his signature from the latest writers' collective protest letter, which applauded the recent execution of Marshal Tukhachevsky and other leading generals. A posse of senior literary functionaries descended on Peredelkino and begged the poet to sign; but he stubbornly refused, also ignoring the pleas of his pregnant wife Zinaida, who threw herself at his feet in understandable fear of the reprisals that seemed certain to follow. His colleagues appended his signature without his consent in the end, and the affair blew over — even though Pasternak, still believing in the possibility of a dialogue between himself and Stalin, had naïvely sent the Leader a letter explaining his refusal. He ascribed it to Tolstoyan convictions that prevented him from acting as a judge in such matters of life and death as the military executions. When telling the story many years later, he commented, "I do not understand to this day why I was not arrested there and then."[4]

How, indeed, did Pasternak escape arrest in the years of fully developed Stalinism from 1930 to 1953, when millions of individuals — innocent even of such political peccadilloes as he had committed — were arbitrarily shot or imprisoned? There has been much inconclusive speculation on the matter. Stalin may have been moved by the poet's postscript, mentioned above, to the authors' letter of condolence sent after his wife's death in 1932. Or perhaps the Leader respected Pasternak's courage, for there are other instances of defiant individuals being spared, however exceptionally. Then again, Stalin may have felt compromised by the persecution of Mandelstam, and may have been unwilling to make the same mistake again. Or perhaps Stalin did not hold a high enough opinion of Pasternak's work to make his death an imperative necessity. Another possibility is that Pasternak's widely admired renderings of Georgian poetry into Russian may have helped to dispose the Georgian dictator in his favour. It may be added that sheer accident was an explanation commonly advanced when individuals — Nadezhda Mandelstam and Ilya Ehrenburg, for example — sought to explain the mystery of their own long-term immunity.

Though Pasternak retained his life, his liberty, his country house, and his town flat, he was now discredited with the authorities, and discounted as a potential poet laureate of Stalinism. Publication of his original verse was suspended, and he entered another period of poetical silence — perhaps because he had no outlet, more probably because he felt choked by the atmosphere of the *Yezhovshchina*. But he still needed to earn his living, and had begun to do so as a translator. His writings of the 1930s include the renderings of Georgian poets, some of them his personal friends, which may have helped to avert Stalin's wrath. Not knowing the language, he worked from line-by-line cribs supplied by others, a common procedure of the era. He also embarked on his widely admired translations of Shakespeare, whom he was well able to understand in the original, though he was modestly unwilling to utter a word of English in the presence of native English speakers.

Akhmatova has left only two lyrics attributable to 1937. Both are outspokenly political, and both were preserved in secret for decades, being first published long after Stalin's death, and then only abroad. The first is a sardonic quatrain in which she says that her "clowning" is likely to earn her "a leaden pellet from the Secretary." The second, "A Little Geography," apostrophizes Leningrad as a former beauty queen among European cities, now converted into a marshalling yard from which massed convicts are freighted east to exile and the GULAG empire. What was once St. Petersburg has been reduced to a mere staging point for the bleak Siberian River Yenisey, for remote Chita,

> For Ishim, for waterless Irgiz,
> For ill-famed Akbasar.
> It's "All change for Freedom Camp
> And rotted bunks' corpse stink."[5]

Apart from the sarcastically entitled Freedom Camp, the place names are all of alien etymology; exotic, harsh, redolent of utter homelessness to a Slav ear, they denote concentration-camp sites or places of exile in Siberia and Central Asia.

Voronezh was no more exempt than any other city of the USSR from the oppressions intensified in autumn 1936, and Mandelstam's exile now entered its harshest phase. With no source of income left, he and his wife escaped starvation only through subsidies from friends. They were also discreetly assisted by the local theatre, which had terminated his employment as literary adviser, but arranged for him to rent a room in a shack overlooking the River Voronezh from the company's wardrobe mistress. The favour was the greater in that helping political exiles was now more dangerous than ever. Meanwhile the local press had denounced Mandelstam as a Trotskyite and class enemy who had "tried to penetrate" the Voronezh branch of the Writers' Union,[6] which — given the poet's loathing both of Trotsky and of officially sponsored literary associations — is a sample of the period's macabre unintended humour. The Trotskyite, class-alien poet and his wife were generally shunned; almost the only person willing to risk meeting them was Natasha Shtempel, daughter of a local schoolmistress. Mandelstam alludes to her in some of his lyrics, and she was to play a large part in salvaging his archive after his death.

The poet's heart complaint and asthma had become more troublesome, and he was now referring to himself as an invalid. Nor can his mental health have benefited from reading, as he did, the voluminous reports of the Moscow show trials in the press. His letters of the period reflect fluctuations of morale. At one time he was "remarkably healthy, full of energy," and ready to start life anew wherever fate might cast him. But there were spells of black despair, as when he wrote to the author Korney Chukovsky begging money to save him from starvation. "Though I've committed no new fault, everything has been taken from me: my right to live, to write, to receive medical care. I've been reduced to a dog, a cur. I'm a ghost, I don't exist, I have only the right to die." He lived in fear of a renewed term of exile, now that his existing sentence had almost ended, and he was ready to commit suicide rather than face such a prospect. And so he asked Chukovsky to write on his behalf to "the one person in the world to whom such an address can and should be directed."[7]

Mandelstam remained conscious, even as he suffered these ills, that this might be his last breathing space on earth, and decided to use it to the full by devoting what might be his last weeks or months to his art.[8] After producing no original verse for seventeen months, he embarked on the most intensive bout of creativity in his life in December 1936, and composed his Second and Third Voronezh Notebooks; the latter was completed in May 1937. Though never a prolific versifier, he was now composing a fresh lyric every two days: nearly seventy in four months. The work is on his highest level, despite the appalling conditions in which it was produced.

When Mandelstam had written about half the lyrics of his second Voronezh Notebook he suddenly swerved aside and composed his so-called Ode to Stalin. This must on no account be confused with the very different "Poem on Stalin" that had led to its author's arrest in 1934. The Ode was, in fact, an attempt to get him out of the trouble that the Poem had got him into in the first place. Far from abusing the Peasant-Slaying Highlander in the Kremlin in the manner of the Poem, the Ode was designed as a fulsome address to the Great Leader and Benefactor of Mankind whom other bards had long been commemorating in their thousands.

The exile of Voronezh braced himself for so daunting a task, and deliberately abandoned his usual method of composition — that of letting his verses take shape in his head, and of committing them to paper only when the creative process was complete. A procedure so casual seemed unsuitable for the Stalin Ode because he did not regard it as a poem at all. And so he solemnly set to work, on 12 January, by commandeering the table in his rented room — he who had always scorned a desk — and by laying out the paper and pencils that were not normally needed until creative work was finished. "Each morning he would sit at the table and pick up a pencil, just like a real writer," his widow tartly recalls. She also adds that he had become "a regular Fedin," a scathing reference to the officially approved novelist and later exalted literary functionary Konstantin Fedin.

The text of the Ode has survived, having been preserved — however reluctantly — by Mandelstam's widow because of its importance as a historical document. It was first published in 1975, in the United States, and forms a cycle of seven stanzas containing seventy-eight lines in all. There are no references to the Kremlin Highlander's greasy fingers and cockroach whiskers, such as are found in the very different Stalin Poem, for the Stalin of the Ode is the smiling, all-wise Father of his People, whose eyes can sunder mountains. He is "The One who moved the Axis of the World, / Honouring the customs of seven score Nations" (the different peoples of the USSR). In another couplet brief biographical hints are combined with an attempt to get on "human" terms with the tyrant by recalling the Georgian surname with which he had begun life, only to exchange it in due course for the alias by which the world knows him.

> Born in the highlands, he knew prison's harsh anguish.
> Rather than *Stalin* would I dub him *Dzhugashvili.*

The Ode is no routine tribute to the Leader of Genius, for all its conformist genuflexions; and it has been well described as "laden with ambiguity throughout." The final quatrain, in particular, is both sinister and ironical. It begins with two lines obliquely referring to the Stalin-sponsored executions of the period and to the poet's own imminent fate; but it ends with what, given such a prelude, loses the whiff of facile optimism that it would otherwise have carried.

> Bulges of human heads recede into the distance.
> Mine dwindles too, and soon I'll disappear from notice.
> Yet in my gentle books, in little children's laughter,
> Shall I be resurrected and proclaim the sunshine.[9]

The harder Mandelstam battled with his insincere Ode, the less could he suppress the true poetry that insisted on bombinating in his brain even as he ransacked it for the cadences of abject sycophancy. The result was the sequence of two dozen lyrics that conclude the Second Voronezh Notebook. Anti-odes rather than odes, they are all in some degree the offspring of the misbegotten eulogy to Stalin, being as it were the legitimate children of a bastard who seemed (until recently) to have disappeared without trace.[10]

Many items of the Second and Third Voronezh Notebooks reflect Mandelstam's usual oscillations from buoyant optimism to abject despair. But some verses do not veer to either pole, and some balance the two elements. These shifting attitudes are amply illustrated in references to the city of Voronezh and its environs. In "I Love the Breath of Frost" the poet revels in the winter scene while describing a small boy, "the little monarch of his toboggan."[11] In a more famous lyric, "You Aren't Dead Yet," the mood is not as cheerful as those words suggest, for this is more a statement of resignation than of joy unconfined. The poet relishes "plains' grandeur, / Their mists, their cold, their blizzards," counselling himself to live calmly, in bountiful indigence, in potent penury. He will enjoy days and nights of bliss, by contrast with those who have abased themselves before the age's pressures and sought concessions from its senior phantom.

> Unhappy he who, shadow-like,
> Fears dogs' bark, whom breeze lays low;
> And wretched he who, half alive,
> Begs charity from shadow.[12]

A third lyric expresses disgust with the local scenery as a sluggish, suffocating panorama of which the poet is heartily sick.

> The sprawling vista gets its second wind.
> Ah, blindfold both my eyes![13]

Yet other verses combine Mandelstam's recurrent dislike of the Voronezh plains with his fear of the future, and of a traitor to humanity who may again be identified as the era's chief bogyman. What, the poet wonders, can be done about these stricken prairies? And whose is that dim figure slowly crawling over them?

> Is it not He of whom we scream in sleep —
> Tomorrow's Judas of the Nations?[14]

Intense loneliness infuses "What Can I Do with Myself This January?" Mandelstam had called on a minor poet of the locality, hoping to find a fellow spirit, but the man had contrived to elude him. Avoided now by almost everyone in town, the unwanted visitor felt positively drunk from knocking on closed doors.

> All these locks and clamps make me want to moo. . . .
>
> Give me a reader! A counsellor! A doctor!
> Someone to talk to on barbed stairway.[15]

The terms of the poet's exile permitted him to travel within Voronezh Province, and he has left a few verses recalling excursions to its outlying regions. He commemorated Zadonsk, which he had visited in summer 1936, evoking the wind's music in the pines and their branches twisted into the semblance of harps and violas. A very different expedition, to the southeast of the area, is recalled in "This Province in Dark Water Season." For once Mandelstam had fallen into line by undertaking an officially approved Creative Mission to an economically significant region, with a view to incorporating the experience in some new literary work destined to hearten the country's toiling millions. But the nearest he came to hymning the collective achievements of the agriculturally important Vorobyovka District was to dwell on a single detail of limited economic purport: a plywood map that had chanced to catch his eye at District Headquarters because it was equipped with little lights to show which of the local Collective Farms were on the telephone network.[16]

Journeying further afield in imagination, Mandelstam takes farewell of St. Petersburg/Leningrad in a short, Blok-echoing lyric that invokes the city's naval associations, and the

> Quiet, quiet, through wan water,
> Warships' thrust.

He also returns in imagination to the Caucasian south with a brief poem on Tiflis, and another recalling a wedding celebration witnessed in Sukhumi in 1930. Nostalgia for the south and the sea is further aroused by recollections of "Curved bays' spans, shingle, deep blue sky, / Slow sail merging in cloud," from which he is now cut off.

> Why is another sand beneath my head?
> Throaty Urals, hefty Volga banks,
> These flat lands — they're all I am allowed.[17]

The longing for parts of the poet's own country now out of bounds to him is complemented by his hankering for Western Europe, to which he had been denied access for a quarter of a century. Uniting two favourite themes, France and architecture, he portrays Laon Cathedral and the light streaming through its famous rose window in the superb lyric that begins "I saw a vertical lake. / With slit rose in wheel / Fish toyed." In other verses he addresses France directly. "As alms and mercy I beg, / France, your earth and honeysuckle." Italy also figures in these poems as Mandelstam commemorates Dante — his favourite poet, an exile like himself.

> From rough stairways, from squares
> With angular palaces
> The circle of his Florence
> Alighieri sang more mightily
> With weary lips.

Mussolini's capital is denounced in "Rome," where the Eternal City is shown to be unworthy of its splendid cultural heritage, since it now toadies to the powerful and is given over to violence.

> You made it murder's nursery,
> You brown-blooded hirelings,
> Italic blackshirts,
> Dead Caesars' vile curs.

The poem ends with a glimpse of the prognathous Benito.

> Above Rome dictating degenerate's
> Ponderous chin sags.[18]

Mandelstam celebrates the visual arts in other verses of his Voronezh exile, touching on the paintings of Brueghel, Raphael, Rembrandt, and Ruysdael. Taking farewell of European culture and art, he also delves back further into the past, evoking the potters of Minoan Crete and "The blueness that was, that was sung / Long, long before Odysseus." One short lyric apostrophizes a Black Figure Greek pot — housed in the Voronezh museum and depicting satyrs, ripening fruit, and flute players as they whistle and rage because the red-black rim is chipped.

> And there's no one to attend
> To you and your mending.[19]

Mandelstam also displays vivacity in descriptions of nature unattached to specific localities or cultures. He is assaulted by the combined smell of blossoms. "Pear and bird cherry have me in their sights, / Have hit me pointblank with scatter shot." Elsewhere he lifts the earth to his lips: "These leaves' sticky promise, / This soil forsworn, / Mother of snowdrops, maples, oaklings." In another lyric he addresses a goldfinch, speaks of cocking his head back as the bird does, and stresses a further feature that they have in common: alertness to danger.[20]

Another lyric evokes a baby's smile as conveying a moment of sudden comprehension. This instant of cognition is comparable to the perception — of something never previously noticed — that lies behind the poet's creative activity. The effect of the child's dawning smile, in which grief and happiness combine, is to

> Stitch that rainbow seam
> Which makes the Seen the fully Knowable.

From this crucial experience in the human infant's brain, the poet abruptly leaps back to the early evolution of the globe, to the time when the first continent "reared from Ocean on paws," and then moves forward to the intermediate era when such primitive forms of life as snails came into being.

> Backboned, arched, continent reared.
> Out crawled snail, smile gleamed.
> Rainbow drew both ends together.[21]

Besides poems — chiefly buoyant in tone — acclaiming the Russian landscape and European culture, there is also material reflecting the poet's isolation, his awareness of imminent death, and his consciousness of the cockroach-moustachioed destroyer of European civilization on whom his fate depended. One lyric takes us back to Kiev in 1919, when Mandelstam had first met his wife, and is particularly tragic in tone. The poet now fears, nearly twenty years after their first meeting, that she may soon be widowed, and evokes this by describing an unnamed Ukrainian woman seeking her lost husband in the ravaged city's streets during the Civil War. Horses drop dead on the main thoroughfare and doom lowers over what had recently been Kiev's most desirable residential area.

> Horses fallen on Kreshchatik,
> Feudal Lipki smelling of death.[22]

The eight-lyric cycle *Unknown Soldier* is one of Mandelstam's finest and most tragic works. Its triple theme is death: in the past, as threatened in the present, as it will occur in the future. Death comes from above: a reminder that the sky still remained an obsession of the poet's. It often figures as a mysterious source of good, and especially of poetry itself; yet it also harbours the latent menace of evil. In *Unknown Soldier* Mandelstam pictures the mass destruction caused by war — especially by the First World War, with its poison gas shells descending from the heavens. As in the past, so too in the future, "Cold, frail men will / Kill, freeze, starve." The poet sees the air as a gigantic, empty tomb — a frozen vault where airmen die alone — as he appeals to his Muse, a swallow now grown helpless.

> Teach me, frail swallow
> Who have forgotten how to fly:
> How with this aerial tomb
> Can I — rudderless, wingless — cope?

Poison-gas pellets fall from the heavens like venomous grapes, while countless unknown soldiers go to their deaths: "Millions slaughtered on the cheap."

> For this did skull evolve,
> Spanning forehead, temple to temple —
> That into precious eye sockets
> Armies could not but flood?

The last poem of the cycle chillingly evokes the era's most typical contribution to the mechanics of mass death — the bureaucratic sanctification of the process in endless forms and documents. "Herded in horde," and "clutching my dog-eared birth year," the poet finds himself whispering through bloodless lips

"I was born on night of Two-Three
January Eighteen Ninety Something,
Unsound year; and the centuries
Ring me with flame."[23]

Whereas *Unknown Soldier* reflects fear for world civilization as a whole, other poems comment on the rift between Western European culture and its antithesis — the static, sluggish, despotic Orient. Evidently still preferring any "fifty years of Europe to a cycle of Cathay," he contrasts Western civilization, as represented by François Villon — a rebellious poet like himself — with the Egypt of the Pharaohs, which he mentally classes with Buddhism, Assyria, and Stalinism as the very negation of the European tradition.

Egypt's governmental shame
Bestowed sundry trash on corpses,
Sprouts trivial pyramids.[24]

Mandelstam defies Stalinism less obliquely in other poems written in Voronezh. Though not named, the dictator is his complacent

Idol, idle inside mountain. . . .
It smiles, broad-mouthed,
Thinks with bone, feels with forehead,
Strives to recall its human image.

Emphasizing the immobility, the inertia, of this fat-encased, Buddha-like figure, Mandelstam repeats the point that he had made when deriding moribund ancient Egyptian civilization. It is now known that his Idol is to be equated with Stalin. But the poet himself somehow remained unaware of this, and spent some time puzzling over the possible identity of the gross figure that had presented itself to his creative imagination. At first he seemed to identify it with Shileyko — Akhmatova's second husband, the eminent Assyriologist. But in the end the equation with Stalin became clear, together with the condemnation of the Stalin era as spiritually stagnant.[25]

One particularly fine lyric shows the poet imagining himself as a future concentration camp inmate, but as one who will never be silenced, even if his enemies should seize him and no one should speak to him again. Even if he were to be "stripped of all on earth, / The right to breathe, to open doors," he would yet

> Pump bare frame into bell,
> Rouse hostile murk's cranny,
> Yoke ten oxen to voice,
> Furrowing gloom with hand's plough.

All quickening, vibrant crescendo, and consisting of a single sustained twenty-three-line sentence, the poem ends by pronouncing anathema on the dictator — here, exceptionally, invoked by name, as "Stalin, bane of Life and Reason."[26]

In May 1937 Mandelstam's three-year sentence of exile expired, and he returned to Moscow with his wife. But they could neither find lodgings nor obtain the necessary residence permits, and were forced to live in nearby provincial towns or villages; they also visited Akhmatova in Leningrad. They still lacked any source of income, and were still suffering from acute poverty, still dependent on the charity of friends.

Mandelstam believed poetry to be endowed with magic potency that might yet save his life, and was vainly seeking to give a recital of his verse under Writers' Union auspices, for he thought that such a performance might lead to paid employment. He also undertook an officially sanctioned Creative Mission to the White Sea Canal, recently constructed by convict labour. But though he dutifully recorded the visit in verse, it was only a feeble landscape description, which remained unpublished; his widow and Akhmatova were to burn the only manuscript copy during the war, confident that the author would not have wished it to be preserved. This was one of several poems written by Mandelstam after his release from exile. Only one humorous trifle, on Charlie Chaplin, survives; the others vanished after confiscation by the security forces.[27]

The Mandelstams' fortunes seemed to have improved in early 1938, when they received, through the Writers' Union, a voucher for a two-month stay at a State rest home or sanatorium at Samatikha, in the depths of the countryside about a hundred miles east of Moscow. They travelled by train on the Murom line to Cherusti, and then about fifteen miles by sleigh to their remote destination. It was the end of a bitter winter, and the forest pines were splitting in the intense cold. Though they could get about a little on skis, they felt uncomfortably isolated. They were also uneasily aware that this was not one of the regular Writers' Union establishments, for the other residents were mostly manual workers. Such a detail could have a sinister significance, and as the weeks went by the suspicion grew that the visit might have been sanctioned for a purpose contrary to the poet's welfare. If he had known more about security procedures, he would have realized that the NKVD's modus operandi provided for the arrest of prominent persons in precisely this way: they would be lured from "the centre" on a plausible pretext, and then picked up at the authorities' convenience, without their associates knowing what had happened to them.

The Mandelstams heard a tap on their bedroom door early in the morning of 2 May, and then two men in military uniform entered with the doctor in charge of the establishment. The poet and his belongings were removed by truck. His wife was left at liberty, but she never set eyes on him again.

The news filtered through some months later that Mandelstam had received a five-year concentration camp sentence for counter-revolutionary activity. He had first been held in the Butyrki prison in Moscow and then consigned to Vladivostok in September with a batch of convicts "herded in horde" — as *Unknown Soldier* has it — by rail to the Far East. He is said to have died on 27 December 1938 at Vladivostok in one of the enormous transit camps feeding convicts to the gold-bearing wastes of the Kolyma. He perished in a pitifully demented condition according to one version, refusing food because he believed it poisoned.[28] But the date and details of his death still remain open to question, while the site of his last resting place lies beyond all computation.

In conformity with a common pattern of the period, Mandelstam's fate caused his widow's friends to shun her through fear of association with the relict of an Enemy of the People. Only a single individual was kind — and courageous — enough to call and commiserate with Nadezhda Yakovlevna over her husband's fate: Pasternak.[29]

14

OLD STYLE, NEW STYLE

A K H M A T O V A became embroiled in the Terror through the second arrest of her son Lyov Gumilyov in 1938. It occurred in Leningrad on 10 March, even as the last and most spectacular of the era's three chief judicial pageants (the Bukharin trial) was taking place in Moscow. As the son of two gifted poets — of a father who had been executed for a political offence in 1921, and of a mother who had long been the target for official disfavour — the young Lyov Gumilyov was earmarked for persecution by his birth. He was further vulnerable through his earlier brief spell in prison, since the rearrest of those previously taken into custody and released had become an almost automatic procedure of the *Yezhovshchina*. Akhmatova's son (aged twenty-five at the time of his second arrest) was held under interrogation for seventeen months in Leningrad.

The blow distressed Akhmatova all the more because she felt guilty for rejecting a maternal role during his boyhood — having left him to be brought up by his grandmother while she herself was writing poems about what a bad mother she was. Now deeply concerned for her son, she regularly joined the long queues of women who waited outside Leningrad's prisons, bearing parcels for their immured menfolk and hoping for news of their fate: parcels that might never arrive, news that might never be received.

Not long after her son's arrest, Akhmatova decided to leave Nikolay Nikolayevich Punin. To be more precise, she left his room — but not the lodgings that they both continued to share with his former wife, the other Anna. On 19 September 1938 the first of Punin's Annas accepted an offer from the second to resume her long-suspended marital status by "changing rooms." The poet thereby re-embraced the single state while remaining under the same roof.[1]

Akhmatova wrote as follows about her separation from Punin, for once admitting herself partly to blame for their incompatibility.

Not for weeks and months — for years
We drew apart. Now strikes at last
True freedom's chill,
As grey hair crowns temples.

No more betrayals or treacheries;
No more do you hear before dawn
The proofs, flowing in torrent,
Of my matchless rectitude.[2]

The closing months of 1938 witnessed a slight but significant decline in the incidence of arrests and executions; they were scaled down, but by no means suspended. Yezhov himself was liquidated and replaced by a new security chief, Beria. Certain officials in the apparatus of oppression (itself already purged several times) were ostentatiously indicted for excess of zeal, and a few cases under current review received favourable treatment, though there was no widespread release of convicts from the camps. Akhmatova's son, whose sentence was commuted from death to exile, was one beneficiary of the new trend.

A few weeks after Akhmatova's rejection of Punin her loneliness was alleviated by a new friendship — with a younger woman, Lidiya Chukovskaya, who became her confidante. She was the daughter of the well-known littérateur Korney Chukovsky, and she was another victim of the *Yezhovshchina*, which had widowed her; she herself also became a distinguished author, whose works include novels published outside the Soviet Union. Through her diaries, which were brought out abroad after Akhmatova's death, Lidiya Korneyevna is the main source on the poet's later years.

These diaries give vivid glimpses of the poet in her late forties — a woman of such overpowering natural elegance that it transcended her sordid surroundings, her neglected appearance, her worn, tattered clothes. Chukovskaya speaks of the old mackintosh; the squashed, faded hat; the darned stockings; the black silk dressing gown with the dragon on the back; the hair, disordered but still with the renowned fringe — now grey — and still surmounted by the famous comb of her prime. The poet's room was permanently untidy, her legless armchair sprouted springs, the floor was rarely swept, cracks in the windows were plugged with newspaper. She smoked endlessly; she could never seem to find her spoons, her forks, her manuscripts; she drank vodka out of a saltcellar without ever becoming drunk. And yet, while suffering hardships such as crippled others, Akhmatova never ceased to radiate the inner strength that made them turn to her for support. She was never to lose the

dignified bearing, the overwhelmingly imposing air that had so deva-
stated Petrograd and its literary smart set when she had been half her
present age. Now, as she cradled in her arms the infant child of a
neighbour (whom she privately believed to be reporting her activities
to the authorities), she looked like a very Madonna. It seemed that
nothing could ruffle her composure: neither fears for her son, nor con-
cern for her own welfare, nor the noisy gramophone of her neighbours,
nor the dire poverty that often left her without tea and cigarettes. She
also suffered from Basedow's disease (a thyroid complaint), and from a
form of neurosis that deterred her from stepping outside her door
because she had convinced herself that the landing had been mysteri-
ously removed, and that she had only to take a pace forward to plunge
to her death. She feared madness — all the more so when a close friend
of her youth, Valeriya Sreznevskaya, actually succumbed to insanity.[3]

This is the portrait conveyed by Lidiya Chukovskaya's diary of
1938–41, when she was the poet's amanuensis as well as her confidante.
She would memorize the verses which now flowed into Akhmatova's
mind; despite the minor relaxations associated with the fall of Yezhov,
it was still unsafe to preserve many of them in written form, lest they
become the basis for an incriminating dossier. Akhmatova was now
writing more poetry than she had for many years, perhaps because she
was stimulated by having a sympathetic listener who was helping to
preserve her work for posterity. There are poems on her fear of insanity,
on the insanity of her era, on her own death, on the death of her youth.
Akhmatova whispered her lines to Chukovskaya in fear of hidden mi-
crophones, or burnt scribbled copies in the stove after they had been
memorized, and in this way she taught her friend the celebrated cycle
Requiem, consisting of fifteen thematically linked lyrics. The first had
been composed in 1935, and has been mentioned above; the rest fol-
lowed in 1939–40. More than twenty years were to pass before *Requiem*
was brought out as a whole, in Munich, with a disclaimer absolving the
author from responsibility for the publication.[4]

The cycle is a lament for the victims of the *Yezhovshchina* and for
the many women who suffered, through their menfolk's imprisonment,
the torment of liquidation by proxy. Not that women were exempted
from arrest, either in their own right or as a corollary to the persecution
of a husband or lover; but they were directly victimized in far smaller
numbers than men.

In *Requiem* Akhmatova affirms her solidarity with her spiritual
sisters who had stood in line with her outside the Leningrad prisons,
waiting for news of their men. It was a time when only the dead smiled,
and when Leningrad was a mere appendage to its prisons.

> Stars of death hung over us,
> While innocent Russia writhed
> Under bloody jackboots
> And Black Marias' tyres.

The poet draws a vivid contrast between her former carefree state as "Tsarskoye Selo's joyous sinner" and the present degraded position of a woman standing

> Three hundredth in line, with parcel . . . ,
> Own hot tear
> Burning new year's ice.[5]

In this cycle embellished with religious imagery Akhmatova compares herself, and other women in her position, to the Mother of Christ — forgotten during the Crucifixion. She is near to madness as she calls for death or for her own arrest; let her see for herself the "blue-topped cap" characteristic of the uniformed NKVD, and her "house manager pale with fear."

> I have known faces slump. . . .
> Have known cuneiform pages
> Chiselled on cheeks by anguish . . . ,
> The shiver of fear in a dry laugh.

She ends with a prayer for all those who have shared her terrible vigil, "In raging cold, in July's oven. / Beneath that blinded red wall."[6]

The very existence of *Requiem* was long kept secret owing to its open allusions to the period's oppressions, but other verses written by Akhmatova during these years were less flagrantly unpublishable. By 1940 literary controls had been relaxed to such an extent that she was able to bring out some recent lyrics in the literary journals of that year. Even more surprisingly, she was also permitted to publish a whole volume of poems, *From Six Books*, consisting largely of reissued early work, but also including more recent material.

The publication of a new book by Akhmatova was a major literary event. Long queues quickly formed outside the Moscow bookshops, Pasternak hastened to inform her, and copies changed hands for huge sums on the black market. But then the publication of *From Six Books* was suddenly proclaimed a mistake, and the volume was withdrawn — on Stalin's personal intervention, according to Akhmatova herself.

Critics obediently endorsed the ban, denouncing the poet — in language familiar since the early 1920s — as "profoundly alien" to the spirit of Soviet society. "New, vital people" were indifferent, it was alleged, to the work of one who had made two cardinal mistakes in life: she had been born too late; she had failed to die early enough.[7]

As in *Requiem,* so too in Akhmatova's other verse of the period death is a prominent theme. It underpins the long poem *Way of All Earth,* which she once described as her most avant-garde work.[8] Here she portrays herself travelling alone by sledge — the vehicle associated with death in Russian tradition — to her last resting place in the city of Kitezh, that legendary elysium of folklore. She also wrote obituary elegies to two recently deceased authors of prose fiction: to Mikhail Bulgakov, who had contrived to die of natural causes, and to Boris Pilnyak, a prominent literary victim of the Terror who (she claimed) had once proposed marriage to her.[9] The poems of doom and destruction also include "Cleopatra," a further addition to her verses about famous women. The Egyptian queen is described as her children are about to be put in chains while she herself seeks death — "casually placing black snake on dusky breast" — to avoid being paraded in a Roman triumph. And yet, "Serene as ever slants that swan-like neck":[10] a line superbly applicable to the poet's own stance throughout the years of persecution.

In another poem on her own doom Akhmatova writes with dry humour, common in her conversation but rare in her verse, comparing herself to a famous Russian martyr of the late seventeenth century — "Morozova the Boyar woman," whose departure into exile for religious dissent is depicted in Surikov's flamboyant painting in the Tretyakov Gallery in Moscow. The poet wishes that she herself could be relegated to the seventeenth century, and says that she would gladly accept exile to so civilized an epoch, "By sledge, in dusk, / Drowning in dung and snow." She ends with a grotesque question.

What crazed Surikov
Shall paint *my* last journey?[11]

In other poems of the period Akhmatova turns back to mourn the passing of her youth. She calls up memories of Tsushima, the great Russian naval defeat by the Japanese in 1905, and of the age when "Landaus smoothly bore / Today's corpses" through St. Petersburg's streets. Her conversation of the post-Yezhov period abounded in bitter references to the same city under its later name of Leningrad. She was sick and tired of the place: of its seals howling in the white nights of summer, when the sun never set; of the windows of the palace where the Emperor Paul had been strangled in 1801; of the Neva and the canals with their black, yellow-glinting water — colours that echo some of Mandelstam's verses on the city. She also believed Leningrad to be "ideally adapted for disaster."[12]

Akhmatova exceptionally commemorates contemporary foreign events in her cycle *In 1940*. The verses are a reminder that this was the first year of the Second World War, which the Soviet Union had so far entered only to the extent of signing a pact with Hitler and invading Poland. They also confirm that she shared Mandelstam's concern for the fate of European civilization as a whole. Akhmatova laments the fall of Paris to the Germans as the funeral of an epoch. And she calls the German air assault on London "Shakespeare's twenty-fourth drama" — one supernumerary to the existing canon (ten histories, thirteen tragedies) and embodying a crisis yet more harrowing that those suffered by Hamlet, Julius Caesar, Lear, and Macbeth.[13]

Such were the tribulations imposed by Soviet political controls, even in their slightly mitigated form of the post-Yezhov years, that one marvels at any citizen of Moscow or Leningrad sparing a thought for the sufferings inflicted on London by German bombs. But Pasternak shared this concern with Akhmatova, as was natural since his father and sisters were now living in England. His thoughts were also directed to England by his latest literary enterprise: translating *Hamlet*. It was the first of the eight Shakespeare plays that he was to put into Russian, and it appeared in a Soviet periodical of 1940. A volume of his verse translations from German, English, and other poets was also published in the same year — a further example of the relaxations permitted after Yezhov's departure, and a sign that the poet was no longer in serious disgrace.

Pasternak responded to Akhmatova's *From Six Books* with a long letter addressing her as the equal of Blok and Pushkin; he also claimed himself "far more indebted to you than is usually thought." The four poets may seem a mutual admiration society at such times, but the impression is modified by the tart comments that Akhmatova privately made about Pasternak's well-meaning missive. She told Chukovskaya that he had never previously read her verse; that he was interested in no one's poetry but his own; that he was wont to single out works which he particularly disliked for exuberant hypocritical praise. For example, he had attempted to flatter Akhmatova by finding Mandelstamian virtues in *Way of All Earth*, while forgetting that he had once told her how much he disliked Mandelstam's writing. Akhmatova derides Pasternak's "occupational disease" of obsession with his own reputation, while claiming herself immune from that common complaint.[14] The evidence of her life bears her out.

Akhmatova also fulminated privately on the defects of Pasternak's second, much disliked, wife Zinaida Nikolayevna, who was described as crude, vulgar, neglectful of her son, and given to playing cards all day. Pasternak's domestic life would be the ruin of him. "He's not writing original verse because he's translating other people's." That there was nothing so destructive of originality as translating she had learnt from her own experience, once comparing it to "eating your own brain."[15] Whether or not Pasternak was indeed so gravely incapacitated by the process, the fact is that he seems to have written little if any original poetry between 1932 and 1941 — apart from the verses on Stalin discussed above and an undistinguished second clutch of lyrics on Georgia, *Travel Notes,* also published in 1936.

Akhmatova might drop caustic remarks about Pasternak, as about almost everyone else, but there was a bond of mutual regard between them, and it must have been a comfort to her to receive a second long letter from him in November 1940. It reached her at a particularly anxious time, when her son was still exiled, when her new book had recently been withdrawn, and when she was still the target for attacks in the press. Meanwhile, as her verses on London and Paris illustrate, Hitler's victories in the West had aroused her misgivings about the fate of European civilization. That both poets derived consolation from religion in these dark years seems clear from the reference to Akhmatova in Pasternak's second letter as one who, being "a true Christian," must realize that she should never give up hope.[16]

After Tsvetayeva's meetings with Pasternak in Paris in summer 1935 her circumstances continued to deteriorate — emotionally, spiritually, and materially. She still suffered acute poverty in the suburbs of Paris, she was increasingly alienated from her husband, and she was finding it harder than ever to place work of any kind with Russian émigré editors, to whom she was more and more a suspect and eccentric figure.

Her poetry of the late 1930s includes a cycle of seven lyrics, *Verses to an Orphan.* They are addressed to Anatoly Shteyger, a young Russian émigré and poet who had sent her some of his work and whom she had briefly met, but who is not named in the verses. While Tsvetayeva was writing them, and also impassioned letters to the same young man, he was recovering from an operation in a Swiss hospital. In language characteristically potent, Marina Ivanovna describes the many ways in which she will clasp the "frail, barely alive, transparent, paper-thin" poet to her bosom. She longs to embrace him like the mountain-girt horizon, like entwining ivy and honeysuckle, like the two arms of a river encompassing an island. The sick man is "desirable in scabs, longed for

from the graveyard ... beloved, desired, pitied, ailing." Mindful perhaps
of Dido and Aeneas, Tsvetayeva threatens to lure Anatoly into the
womb of a cave as a preliminary to admitting him to the cave of her
womb. Above all she cherishes him because

> At last I have met
> Someone that I need,
> Someone with a desperate
> Need of me.

The second clause of this statement unfortunately proved untrue, for it
soon became clear that the young man had no need of her at all. He
formed yet another link in the long chain of attachments conceived
by Tsvetayeva for individuals who could not reciprocate, wilting as
they invariably did in the white heat of her intensity. In the present
instance an extra resonance was contributed to a familiar situation
when Tsvetayeva's beloved poet turned out to be a homosexual.[17]

Tsvetayeva's troubles were further aggravated in early 1937 when
her twenty-five-year-old daughter Ariadna returned to her native land,
which she had quitted with her mother fifteen years previously. To
journey to the USSR at a time when the merest hint of association with
the non-Soviet world often led to arrest for espionage — it seems an act
of folly attributable to apathy, despair, or total ignorance of conditions.
Yet Ariadna's father soon followed her, disappearing from France later
in the same year. By contrast with his daughter, he had a pressing motive
for leaving, since he faced arrest and prosecution for his part in an
unsavoury political conspiracy in Western Europe.

After serving as a White officer in the Civil War, Sergey Efron had
not only switched his allegiance to the Red cause in emigration, but had
even taken to collaborating with Stalin's secret service in attacks on
prominent anti-Soviet Russian political émigrés and defectors on for-
eign soil. After one notable refugee and former OGPU agent, Ignace
Reiss, had been found riddled with bullets on a road near Lausanne, the
subsequent murder trial had included evidence from a female accessory
to the effect that Efron had recruited her to the assassination plot; he was
also accused of complicity in causing the death of a son of Trotsky. But
before the police could capture him he had slipped out of Paris on his
way back to the USSR, while Tsvetayeva herself began to attract the
violent indignation that his activities naturally aroused among Russian
émigrés. The poet flatly refused to believe that her husband could have
been a Stalinist agent, and her sincerity need not be doubted. But her
fellow émigrés thought otherwise, treating her as guilty by association.

The result was to isolate her still more from the Russian community in France that supplied her main readership.

In this context her thoughts turned more and more to the past, as she continued to contribute literary reminiscences in prose. The essay *An Evening Elsewhere* commemorates Mikhail Kuzmin, an older contemporary renowned both for his poetry and his homosexual enthusiasms. Tsvetayeva invokes Kuzmin and the pre-Revolutionary Russian literary coteries of his day, while stressing the inspiration that she herself had derived from Akhmatova's poetry. Never rivals, only fellow zealots, the two women poets had shared with Kuzmin the common fate of "serving terms of life imprisonment" within the solitary confinement of the self — a dungeon more secure (says Tsvetayeva) than the notorious casemates of St. Petersburg's historic St. Peter and St. Paul Fortress.[18]

Her next important essay, *My Pushkin,* traces the impact of Russia's premier poet on herself in early infancy. The article is characteristically exuberant in its re-creation of childhood, and valuable for its comments on her life in general.

The first details that the infant Marina had ever learnt about Pushkin were that he had been "murdered" (in the duel of 1837), that he was a poet, and that he was what she called a "Negro": to be more exact, he was an octoroon. This last point had been stressed by Pasternak in his verses on Pushkin contained in *Themes and Variations.* Tsvetayeva emphasizes her own childish obsession with the murder of the "Negro and Poet" Pushkin. She uses "Negro" as the symbolic equivalent for what the cant of a later age has called "the underprivileged," and goes on to ask two rhetorical questions: "What poet, dead or living, is *not* a Negro? What poet has *not* been murdered?" (The remark is a variant to her statement, quoted above, that "All poets are Yids.") Pushkin was himself black, and his famous statue in Moscow, which Marina had often visited on her childhood walks, was black too. Faced so early in life with a symbolic choice between optimism and pessimism, wealth and poverty, happiness and misery, she had deliberately decided on "Black, not White: Black thoughts, Black fate, Black life." This was not a case of inverted colour prejudice, but of the child deciding once and for all — despite her birth and upbringing in a moderately affluent professional family — that her place was with the poor and downtrodden.

The Pushkin memoir also records the infant Marina's reaction to Pushkin's verse novel *Eugene Onegin.* That tale of doubly unrequited passion had aroused her appetite for unhappy, unreciprocated, impossible love. "I conceived the desire not to be happy, thus dooming myself to *nonlove.* " In affairs of the heart, as she now retrospectively noted, she had always been the one to take the initiative. The objects of her passion had all deserted her, but never had she "held out her hands to them or turned back her head" at the time of parting. All this, she tells us, was due to the influence on her of Tatyana, the heroine of Pushkin's *Eugene Onegin.*[19]

Tale of Sonechka is Tsvetayeva's last major prose work. It was inspired by the news that a close friend of pre-emigration days, Sonechka Holliday, had recently died in Russia. Tsvetayeva had first met this tiny, childlike actress during the Civil War years in Moscow, and the result had been a "crush" so violent that the poet had no difficulty in re-creating it in full vigour in an extensive memoir written nearly twenty years later. In long conversations, reported verbatim and based on diary quotations, the two heroines address each other as if they had been fixed for all time in some Slavonic counterpart of the Fifth Form at St. Monica's. Of their speeches, littered with "Akh, Sonechka"'s and "Oo, Marina"'s, the following (from the perpetual fourteen-year-old Sonechka) is typical. "Akh, Marina! How I love to love! How wildly I do love being the one who loves. . . . Do you ever forget loving when you love? I never do. It's like toothache, only the opposite."[20]

Enough is enough. When a major writer miscues, as in this emotionally incontinent effusion, the results are liable to be more pyrotechnically bathetic than anything that mere literary mediocrity can ever hope to achieve by meritorious persistence with indifferent writing. This helps to explain why the émigré journal *Russkiye zapiski* discontinued publication of the memoir after bringing out the first of its two parts in early 1938. But the decision now seems regrettable in view of Tsvetayeva's stature as an author — one whose very aberrations are more significant than many another writer's levelheadedness. There is also the point that *Tale of Sonechka,* first issued in full in 1976, contains valuable evidence on the poet's life.

The discontinuation of *Tale of Sonechka* in mid-career further emphasized the decline in Tsvetayeva's reputation among the Russian émigrés who were virtually her only readers. After *Verses to an Orphan,* also published in early 1938, no more of her work was to be brought out in Paris during her lifetime. A further break with her dwindling readership is marked by the end of the occasional recitals of her verses that she had been accustomed to give to small audiences in the French capital.

Tsvetayeva's last literary contributions of note are two vigorous poetic cycles grouped together as *Verses to Czechia.* The first of them, *September,* laments the dismemberment of Czechoslovakia under the

Munich Agreement of 1938, while the second, *March*, denounces the occupation of Bohemia and Moravia by Hitler's forces in the following spring. The verses commemorate the country's past glories, together with its two decades of independence and prosperity between 1918 and 1938. Written from the heart by a poet who retained grateful memories of her life in Bohemia in the early 1920s, they show her continued mastery of vituperation and her sympathy for the Czechs in an era when "Prague is remoter than Pompeii." There is also a brief vignette of Hitler as she had seen him photographed looking out of a window of the Hradčany in Prague,

> Framed in icy window
> To drums' thrum —
> *Hun, Hun, Hun!*[21]

Though Tsvetayeva affirms her faith that the humiliated country will arise again, she was deeply troubled by the advance of world Fascism in the late 1930s: in Abyssinia, Spain, and Albania as well as in Czechoslovakia. This was another factor contributing to her fatal decision to return to her homeland.[22]

What was there to keep her in Paris? She was shunned by the local Russians, she had no readers for her work, no one to listen to her recitals, no publishers, no way to earn her living. Her fourteen-year-old son Georgy hated France, longing for the land which he had never seen but thought of as his own, and to which his father and sister had returned two years earlier. Tsvetayeva was more and more convinced that there was no future for her son in Paris, and she also knew that there was some prospect of her obtaining translation commissions in the Soviet Union, even though she might never be permitted to publish any original writings. She could get no paid work of any kind in France. With these considerations in mind — and anything but blind to what might await her — she left Paris with Georgy on 12 June 1939, travelling via Le Havre by sea to Poland, and thence by rail to Moscow.

> *atqui sciebat quae sibi barbarus*
> *tortor pararet.*

Marina Ivanovna was duly reunited with her husband Sergey and her daughter Ariadna in Moscow, but only to be parted from them after a few weeks. By early autumn both Sergey and Ariadna had been arrested. This had been predictable, since the slightest taint of association with any foreign country or individual was basis enough for a charge of espionage. Moreover, no one was more vulnerable than those who, like Sergey Efron, had been undercover agents operating abroad on behalf of the Stalin régime. So far as can be ascertained, Tsvetayeva's husband died or was executed quite soon; her daughter had embarked on sixteen years of concentration camps and exile.

It seems remarkable that the poet herself was never taken into custody. She was even permitted to earn a little from translation, publishing renderings from the Hebrew and Yiddish writer Isaac Leib Perets based on literal versions of his work supplied to her. She also used line-by-line cribs to translate the Georgian poet Vazha Pshavela, some of whose work had been put into Russian by both Mandelstam and Pasternak, using the same method. Like the other three poets, Tsvetayeva found translating uncongenial and arduous, which is perhaps why she was no longer writing original verse. For whatever reason, she had now "written herself out," as she admitted. Nor was she able to find a satisfactory home for herself and her son. Attempts to settle in metropolitan Moscow failed, and she soon found herself as exasperated by that city — its subways, escalators, trams — as formerly by the hated Paris. And she failed to establish a satisfactory home in any of the provincial and suburban lodgings in which she and her son found temporary refuge.

Her few surviving letters and jottings of the period consist chiefly of complaints about such matters, delivered without self-pity by one who had repeatedly contemplated her own death since early adolescence, and whose thoughts were now firmly fixed on suicide. On 5 September 1940 she wrote that she had spent the previous twelve months vainly searching for a hook from which to hang herself. "I've been measuring myself for death for a year." She also wrote that she was not brave, as many thought, but afraid of everything — of herself most of all. She feared to take poison, or jump to her death. She did not want to die, she simply wanted not to be. She also wrote, no less poignantly, that she — grey-haired, in her late forties — had lost all the feminine appeal that had helped to preserve her morale in the many dark days of her younger life.[23]

Though passages in the letters show a Tsvetayeva drained of vitality, her old self was vividly revived in early 1940 by two long meetings with Akhmatova in Moscow. It is astonishing that Russia's two most celebrated women poets — of almost the same age, of comparable renown — should never have come face to face before. And it is regrettable that we know so little of what passed between them. Akhmatova has said that Tsvetayeva spoke brilliantly, so outshining the former toast of St. Petersburg as to make her feel "dull and cow-like."[24] An Akhmatova rendered bovine! There was a prodigious feat.

Akhmatova commemorated Tsvetayeva's return to Russia with a lyric of March 1940 portraying the other poet looking down from a tower as she laments that an abyss has swallowed her loved ones, that her parents' home has been looted. Continuing in her own name, Akhmatova imagines herself and her friend walking through Moscow at night.

You and I, Marina,
Walk the capital this midnight. . . .
Funeral bells ring round us;
Wild groans of Moscow's
Blizzard cover our tracks.[25]

Later in the same year Tsvetayeva read Akhmatova's newly published collection *From Six Books,* but was disappointed. Once an admirer of the other poet's work, she described these lyrics from all periods of Akhmatova's life as "dated and feeble," noting how often they seemed to end unsatisfactorily and taper off into nothingness. It is here that Tsvetayeva discusses "Lot's Wife," quoting its last lines and suggesting how they could have been better written. Her criticism of this aspect of an otherwise impressive lyric is absolutely correct; nor can one entirely reject her general condemnation of Akhmatova's habit of "tailing off."[26]

Tsvetayeva was more closely linked to Pasternak than to Akhmatova. The two poets had met only a few times — in Russia before 1922 and in Paris in 1935; but they had corresponded over a long period and admired each other's work. Pasternak had credited Tsvetayeva with ten times the talent necessary to establish her as a major poet, proclaiming her the finest of all poets, while Tsvetayeva claimed to regard him as being, with Rilke, her only equal in poetic and human strength.

Since Tsvetayeva and Pasternak had so rarely met, and since she was apt to invest so much emotion in her relationships with absent friends, their encounter in the flesh after her return to Russia was bound to disappoint. Pasternak felt responsible for Tsvetayeva's fate owing to his failure to dissuade her from returning to her homeland during their Paris meeting, but he was able to help her shortly after her arrival in Russia by introducing her to the State publishing concern Goslitizdat. He could not give her even the most temporary refuge at Peredelkino, as she would have wished, owing to the predictable opposition of his wife Zinaida Nikolayevna, to whom Marina Ivanovna presumably presented a political rather than a sexual threat; it is perhaps regrettable that Boris Leonidovich, who so often went against his second wife's wishes, chose not to do so in this instance.

As for the prospect of any closer rapprochement between a man and woman so intimately linked by mutual esteem expressed at a distance, reference has already been made to Pasternak's blunt assertion that he could never have married Tsvetayeva, since she combined in one person every possible form of female hysteria. Olga Ivinskaya, the companion of Pasternak's declining years, has written as follows on the temperamental contrast between the two poets. "Marina was mannish, brusque, peremptory, while Boris Leonidovich was softly feminine in his life style — or, as M. Ts. herself put it, 'gentle, with complications.' "[27]

Two years after Tsvetayeva's return to Russia a new affliction struck her and her country — the massive German invasion that tumbled Russia into the Second World War. As Hitler's armies converged on Moscow in summer 1941, the poet and her son were evacuated eastwards by river steamer to the Tatar Autonomous Republic, where other writers were also being assembled. The more favoured were able to find refuge in Chistopol, a small town on the Kama. Chistopol ("Purgeburg"!) was a repellent backwater even at the best of times, and less hospitable than ever under wartime conditions. But Tsvetayeva was not permitted to rest even here, being compelled to continue her journey further east up the Kama to Yelabuga — a smaller, still more lugubrious version of Chistopol. After once briefly revisiting that centre in a vain search for lodgings, employment, and moral support, she retired to Yelabuga utterly weary and desperate. She had a little money and some food, and she settled down with her son in a screened-off section of a local hut, declining the only employment offered to her, as dishwasher in a canteen.

On Sunday 31 August Marina Ivanovna hanged herself from a hook in the lobby of her humble lodgings. The townspeople had never heard of her or her poetry, and no one, not even her son, attended her burial in the local cemetery. Nor has the precise location of her grave ever been identified, and so Pasternak was not literally accurate in the second of the following lines from his obituary elergy to Tsvetayeva of 1943.

> Ah, Marina, it is high time,
> Besides being no great trouble,
> To transfer your neglected dust
> From Yelabuga to rest in peace.[28]

The poet's son Georgy Efron was to be killed during the war, probably while still in his teens. His sister Ariadna was to survive her sixteen years of camps and exile, returning to work on her mother's literary archive and compose a valuable memoir of Marina Ivanovna in life; there is also a memoir from another convict, the poet's younger sister Anastasiya.

In 1960, after serving her time, Anastasiya Tsvetayeva had a metal cross erected in Yelabuga cemetery with an inscription in which the dates of her sister's birth and death were scrupulously recorded in accordance with the calendars (Old Style and New Style) in force in Russia at the relevant periods; as has been noted, the poet herself would have none of the New Style calendar — or of New Style spelling either — and rigorously banished both from her publications wherever possible. The inscription read as follows.

ON THIS SIDE OF THE GRAVEYARD IS BURIED

M A R I N A   I V A N O V N A   T S V E T A Y E V A

BORN MOSCOW 26 SEPTEMBER 1892 OLD STYLE

DIED YELABUGA 31 AUGUST 1941 NEW STYLE[29]

Born Old Style, died New Style!

Whether the effect was intended or not — does it ever happen, in Russia, that such effects are *not* intended? — the last two words pierce the heart as if they had come from one of the dead woman's poems. But they were not to do so for long. A few years later the Union of Writers arranged for the ideologically embarrassing cross, together with the epigraph so poignantly twisted, to be replaced by a small engraved tombstone more in keeping with official notions of decorum.

15

TWO VOICES CALLING

AKHMATOVA and Pasternak were to outlive their two colleagues by twenty and more years, but the story of the poets as a quartet of closely linked individuals has been brought to an end by the deaths of Mandelstam and Tsvetayeva.

During their remaining years Akhmatova and Pasternak were to live through the Soviet Union's early wartime defeats, and through nearly four years of bitter struggle followed by the Allied victory over Germany in 1945. They were then to suffer the eight appalling years of Stalin's postwar rule before they could at last celebrate his death in March 1953. Then they witnessed the uneasy relaxations of cultural oppression called the Thaw, and the limited, carefully calculated campaigns of de-Stalinization and re-Stalinization promoted by Stalin's successor, Khrushchev. When Pasternak died in 1960 Khrushchev was still in the ascendant, but Akhmatova survived his political downfall in 1964, and herself died two years later.

In these decades of war and peace each poet went through a long, complex evolution which can only be indicated in outline.

Paradoxical as it seems, the war against Germany brought general relief, since the presence of an identifiable enemy diverted Soviet citizens from destroying each other to destroying the invader. Life was more hazardous than ever, but there was less mutual suspicion and fear. There was, rather, an upsurge of national morale fostered by an official policy of relaxing political controls. Patriotism now rivalled or even took precedence over Marxism-Leninism as the nation's most actively promoted credo, and the Orthodox Church was restored to favour after many years in which religion had been repressed and persecuted. The general effect of these developments — and above all of the savage German onslaught and of German cruelty in the huge occupied areas — was to unite the USSR around Stalin as a leader more acceptable to the population than he had ever been in peacetime. Pasternak has one of the characters in *Doctor Zhivago* sum up the change of atmosphere as follows. "When war flared up, its real horrors and real dangers, the threat of a real death, were bliss compared to the inhuman reign of fantasy, and they brought relief by limiting the magic force of the dead letter."[1]

The German invasion forcibly reminded the two surviving poets that they were ardent patriots. Both rallied to the national cause, and both published patriotic verses in the press after being evacuated to the east — Akhmatova to Tashkent and Pasternak to Chistopol, near the scene of Tsvetayeva's death. In each case, as was to be expected, their wartime verses strayed far beyond the theme of national assertiveness. Both were able to publish volumes of poetry during the war years: Akhmatova's *Selections* was brought out in Tashkent in 1943, and Pasternak's *In Early Trains* and *Earth's Spaciousness* came out in Moscow in 1943 and 1945, respectively. Pasternak also published, in *Pravda* of 15 October 1943, the remarkable poem *Afterglow,* in which patriotic sentiment is combined with an appeal for victory to be rewarded by political relaxations — and even with the suggestion that such relaxations will be *demanded* by the victorious people. He had once again overstepped the limits by invading the area sacred to Stalin and his high flunkeys. And in any case, once victory had been achieved, the hopes were to prove as vain as their expression was to seem retrospectively hazardous.

With the onset of peace and the poets' return to their homes — of Akhmatova to Leningrad and of Pasternak to Moscow — their troubles began again, as each became re-alienated from the society with which they had felt themselves intimately linked in wartime.

Akhmatova's postwar misfortunes may be traced back to a disturbing contretemps in which she had become involved during the last year of the conflict. While in Moscow in May 1944 (on her way from Tashkent to Leningrad) she had unwisely consented to recite her verses at a public gathering in the city's Polytechnic Museum. Such was her fame — as incubated largely in secret, for she received little officially sanctioned publicity — that those present greeted her appearance on the rostrum by rising to their feet and applauding vigorously. But Akhmatova herself was quick to realize that only harm could come from this display of spontaneous enthusiasm, and for an object not selected by political authority as appropriate for adulation. She therefore did her utmost to preserve the lowest possible "profile" while on stage, assuming her demurest posture and seeking to restrain her hearers from further demonstrations of rapture.

Her apprehensions proved well founded when it was later discov-

ered that Stalin had been informed of the episode and had been pro-
voked to ask a particularly sinister question: "Who *organized* this stand-
ing ovation?" Pasternak chanced to learn of his reaction and shrewdly
noted it as so typical of the dictator that it could not possibly have been
invented. "To conceive of anyone achieving popularity except through
an *apparatus* specializing in mass publicity campaigns — that was be-
yond the Boss's wildest dreams."[2]

According to one plausible version of events Akhmatova's standing
ovation was exploited by one of Stalin's satraps, Zhdanov, to discredit
another, Malenkov, for having once favoured the publication of her
subsequently banned verses. If the story is true, it may help to explain
how Stalin came to sanction the Union-wide hate campaign mounted
against Akhmatova by the Soviet media two years later. This persecu-
tion — in which Mikhail Zoshchenko, the well-known Leningrad
writer of prose fiction, was bracketed with Akhmatova as a victim
— was unleashed by the Party Central Committee's notorious decree
on literature of 14 August 1946. Long-familiar accusations — of writing
unduly personal, emotionally self-indulgent verse, of propagating Art
for Art's sake, of failing to reflect the era's heroic collective triumphs,
and the like — were revived and orchestrated *fortissimo.* The poet her-
self, now described as "half nun, half whore," first learnt that she had
become the Soviet Union's literary Public Enemy Number One when
she chanced to read a page of newspaper wrapped round some salt
herring that she had brought home from the shops.[3]

The two chief victims and their supposed misdemeanours were
incidental to this campaign, since the purpose of singling them out for
abuse was to serve notice — on the educated, cultured, professional,
intellectual, and artistic world as a whole — that wartime relaxations
were over, and that a renewed period of harsh political discipline had
been ordained.

From now until Stalin's death the atmosphere was to be in many
ways yet more oppressive than that of the *Yezhovshchina.* Akhmatova
herself was not arrested, but was expelled from the Writers' Union, had
some unpublished verse pulped, was deprived of her ration card, and
incurred social ostracism. Pasternak hastened to help her with a sizeable
loan of money; he was one of the few who did not turn their backs on
her, just as he had been the only individual to visit Nadezhda Mandel-
stam after her husband's death.

Akhmatova's severest sufferings of the period came through the
renewed persecution of her son, who was arrested for the third time in
1949 and sent to the concentration camps. Hoping to save him, she
forced herself to write a cycle of fifteen conformist lyrics entitled *Glory*

to Peace and published in 1950. Here she has the grateful People's voice proclaiming that

> Where Stalin is, there too are Freedom,
> Peace, and Earth's Grandeur.[4]

Akhmatova can only be respected for so humiliating herself in what proved a vain attempt to induce the dictator to release her son.

Though Pasternak escaped the press onslaughts of 1946 relatively unscathed, he became the object of vicious attacks soon afterwards — not least through a scurrilous article of March 1947 by the minor poet and leading literary functionary Aleksey Surkov. Then, in the following year, Pasternak too found himself embroiled in a poetry recital, and in the same Polytechnic Museum that had witnessed both the ill-omened standing ovation to Akhmatova of 1944 and Tsvetayeva's scandalous declamations as chaired by Bryusov in 1921. Pasternak's contribution to this chain of historic performances took place in February 1948, and has been vividly described by Max Hayward, who was present.[5]

In accordance with the publicity methods of the time, a score of poets had been assembled to declaim propagandist verses supporting Stalin's so-called Peace Campaign — an operation designed to pillory all opponents of his foreign policy as ipso facto rabid sabre rattlers. The evening's slogan was DOWN WITH THE WARMONGERS! FOR A LASTING PEACE AND PEOPLE'S DEMOCRACY! Such was the era's duckspeak, and there was nothing unusual about it. How amazing, though, to find Pasternak, of all people, billed as one of the reciters. He was known to be under a cloud, and he had rarely been heard to mouth political claptrap. What, then, could he possibly be doing here? Had he decided to capitulate, confess his shortcomings, and seek favour with the authorities? Speculation on this point, and Boris Leonidovich's enormous, officially unblessed reputation, combined to pack the auditorium with addicts of that intoxicating mixture, poetry and public impropriety.

The evening began in an atmosphere of anticlimax, since Pasternak turned out not even to be present among the score of tamed bards corralled on the dais. Nor were the proceedings greatly enlivened when one of their number — his archenemy Surkov — began reciting conformist verses in which Winston Churchill was condemned as the Evil Genius of the Cold War. This section of the liturgy was received tepidly. But then, suddenly and in mid-flow, Surkov was deafened by a storm of frenzied applause that somehow did not seem directed at him or his verse. Nor indeed was it: looking over his shoulder, the unfortunate reciter saw that the cause of the uproar was Pasternak. He had made his entrance by a back door, and was taking his seat among the other poets.

From now on the audience had eyes and ears for Pasternak alone, especially as he was stage managing his performance with an unerring sense of drama. When his turn came to declaim he blandly dissociated himself from his peace-loving fellows by disdaining the available microphone, stepping down into the body of the hall, and announcing that he personally had never written any poems on the subject of the evening. But he did confess to having composed certain other sorts of verse before the war, and some of these he now proceeded to recite to a torrent of mounting acclamation. The lines were nonpolitical in content, but were given a strong political accent by the setting in which they were spoken, and were greeted with tumultuous applause. Whenever the poet forgot his words (as he commonly did when reciting) members of the audience leapt up to supply them from memory, and they were soon calling for their favourites like opera lovers screaming for encores at a concert by a Caruso or Chaliapine.

This was probably the nearest approximation to an anti-Stalin demonstration ever staged in postwar Moscow, and it threatened to develop yet more alarming dimensions when particularly daring spirits began shouting *"Shestdesyat shestoy davay!"* ("Give us the Sixty-Sixth!") They were asking for Pasternak's rendering of Shakespeare's Sixty-Sixth Sonnet, as published in a volume of the Russian poet's selected translations dated 1940. The request owed its special pungency to the fact that Shakespeare might almost have had Stalin's Russia in mind when he wrote this particular poem. He begins, "Tired with all these, for restful death I cry," and goes on to specify "all these" as follows.

> Art made tongue-tied by Authority,
> And Folly, doctor-like, controlling Skill,
> And simple Truth miscall'd Simplicity,
> And captive Good attending captain Ill.

Though the audience was bellowing for these lines as if desirous of being freighted to the Kolyma en masse, Pasternak had the good sense to decline the request. Enough was enough, and the risks that he had already taken were sufficient for a thousand evenings. Had he not single-handedly sabotaged an occasion dedicated to the sacred cause of equating a love of peace with love of Stalin's foreign policy? That so grave a misdemeanour did not provoke the poet's arrest may have been due to chance or to a decision consciously taken by Stalin on the basis of considerations previously discussed.

Spared in his own person, Pasternak was persecuted by proxy when the beloved mistress of his autumnal years, Olga Ivinskaya, was arrested in 1949 and sent to the camps. The poet was grievously distressed by this victimization of the person dearest to him; but he was not deterred from continuing work on *Doctor Zhivago,* which he had begun in 1946 and which was more or less completed by 1953, the year of Stalin's death and Ivinskaya's release.

Stalin's death marked the end of yet another era, and the beginning of one in which authority was asserted less rigorously. Many political prisoners, Akhmatova's son among them, were released from the camps. But the system of Stalinist controls was still retained — admittedly in milder form — under the new régime, of which Khrushchev became unchallenged head in 1957.

In the same year Pasternak took over the role of literature's Public Enemy Number One that had been foisted on Akhmatova (with Zoshchenko) in 1946. Unlike them, he had deliberately courted disaster — by handing over a typescript of *Doctor Zhivago* to an Italian publisher's emissary who was visiting him at Peredelkino. As he did so he remarked: "You have invited me to my own execution."[6] His act was an open challenge to the Soviet government such as none of the other three poets ever chose to make, and it would have been inconceivable during the Stalin dictatorship. The novel was first brought out in Russian (Milan, 1957), appearing shortly afterwards in all the world's major languages. It soon became an international best seller and, in 1965, the basis for a successful film.

Loathing the role of world celebrity, Pasternak had consciously assumed it as a matter of duty by releasing his manuscript for publication in the West. In doing so he was acting out the role for which he had cast himself back in 1946, when he had written the first of the poems later to be appended to the novel: "Hamlet," perhaps the most famous of all his lyrics. In it the poet prays to be excused from playing his designated role on the stage of history, but only to accept his terrible fate — with great reluctance — in the end.

> The acts' deployment has been planned.
> And journey's end can't be escaped.
> I am alone. All drowns in cant.
> Life's not an easy row to hoe.[7]

The publication of Pasternak's novel in the West was followed by a Soviet press campaign directed against him and drastically intensified when he was offered the Nobel Prize for Literature in October 1958. He first accepted it, but then withdrew through fear of being refused re-entry to his homeland should he journey to Stockholm to accept the award. He was also conscious of the potential danger to Olga Ivinskaya, who had already earned four years in the camps through her association with him. In great confusion of spirit he therefore sent to *Pravda* a letter which amounted to a qualified apology for his novel — but not to an abject recantation of the type that errant writers were expected to supply in such a context. Meanwhile the campaign of harassment continued with scurrilous press attacks. Other forms of nerve warfare directed against Pasternak included expulsion from the Writers' Union and the loss of income from literary sources. His private reactions to the persecution are expressed in the lyric "The Nobel Prize," in which he compares himself to a hunted beast at bay with all escape cut off, also affirming his faith that the Spirit of Good may eventually overcome the forces of meanness and malice.[8] As the lyric illustrates, he had now renounced the complex manner of his early verse and early prose. In its place he was cultivating the simple approach of which the narrative of *Doctor Zhivago*, the poems appended to that novel, and the cycle *When the Skies Clear* (1956–59) remain the best-known examples.

Eloquently preaching the futility of preaching, *Doctor Zhivago* affirms the primacy of personal and private living over all the political and public considerations in the world. It is less a novel of character and plot than a philosophical, poetical, and atmospheric study that should, perhaps, never have been called a novel at all. The author himself has admitted that his characterization might be somewhat thin, and the work indeed does show him less adept at creating individual human beings than at asserting the overriding importance of the individual human experience. Anything but a vain man, Pasternak was ready — even eager — to admit that *Doctor Zhivago* might have any number of faults. But on one point he remained firm: the novel was his supreme achievement, beside which all his other writings were of only secondary importance.

From the Soviet authorities' point of view *Doctor Zhivago* contains the most subversive of all possible political messages — that neither politics nor even antipolitical "messages" matter at all in the last analysis, and that human beings should *live,* and not (as Soviet and other politicians would make them) *prepare for life.* So radically does this bold assertion undercut totalitarian presumptions that the author Konstantin Paustovsky must surely have been wrong in claiming that the novel would have been published without difficulty in the USSR, if only those who might have sanctioned its appearance had not been overanxious to prove their loyalty to the system.[9] The ban certainly helped, as widely advertised censorship so often does, to boost the condemned item and to earn it the widest possible publicity.

That the matter had been grossly mismanaged by his minions was the opinion of Khrushchev himself — that is, if credit may be given to the story of his sending for Aleksey Surkov (now First Secretary of the Writers' Union), seizing him by the collar, and giving him a thorough shaking for failing to point out in time that Pasternak was an internationally famous author.[10] Khrushchev was suggesting, through this characteristic overreaction, that he personally would have done more to avert the scandal had he been briefed that it was liable to attain such enormous dimensions. Would he have sanctioned publication if he had been better informed? It seems probable, from the regret that he is reported as expressing (after his enforced retirement) at the failure to bring out Pasternak's novel in a Soviet edition.[11]

One of *Doctor Zhivago*'s virtues is the eloquent silent contrast that it offers to run-of-the-mill Socialist Realist novels depicting heroic Soviet supermen armed with the philosophical certainties of Marxism-Leninism and locked in conflict with the forces of Evil — be they Whites, Germans, Americans, or wicked capitalists in general. Zhivago hates philosophical certainties, and could not be further from seeking a great cause to which he might sacrifice his life, his main aim during Revolution and Civil War being to muddle through the business without harm to himself and his family. He shuns politicians' claptrap and dedicates himself to the routine of everyday domestic existence. But even in that humdrum area he is a failure, for he loses his wife, his child, and his mistress — and does so as much through his own hesitancy and ineptitude as through the pressures of his terrible era. A heart attack in a Moscow tram in the year 1929 spares him the ordeals of the collectivization period and of the *Yezhovshchina*, disposing of one chiefly memorable for remaining so eloquently unmemorable.

As a non-novel about a non-hero, *Doctor Zhivago* should perhaps have been given the same title as Akhmatova's most notable work of the period, *Poem Without Hero*, especially as it is in Zhivago's special role as a poet that the inner significance of Pasternak's book must be sought. The novel's deliciously modulated non-events and non-characters have an exhilarating and life-enhancing impact; but this will not surprise those who remember how devastatingly life-denying are the long-forgotten optimistic, affirmative, and conformist idylls which were winning their Stalin Prizes even as *Doctor Zhivago* was being composed in secret.

Pasternak valued *Doctor Zhivago* as an attempt to do justice to a century in which human life has become more significant than ever, while literature has completely failed to keep pace. To catch up with life had been his aim in writing it, he claimed; but he did not claim to have succeeded, and he was to die within three years of the novel's publication — on 30 May 1960, at Peredelkino, where he is buried.

The creative evolution of Akhmatova's declining years was diametrically opposed to that of Pasternak. She had been by far the easiest to understand among the four poets in youth, but she was now developing a more obscure and elusive technique. It is most effectively deployed in her long *Poem Without Hero*, written over a twenty-two-year period and completed in 1962. Pasternak — himself deeply committed to simplicity in later life — told Ivinskaya that he disliked Akhmatova's later verses, and could not make sense of the draft of *Poem Without Hero* that he read. But other judges place it among its author's finest achievements. It has been well described as "a requiem for the whole of Europe."[12]

The work's difficulties derive from the mystification deliberately cultivated by a poet who was now lavishly employing allusions inaccessible to all but the most dedicated textual commentator. There are, in her later verses, more mysterious mirrors and boxes with hidden compartments than those to which she specifically refers in her lines. Besides, she kept emending a text that has ended up embellished with an astonishingly large array of epigraphs and dedications, and of which no undisputed canonical version has yet been established.

This work and others of Akhmatova's later years abound in cryptic allusions to individuals, principally male, whom she had met either before the First World War or during the Second, and who had come to play a major part in her fantasies of the last half century. Among them are two Russian poets whom she had known in youth: Aleksandr Blok and Osip Mandelstam. To these were added two distinguished foreigners encountered in the 1940s: the Polish artist Joseph Czapski and Isaiah (now Sir Isaiah) Berlin.

All these were individuals whom the poet had met at some time in the past. But by now she was less obsessed by meetings that had actually taken place than by encounters yet more portentous that had failed to take place at all. She presumably derived this concept of the ultrasignificant non-meeting from Tsvetayeva, whose catalogue of unions unimplemented had gone back to Homer's Helen and Achilles, besides also including her own non-meetings with Pasternak and many others. Whatever the debt to Tsvetayeva may have been, Akhmatova too has conjured haunting poetry out of consummation frustrated.

Though Akhmatova and Pasternak had never been the closest of friends, they remained in amicable contact during their last years. In January 1954 she spoke of him to Chukovskaya as follows. "I adore the man, though it's true he's quite unbearable. He rushed in here yesterday to tell me he's a nonentity." This typical expression of insecurity prompted the ever secure Akhmatova to tell him that he would still be one of twentieth-century Europe's greatest poets even if he had written nothing at all in the last decade.[13]

Lidiya Chukovskaya's diaries show how far Anna Andreyevna was from being struck dumb with awe in the presence of Boris Leonidovich. She was convinced that he was a great poet. But she also thought him a figure of fun, and often spoke of him in the *de haut en bas* style that was so much her own. "How good-looking he is now he's had his front teeth out! That horsy quality did give his face a piquant look of course, but he's so much nicer like this — pale, handsome, with such a noble head."[14]

Akhmatova was apt to deride the mildly sensuous love poetry of Pasternak's later years as inappropriate to a man in his seventh decade. She objected, for example, to the lyric "Intoxication," in which he first describes himself standing and embracing his mistress under a cloak and an ivy-entwined willow tree, and then suggests that they spread the cloak out so that the exchange can continue more profitably from a prone position. Akhmatova also takes exception to the following quatrain invoking Pasternak's beloved in the lyric "Autumn."

> Thou shedst thy dress
> As coppice sheds leaves,
> Falling into my arms
> And silk-tasselled dressing-gown.[15]

Akhmatova found these delightful lines embarrassingly outspoken. "I can't stand that tasselled dressing gown stuff, her falling into his arms, and that lying down in coppice business. These aren't subjects for a man of sixty."[16] She obviously thought it downright improper that his amorous vigour had not decently tapered off with advancing age, as had her own.

Akhmatova also criticized Pasternak's love poetry as a whole for evoking only the image of Love, never that of the Beloved. But when Chukovskaya protested against this, Akhmatova grudgingly yielded ground. "He *has* learnt," she conceded. "But nothing ever came harder to him. In the old days he could only manage nature, love, and art. Not people."[17]

Akhmatova's declining years were relatively calm, troubled more by illness than by that potentially worse pest — officials of the Writers' Union, to which she was eventually readmitted, after her expulsion in 1946. In 1964 she was permitted to travel to Sicily to receive a literary prize, and so came to make her first journey to a foreign country for more than half a century. The following year saw her in Oxford, where she received an honorary degree and was compared to Sappho by the university's Public Orator.

During her last decade Akhmatova spent long periods in the tranquillity of the dacha assigned to her at Komarovo, near Leningrad, where she wrote the lyric "Four of Us (Komarovo Fragments)" in 1960. It is the only work by any of the four poets in which the others are all invoked, and it carries three epigraphs — one from each of the other three. Each epigraph consists of material from verses that they had dedicated to Anna Andreyevna; there is also an allusion in the body of the text to Pasternak's short story of 1924, *Aerial Paths*. At the time when Akhmatova grouped these quotations together, prefacing them to the three commemorative stanzas of her own, she was the sole survivor among the four poets.

Four of Us (Komarovo Fragments)

Lithe Gipsy — can she too be destined
To suffer all the agonies in Dante?
                    (o. m.)

As such I see your image and your glance.
                    (b. p.)

O Muse of Lamentation. (m. ts.)

And here I have renounced all,
All earthly bliss.
This place's guardian spirit is now
A gnarled forest stump.

We're all life's guests, more or less.
Living's only habit.
I seem to hear on Aerial Paths
Two voices calling to each other.

Two? See, by eastern wall,
In sturdy raspberry brakes,
Fresh, dark elder bough —
A letter from Marina.[18]

Anna Andreyevna died in Moscow on 5 March 1966, and was buried at her beloved Komarovo. With her death this account of the pathology of Nightingale Fever, as it afflicted four outstandingly gifted Russian poets, has run its course.

APPENDIX

Translation Policy

Since all the Russian material quoted in this volume appears in my own words, some brief remarks on translating policy are in order. They apply only to the renderings of verse; the prose translations have presented no special problems.

Russian poetry has been rendered to conform with a text in which translated verse forms part of a continuous English narrative. This means that it is frequently cited in odd lines and short fragments — as is unavoidable, but also regrettable. Where considerations of space have made it possible to give the whole of an individual lyric this is indicated in the Reference Notes by the designation "in full."

The general approach has been to follow the originals as closely as is consistent with an attempt, however vain, to convey spirit and quality as well as meaning. In no sense are the translations "literal." Nor, with respect to the late Vladimir Nabokov — novelist and translator of Pushkin's *Eugene Onegin* [1] — is poetry susceptible of being rendered literally, as is, for instance, a schedule of instructions for operating a hydraulic pump.

The integrity of the originals is preserved to the extent that each line of Russian is, whenever syntactically possible, rendered by a single line of English. Where translated Russian verse is quoted as part of continuously printed text, oblique strokes are used to indicate the line breaks of the original. Where verse translations are printed free-standing (line by line), the stanzaic breaks of the original are preserved, except when a given quotation is so fragmentary as to rob these of significance. Original metres have not been preserved, except that there has been a tendency for Russian iambics to provoke English iambics. On occasions when it has seemed appropriate noniambic metres have also been reproduced, or approximately echoed. In general, however, the originals — couched, as they usually are, in strict metre — are done into free verse which some readers may choose to regard as indistinguishable from prose. I hope not, since I have always reacted in my heart and mind — if not always on paper — to the drumbeats and resonances of the original.

Rhyme happens to be prevalent in Russian verse (other than folk ballads) of most periods, and it is the norm in the work of all four poets, especially if near-rhyming echoes are not excluded. Rhyme is not, however, employed in the translations; nor was it at any stage contemplated, for it has a tendency — marked, but far indeed from being universal — to turn Russian magic into English doggerel.

Literary history bristles with warnings on the impossibility of shifting poetry from language to language. There is Bentley's oft-quoted scathing dismissal of a notable English version of the *Iliad:* "It is a pretty poem, Mr. Pope; but you must not call it Homer." And there is the discouraging sonnet of 1904, "To the Translator," in which the Russian poet Vyacheslav Ivanov writes that it is impossible "to lure free birds to alien cage." He further develops the zoological image in four lines which are now rendered, in full awareness of the irony involved in any attempt to translate poetry claiming poetry to be untranslatable.

> Foreign verse is slippery, Protean.
> Neither clutch nor nerve can grab it.
> You hold the fish's tail — but flowing, liquid,
>
> It slithers streaming from your flimsy nets.[2]

And yet — have all the fish indeed slithered away? Surely Catullus caught Sappho by the tail with his *Ille mi par esse deo videtur.* Goethe's *Über allen Gipfeln* has been twice netted in Russian: first by Lermontov and secondly by Annensky, both master anglers. More recently there has been Ezra Pound's corpus of translations from Latin, Anglo-Saxon, Chinese, Provençal, Italian, and other languages — a swarming aquatic carnival, a whole cavorting oceanarium, that again and again sets Vyacheslav Ivanov's caution at naught. These instances show what the possibilities are. And though this book is not in competition with Catullus, Pope, Lermontov, Annensky, Ivanov, or Pound — major poets and fine translators all — it is to be hoped that anything approximating the notorious "howlers" in Pound's *Homage to Sextus Propertius* has been avoided. But I also hope not to have been immune from the occasional gust of Poundian lunacy, without which there is no point in anyone's reading or writing poetry at all.

Though "free" in the sense of stalking the sense and tonality of the original without attempting to reproduce all its formal features, the renderings are more rigorous than may appear. They are certainly not casual. Translating a language studied for forty years into my native tongue has proved yet more taxing than putting English verse into the language and metre of Euripides, Virgil, Horace, or Lucretius was in years gone by. But without that prolonged and immensely satisfying discipline of the past, the present book could not have been attempted.

Texts and Sources

Owing to the special conditions with which Russia faces both the poet and the scholar, the textual history of the works discussed in this book is of alarming complexity. Alternative readings, scribes' errors, lost manuscripts, the awesome intricacies of cultural transmission in the Soviet context — all these features occur again and again. The problem is remarkably similar to that of the classical scholar, and it is perhaps time that someone did for modern Russian studies what L. D. Reynolds and N. G. Wilson did for the ancient world with their admirable *Scribes and Scholars: A Guide to the Transmission of Greek and Latin Literature.*

As far as possible the reader has been spared exposure to the rugged Russian politico-textual hinterland, fascinating though its topography happens to be. But its complexities are inevitably reflected in the Reference Notes. They are based, in combination with the Bibliography, on an elaborate — but mercifully economical — coding system designed to cover the overlapping and competing editions of the poets who form the subject of this study. Without some such device it would have been impossible to provide a systematic account of the sources.

Another complication is that abundant new material on the subject of this study, including many newly discovered poems, has been appearing in print during the entire period of my labours. An attempt has been made to keep pace with this most welcome evidence of the vogue now enjoyed by twentieth-century Russian poetry.

Though debts to individual scholars are baldly on record in the Reference Notes, it is proper to pay special tribute here to certain authorities who appear there, and whose works are also cited systematically in the Bibliography. Most particularly is a debt acknowledged to the labours of G. P. Struve and B. A. Filipoff in jointly producing their fine editions, exclusively published and available in the West, of Akhmatova, Mandelstam, Pasternak, and Gumilyov, to which Professor Struve's editions of certain poems by Tsvetayeva must be added. It has been chiefly through these publications of the 1960s and early 1970s that the poets studied in this volume have become known even to limited groups of specialists, let alone to the world in general.

The Struve-Filipoff editions of Akhmatova, Mandelstam, and Pasternak have been followed by comprehensive editions of the same poets (and also of Tsvetayeva) published in Leningrad and/or Moscow from 1965 onwards in the one-volume Biblioteka poeta (bolshaya seriya) editions. These have the disadvantage that censorship considerations have patently influenced both the choice of contents and the deployment of editorial matter. Fortunately, however, such familiar nonliterary pressures have caused less harm than might have been feared. In particular, the volumes of Akhmatova and Pasternak have been relatively little impaired; those of Mandelstam and Tsvetayeva — writers less decorous in a political sense — have naturally fared worse. The Biblioteka poeta editions have an advantage in that the editors concerned — devoted, sensitive, and highly competent within the severe limits imposed on them — have enjoyed access to extensive archive material not available to Western scholars; they have of course also benefited as latecomers (but without being permitted to acknowledge their debt) from the pioneering work done on the texts of Akhmatova, Mandelstam, and Pasternak by Struve and Filipoff.

It is, accordingly, to the Biblioteka poeta texts that recourse has been had in the first instance, the Struve-Filipoff editions and others being invoked on the many occasions when an item has been omitted from the relevant Biblioteka poeta edition (whether for editorial or censorship reasons), or when a superior reading appears to be available elsewhere. The result is that, wherever a quotation is attributed to Struve and Filipoff, the passage in question will usually prove to have been omitted (for whatever reason) from the relevant Biblioteka poeta volume. Despite the need to mediate between these parallel sets of editions — the non-Soviet and the Soviet — they complement each other as well as could be expected where later editors are compelled by pressures independent of literary scholarship to write as if their most important predecessors had never existed. An ideal solution would only be achieved if some supranational team were in a position to collate the rich material available on both sides of the Bering Straits and re-edit the complete works of all the poets from scratch.

As will be evident to those who con the apparatus, the text of Tsvetayeva's verse presents problems more acute than those, by no means negligible, presented by the other poets studied here. The recent issue of Volume One, dated 1980, of a new five-volume edition of her verse by Russica Publishers (New York) is therefore particularly welcome.

Besides being indebted to editors I am also much beholden to the many scholars and critics who have tackled the detailed exegesis of poets all capable of baffling determined efforts to penetrate their meaning. Given the general nature of the task, no attempt could have been made here to rival such a prodigious feat of elucidation as Professor Kiril Taranovsky's analysis of the poem by Mandelstam from which the title of this book is taken. In his *Essays on Mandel'štam* this lyric of a mere sixteen lines receives some six thousand words — none wasted — of admirably marshalled exposition.[3]

In addition to the benefits derived from the technically complex elucidations of Mandelstam by Taranovsky, Baines, Broyde, and fellow Mandelstamians — not to mention discussions of the other poets by scholars and critics too numerous to specify here — valuable guidance has also been found in works of more general scope. Particularly useful have been the discussions of Pasternak in Max Hayward's introductions to the English editions of Gladkov and Ivinskaya cited in the Bibliography, as also the books by Amanda Haight, Clarence Brown, Henry Gifford, and Simon Karlinsky on Akhmatova, Mandelstam, Pasternak, and Tsvetayeva, respectively. As for memoir material, Nadezhda Mandelstam's two volumes are paramount, being fundamental to the cultural history of her epoch. They are admirably supplemented by the accounts of Lidiya Chukovskaya, Olga Ivinskaya, and others. Where would

Russia be without its lady amanuenses? Their accounts are admirably supplemented by one that has only become available after work on this typescript had been completed: Sir Isaiah Berlin's recently published memoir, to which reference is made in the Acknowledgements.

TITLES

In printing the translated titles of Russian works in the text normal practice has been abjured to the extent that designations of short stories, articles, cycles of lyrics, and *poemy* (long poems) are italicized. The purpose is to differentiate what are relatively substantial items from the *stikhotvoreniya* (short poems or lyrics), which are the main subject of study; for the titles of those the usual convention (roman in quotation marks) is followed.

OMISSIONS

Sequences of three dots (four, if a full stop is involved) will be found only in quotations, where they are used to indicate that material has been omitted by myself; they do not reflect any indication of omissions — or any other punctuation device — to be found in the originals.

TRANSLITERATION

Russian names are transliterated as in *The Oxford Chekhov* (London, 1964–80), edited by myself; see especially vol. 3, pages xi–xii. With Ehrenburg, Khrushchev, Mandelstam, Wrangel, and certain other names, common usage is followed in defiance of transliterational consistency.

DATES

Dates preceding 1 February 1918 are given according to the Old Style calendar current in Russia. This lagged behind the Western European calendar by twelve days in the nineteenth century and by thirteen days in the twentieth century. After 1 February 1918 there is no conflict in dating, except that Marina Tsvetayeva refused to recognize the calendar change in many of her later publications; this explains the use of certain Old Style dates in the context of her post-1917 activities.

REFERENCE NOTES

References are by authors' or editors' surnames, as listed in alphabetical order in the Bibliography. "Gladkov" and "Ivinskaya" refer to the Russian editions except where otherwise specified.

The following abbreviations have been employed, and are repeated in the relevant entries of the Bibliography, where the titles concerned are quoted in fuller detail.

A.   Akhmatova, Anna

A.bp   Akhmatova, Anna, *Stikhotvoreniya i poemy* (Leningrad, 1976)

A.s   Akhmatova, Anna, *Sochineniya* (Washington, D.C., 1967–68)

bp   Biblioteka poeta (bolshaya seriya) edition

M.   Mandelstam, Osip

M.bp   Mandelstam, Osip, *Stikhotvoreniya* (Leningrad, 1973)

M.s   Mandelstam, Osip, *Sobraniye sochineniy* (Washington, New York, 1967–71)

N.   Mandelstam, Nadezhda

N., 1   Mandelstam, Nadezhda, *Vospominaniya* (New York, 1970)

N., 2   Mandelstam, Nadezhda, *Vtoraya kniga* (Paris, 1972)

P.   Pasternak, Boris

P.bp   Pasternak, Boris, *Stikhotvoreniya i poemy* (Leningrad, 1965)

P.s, 1   Pasternak, Boris, *Stikhi i poemy, 1912–1932* (Ann Arbor, Mich., 1961)

P.s, 2   Pasternak, Boris, *Proza, 1915–1958* (Ann Arbor, Mich., 1961)

P.s, 3   Pasternak, Boris, *Stikhi, 1936–1959* (Ann Arbor, Mich., 1961) s   edited by G. P. Struve and B. A. Filipoff

T.   Tsvetayeva, Marina

T.bp   Tsvetayeva, Marina, *Izbrannyye proizvedeniya* (Moscow-Leningrad, 1965)

INTRODUCTION (pages xi–xiii)

1. Taranovsky, 81;   2. M.bp, 108;   3. J. Berryman, cited in Gifford, 5;   4. N., 2:283;   5. A., *Pamyati Anny Akhmatovoy*, 188.

PART ONE: PEACE AND WAR (1889–1921)
1. *Motive for Murder* (pages 5–17)

1. A., *Pamyati Anny Akhmatovoy*, 120;   2. P.s, 2:4;   3. Markov (1966), lxvi; 4. Ibid., lxxviii;   5. Blok, 5:247;   6. N., 1:167;   7. Gumilyov, 1:xli;   8. Karlinsky, 5;   9. Brown, C., 3;   10. R. Jakobson, in Brown, E., *Major Soviet Writers*, 30;   11. N., 2:337.

2. *Torture by Happiness* (pages 18– 44)

1. Haight, 25;   2. A.bp, 179;   3. A.bp, 146;   4. Haight, 30, 203; Blok, 3:143, 550; M.s, 1:37;   5. A.s, 2:303;   6. A.bp, 333;   7. Haight, 6–7;   8. Zhirmunsky, 40;   9. A.bp, 25;   10. Eykhenbaum, 120;   11. A.bp, 30, in full; 12. A.bp, 28, in full;   13. A.bp, 31;   14. A.bp, 56–7, in full;   15. Eykhenbaum, 114;   16. A. Kollontay, cited in Zhirmunsky, 41; Haight, 2;   17. A.bp, 26–7, in full;   18. A.bp, 81, in full;   19. Chukovskaya, 160;   20. A.bp, 57; 21. M.bp, 183;   22. S. Andronikova, cited in Brown, C., 51;   23. Brown, C., 52;   24. M.s, 2:89;   25. Brown, C., 25–37;   26. N., 2:289–90;   27. N., 1:264;   28. M.bp, 58–9, in full;   29. M.bp, 57, in full;   30. M.bp, 62, in full; 31. M.bp, 59–60, in full;   32. Gumilyov, 4:363–4;   33. M.bp, 71, in full; 34. Brown, C., 179;   35. M.bp, 74;   36. M.bp, 79, in full;   37. M.s, 1:291–2; 38. M.bp, 85–6, in full;   39. Brown, C., 24;   40. T., *Nesobrannyye proizvedeniya*, 29;   41. T., *Izbrannaya proza*, 2:184, 187;   42. Ibid., 2:35;   43. Ivinskaya, 170–1, 182;   44. T., *Nesobrannyye proizvedeniya*, 9;   45. Ibid., 31; 46. Ibid., 35, 46;   47. Ibid., 36–7, 44;   48. Ibid., 10, 63;   49. T., *Neizdannoye*, 46;   50. Ibid., 5, 8–9;   51. Ibid., 19–20;   52. T., *Nesobrannyye proizvedeniya*, 9;   53. T., *Izbrannaya proza*, 1:136;   54. P.bp, 107;   55. P.s, 2:33; P.bp, 620; 56. Markov (1969), 236–7.

3. *Cloudburst of Light* (pages 45–71)

1. P.s, 2:205;   2. Markov (1969), 384;   3. P.s, 2:32;   4. Gifford, 37; W. Weidlé, in P.s, 1:xxxviii–xl; Markov (1969), 269–70, 409;   5. P.s, 2:41;   6. P.bp, 114–15;   7. Markov (1969), 269;   8. P.bp, 86;   9. T., *Izbrannaya*

proza, 1:143; 10. P.bp, 136; 11. P.bp, 65, 621; 12. P.bp, 113; 13. P.bp, 116; 14. I. Berlin, in Erlich, 39; 15. P.bp, 94; 16. P.bp, 148; 17. T., *Izbrannaya proza*, 1:137; 18. Chukovskaya, 129; 19. P.bp, 73, 583–4, 624; 20. P.bp, 107–9, 594, 629–30; 21. P.bp, 140; 22. P.bp, 126; 23. P.bp, 149; 24. P.bp, 74, 82, 90, 95, 111, 123, 132, 146, 154; 25. P.bp, 75; 26. P.bp, 67, 70, 72; 27. P.bp, 66; 28. P.bp, 88; 29. P.bp, 112–13; 30. P.bp, 72; T., *Neizdannyye pisma*, 268; 31. P.bp, 111–12; 32. Gifford, 59; 33. A.bp, 106, in full; 34. A.bp, 106; 35. A.bp, 84, in full; 36. A.bp, 105; 37. A.bp, 177; 38. A.bp, 115; 39. A.bp, 109, in full; 40. A.bp, 88; 41. N. Nedobrovo, cited in Zhirmunsky, 42; Haight, 44; 42. A.bp, 94; 43. A.bp, 91; 44. A.bp, 463; 45. A.bp, 119, in full; 46. A.bp, 107, in full; 47. A.bp, 144, in full; 48. A.bp, 99; 49. A.bp, 89, 120, 138; 50. A.bp, 115, in full; 51. T., *Neizdannoye*, 85; 52. Ibid., 59–60; 53. T.bp, 736; 54. T., *Neizdannoye*, 81; 55. T., *Vyorsty*, 75–7; 56. Ibid., 82; 57. T., *Stikhi k Bloku*, 11; 58. T., *Neizdannoye*, 60; 59. T., *Psikheya*, 19 ff.; 60. T.bp, 84; 61. T., *Vyorsty*, 37, 41; 62. T.bp, 734; 63. T., *Vyorsty*, 47, in full; 64. Ibid., 38; 65. M.bp, 271; 66. T., *Vyorsty*, 12–14; 67. M.s, 3:321–8; 68. T., *Vyorsty*, 10, in full; 69. M.s, 3:342–3; 70. M.s, 3:337–41; 71. M.bp, 99, 271; 72. M.bp, 225, 310; 73. M.bp, 97–8, 270; 74. M.bp, 100–1; 75. M.bp, 92, in full; 76. M.bp, 223, 309; 77. M.bp, 96–7.

4. *My Craft Adrift* (pages 72–83)

1. M.bp, 103–4; 2. M.bp, 107–8; Taranovsky, 68 ff.; 3. M.bp, 98, in full; 4. Broyde, 66; M.bp, 98, in full; 5. M.bp, 108; 6. Brown, C., 70; 7. M.s, 1:142; 8. M.s, 1:72; M.bp, 109–10; 9. M.s, 1:67; 10. M.bp, 107; 11. A.s, 2:175; M.s, 1:67; 12. N., 2:249–50; 13. A.bp, 133, 468; 14. A.s, 1:378, in full; I. Berlin, cited in Haight, 142; 15. A. Lezhnev, in Davie, 97; 16. P.bp, 77; 17. P.bp, 625; 18. P.bp, 124; 19. P.bp, 133–4, 637; 20. A. Sinyavsky, in Davie, 202; 21. T., *Izbrannaya proza*, 1:143; 22. P., *Doktor Zhivago*, 148; 23. Ibid., 187, 198; 24. Ibid., 185; 25. T., *Lebediny stan; Perekop*, 37–40; 26. Ibid., 41–2; 27. Ibid., 43; 28. Ibid., 46–52; 29. Ibid., 45, 69, 74.

5. *Black Velvet* (pages 84–102)

1. A.s, 2:172; 2. T., *Izbrannaya proza*, 1:433; 3. T.bp, 156; 4. T., *Lebediny stan; Perekop*, 61; 5. T.bp, 779; 6. T., *Izbrannaya proza*, 1:50ff.; 7. See above, p. 64; 8. T.bp, 153–4; 9. T.bp, 148; 10. T., *Psikheya*, 16; 11. Ibid., 15; 12. T.bp, 151; 13. T.bp, 130; 14. T.bp, 168–9; 15. T., *Tsar-devitsa*, 22; 16. Ibid., 95; 17. T.bp, 765; 18. A.bp, 153, in full; 19. A.bp, 153–4; 20. A.bp, 155, 166, 170; 21. A.bp, 166, in full; 22. N., 2:24; 23. M.bp, 112–13; 24. N., 2:579; 25. See above, p. 81; 26. M.bp, 115–16; 27. M.s, 2:116, 120; 28. M.bp, 119–20; 29. Broyde, 92–3; M.s, 1:85–6, 454; 30. M.bp, 121–4; 31. M.bp, 120; 32. N., 2:70; 33. M.bp, 121; 34. T., *Neizdannyye pisma*, 267; 35. P.bp, 157–8; 36. P.bp, 160–1;

37. P.bp, 161–3;   38. P.bp, 162–3;   39. P.bp, 165;   40. P.bp, 170;   41. P.bp, 173–7;   42. P.bp, 193.

PART TWO: BETWEEN CONVULSIONS (1921–1930)
6. *Herbs for Alien Tribe* (pages 105–15)

1. Gumilyov, 1:xli;   2. A.bp, 168, 172, 174;   3. A.bp, 171–2, in full;   4. A. bp, 160; T., *Neizdannyye pisma*, 631;   5. A.bp, 152, in full;   6. A.bp, 182; 7. M.bp, 127, in full;   8. Taranovsky, 153;   9. M.bp, 131–2;   10. M.bp, 140; 11. M.bp, 139;   12. M.bp, 134–5;   13. M.s, 2:330, 351;   14. M.s, 2:327–8, 345, 347;   15. Trotsky, 30–1.

7. *Rebel in Head and Womb* (pages 116–31)

1. T., *Izbrannaya proza*, 1:199;   2. Ibid., 1:204–5;   3. T., *Remeslo*, 7;   4. Ibid., 65;   5. Ibid., 51, 89–90;   6. Ibid., 56;   7. Ibid., 122–3;   8. Ibid., 77–8;   9. Ibid., 83;   10. Karlinsky, 209–10;   11. T.bp, 441–2;   12. N., 2:515–16;   13. N., 2:517–21;   14. T., *Neizdannyye pisma*, 274;   15. Marc Slonim, "O Marine Tsvetayevoy," *Novy zhurnal* (New York, 1970), No. 100, p. 167;   16. N., 2:514;   17. T.bp, 444–9, 767;   18. T.bp, 471;   19. T.bp, 463;   20. T., *Posle Rossii*, 78–9;   21. Ibid., 22;   22. Ibid., 135–6, 139; 23. Ibid., 133;   24. Ibid., 61–2;   25. Ibid., 77–8;   26. Ibid., 60; P., *Doktor Zhivago*, 532;   27. T., *Neizdannyye pisma*, 264–5, 310–13; T., *Posle Rossii*, 62; 28. Ibid., 72–3;   29. Ibid., 128–30;   30. T., *Izbrannaya proza*, 1:240.

8. *Time's Great Dislocation* (pages 132–146)

1. Ivinskaya, 72;   2. P.s, 3:215–16;   3. P.bp, 243–4;   4. P.bp, 246, 655; 5. P.bp, 236–40;   6. P.s, 3:215;   7. P.bp, 245;   8. P.bp, 247–8;   9. W. Weidlé, in Davie, 124; P.bp, 249;   10. P.bp, 251–4;   11. P.bp, 302;   12. T., *Neizdannyye pisma*, 307–8;   13. P.s, 2:151;   14. P.bp, 311;   15. T., *Neizdannyye pisma*, 266;   16. Gifford, 121–3;   17. P.s, 2:234;   18. P.bp, 201; 19. P.bp, 199–200;   20. A.bp, 185;   21. A., *Pamyati Anny Akhmatovoy*, 99; 22. Haight, 85; Chukovskaya, 162;   23. Gumilyov, 1:xl; M.s, 3:255–6;   24. M.bp, 144; N., 2:239;   25. M.s, 2:607;   26. M.s, 2:182.

9. *Loving and Lopping* (pages 147–54)

1. T.bp, 477–81;   2. T.bp, 499;   3. T.bp, 506–9;   4. T.bp, 514–23; 5. T.bp, 518–19;   6. Karlinsky, 232–3;   7. T.bp, 674;   8. T., *Nesobrannyye proizvedeniya*, 432;   9. Karlinsky, 72–3; T., *Nesobrannyye proizvedeniya*, 483; 10. T.bp, 539–42;   11. T.bp, 544–7;   12. T.bp, 548–52;   13. T., *Lebediny stan; Perekop*, 82, 92, 110, 120;   14. T., *Nesobrannyye proizvedeniya*, 547ff.; Karlinsky, 235.

PART THREE: TERROR AND BEYOND (1930–1966)
10. *Frolics and Pitfalls* (pages 157–73)

1. Conquest, 23; 2. Brown, E., *Mayakovsky*, 12–26; 3. P.bp, 356; 4. T., *Nesobrannyye proizvedeniya*, 566–7; 5. Mayakovsky, 7:105; 6. T., *Nesobrannyye proizvedeniya*, 569–70; 7. Mayakovsky, 1:195–6; T., *Nesobrannyye proizvedeniya*, 571; 8. A.bp, 199; 9. N., 1:342–5; 10. M.s, 1:169; Baines, 5; 11. M.bp, 145–50; 12. M.s, 2:143; M.bp, 146; 13. M.bp, 145–9; M.s, 2:169; 14. M.bp, 150; 15. M.bp, 161–2, 290; 16. P.bp, 370; 17. P.bp, 369; 18. P.bp, 346, 352, 369; 19. P.bp, 343; 20. P.bp, 349; 21. P.bp, 350; 22. P.bp, 371–2, 379; 23. P.bp, 199; 24. Pushkin, 2:342; P.bp, 377; 25. M. Hayward, in Gladkov (English edition), 15; 26. Ibid., 16; N., 2:268; 27. P.bp, 371; 28. P.bp, 351; 29. P.bp, 365; 30. Chukovskaya, 134.

11. *Harder to Breathe* (pages 174–88)

1. N., 1:165; N., 2:343, 484; 2. M.bp, 150–1; N., 1:289; 3. M.s, 1:160; Baines, 16; M.bp, 151; 4. N., 1:250; 5. M.s, 1:168; 6. M.bp, 153; 7. M.bp, 153; 8. M.s, 1:165–6; 9. M.s, 1:189–90; 10. M.bp, 164; 11. M.s, 1:195; M.bp, 296; 12. M.bp, 171, 296, in full; 13. M.bp, 140; 14. Ye. Tager, cited in M.s, 1:lxii–lxiv; 15. Baines, 103; 16. M.s, 1:195; Baines, 74; 17. N., 2:469; 18. N., 1:157–8, 296–7; 19. M.s, 1:196; 20. Hughes, 114; N., 1:159; 21. N., 1:166; 22. M.s, 1:202, 511; 23. N., 1:88; 24. Ivinskaya, 75–6; 25. N., 1:26, 34–5; 26. N., 2:242–3; 27. M.bp, 173–4; 28. Brown, C., 128; 29. N., 1:236; N., 2:257; 30. A.bp, 191, in full; 31. A.s, 2:181 ff.; 32. N., 1:12, 289; 33. N., 1:25; 34. N., 1:80–1; 35. A.s, 2:182; N., 1:152 ff.; Ivinskaya, 75 ff.; 36. N., 1:155; 37. N., 1:35, 59.

12. *Doom's Black Whisper* (pages 189–206)

1. M.s, 214–19; Baines, 123; N., 1:57; 2. M.s, 1:219; N., 1:55; 3. N., 1:62, 65, 68; 4. N., 1:63; M.s, 1:217; 5. N., 1:100; 6. Brown, C., 1; N., 2:12; 7. A.bp, 190; 8. M.bp, 176, 180; 9. M.bp, 180–2; Baines, 127–8; 10. M.s, 1:214, 222; 11. M.bp, 174; Baines, 108–9; 12. M.bp, 155–6; Baines, 141–3; 13. N. Bukharin, cited in Ivinskaya, 83; 14. Ivinskaya, 83; P.s, 3:217; 15. P.s, 3:217–18; 16. Hughes, 136–7; 17. Charters, 367; P.s, 2:44; 18. Ivinskaya, 86; 19. Ibid.; 20. Karlinsky, 82, citing N. Gorodetskaya and G. Ivask; 21. T.bp, 304–5; 22. T.bp, 294–6; 23. T.bp, 280–313; 24. T.bp, 289; 25. T., *Izbrannaya proza*, 1:454–5; 26. P.s, 2:46–7; 27. A.bp, 198, in full; 28. A., *Rekviyem*, 11; Chukovskaya, 209; Haight, 92; 29. A., *Pamyati Anny Akhmatovoy*, 10; 30. A.bp, 187; 31. A.s, 2:179–80; 32. N., 1:151; A.bp, 188; 33. P.s, 3:138; 34. P.bp, 554; P.s, 3:241; Hughes, 102–3; 35. Ivinskaya, 95; 36. P.s, 3:218–22; 37. P.s, 3:223.

13. *All Change for Freedom Camp* (pages 207–20)

1. A. Solzhenitsyn, cited in Sakharov, 131; 2. P., *Doktor Zhivago*, 519; 3. Hughes, 150; Gladkov, 11; 4. Ivinskaya, 145–6; 5. A., *Pamyati Anny Akhmatovoy*, 11, 24; 6. M.s, 3:286; 7. M.s, 3:278–85; 8. N., 1:213; 9. M., "Mandelstam's Ode to Stalin," 683–91; M.s, 1:233; 10. N., 1:216 ff; Baines, 174 ff.; 11. M.s, 1:242; 12. M.bp, 187–8; 13. M.s, 1:238; 14. M.s, 1:238; 15. M.bp, 191–2; Baines, 187; 16. M.s, 1:230–2; Baines, 164; 17. M.bp, 192–3, 227; Baines, 192; 18. M.bp, 190, 196–7; M.s, 1:254; 19. M.s, 1:262–3; Baines, 222; 20. M.bp, 183, 199, 201; 21. M.s, 1:234; 22. M.bp, 200; 23. M.s, 1:245–9; 24. M.s, 1:261; 25. M.s, 1:227; Baines, 158–60; 26. M.s, 1:253–4; 27. M.s, 263–4; Baines, 234–5; 28. G. Stukov, cited in M.s, 1:lxxiii; N., 1:389–95; 29. N., 1:139.

14. *Old Style, New Style* (pages 221–35)

1. Chukovskaya, 15; Haight, 97; 2. A.bp, 198; 3. Haight, 114; Chukovskaya, 14–144; 4. A., *Rekviyem*, 4; 5. Ibid., 10, 14; 6. Ibid., 18, 21; 7. Haight, 111–12; Chukovskaya, 113; 8. Haight, 116; 9. A.bp, 191–2, 289; A., *Pamyati Anny Akhmatovoy*, 186; 10. A.bp, 194; 11. A.bp, 288–9, emphasis added; 12. A.bp, 195; Chukovskaya, 20, 47; 13. A.bp, 208–9; 14. Chukovskaya, 90–2, 147; 15. A., *Pamyati Anny Akhmatovoy*, 65; 16. Haight, 113; 17. T.bp, 319–21; Karlinsky, 90–2; 18. T., *Izbrannaya proza*, 2:141; 19. Ibid., 2:249–52, 262; 20. T., *Neizdannoye*, 241; 21. T.bp, 332–3; 22. T.bp, 762–3; 23. T., *Neizdannyye pisma*, 613, 630; 24. Haight, 108–9; 25. A.s, 1:342; 26. T., *Neizdannyye pisma*, 631; 27. Ivinskaya, 181; 28. P.bp, 567; 29. T., *Neizdannyye pisma*, 638.

15. *Two Voices Calling* (pages 236–47)

1. P., *Doktor Zhivago*, 519; 2. N., 2:422; 3. Haight, 145; 4. A.s, 2:151; 5. M. Hayward, in Gladkov (English edition), 20–4; 6. Ivinskaya, 218; 7. P., *Doktor Zhivago*, 532; 8. P.s, 3:107–8; 9. K. Paustovsky, cited in Ivinskaya, 386; 10. Dewhirst, 13; 11. N. Khrushchev, cited in Ivinskaya (English edition), 431; 12. Ivinskaya, 160; I. Berlin, cited in Haight, 142; 13. A., *Pamyati Anny Akhmatovoy*, 95; 14. Ibid., 69; 15. P.bp, 432–3, 436; 16. A.,*Pamyati Anny Akhmatovoy*, 174; 17. Ibid., 174–5; 18. A.bp, 264, 493.

Appendix (pages 248–52)

1. Nabokov, 1:x; 2. V. Ivanov, in Markov (1966), 140; 3. Taranovsky, 68–82.

BIBLIOGRAPHY

This bibliography consists principally of the works cited in the Reference Notes (in certain cases by the abbreviations given below, to the left of the relevant title) and also lists works to which direct allusion is made in the text.

Cited as

A. Akhmatova, Anna
  ———*Rekviyem* (Munich 1963)
A.s ———*Sochineniya*, 2 vols., ed. G. P. Struve and B. A. Filipoff (Washington, D.C.: vol. 1, 2nd ed., revised and enlarged, 1967; vol. 2, 1968)
A.bp ———*Stikhotvoreniya i poemy*, ed. V. M. Zhirmunsky (Biblioteka poeta, bolshaya seriya, Leningrad, 1976)
  ———*Pamyati Anny Akhmatovoy: stikhi; pisma;* L. Chukovskaya: *Zapiski ob Anne Akhmatovoy* (Paris, 1974)
Baines, Jennifer,*Mandelstam: the Later Poetry* (Cambridge, 1976)
Berlin, Isaiah,*Personal Impressions* (London, 1980)
Blok, Aleksandr,*Sobraniye sochineniy v vosmi tomakh* (Moscow-Leningrad, 1960–63)
Brown, Clarence,*Mandelstam* (Cambridge, 1973)
Brown,Edward J. (ed.), *Major Soviet Writers: Essays in Criticism* (London, 1973)
Brown, Edward J.,*Mayakovsky: A Poet in the Revolution* (Princeton, N.J., 1973)
Broyde, Steven,*Osip Mandel'štam and His Age: A Commentary on the Themes of War and Revolution in the Poetry, 1913–1923* (Cambridge, Mass., 1975)
Charters, Ann and Samuel,*I Love: The Story of Vladimir Mayakovsky and Lili Brik* (London, 1979)

CHEKHOV, ANTON, *The Oxford Chekhov*, 9 vols., ed. and tr. Ronald Hingley (London, 1964–80)

CHUKOVSKAYA, LIDIYA, *Zapiski ob Anne Akhmatovoy*, vol. 1, 1938–1941 (Paris, 1976)

CONQUEST, ROBERT, *The Great Terror: Stalin's Purge of the Thirties* (London, 1968)

DAVIE, DONALD and ANGELA LIVINGSTONE (EDS.), *Pasternak: Modern Judgements* (London, 1969)

DEWHIRST, MARTIN and ROBERT FARRELL (EDS.), *The Soviet Censorship* (Metuchen, N.J., 1973)

EFRON, ARIADNA, *Stranitsy vospominaniy* (Paris, 1979)

ERLICH, VICTOR (ED.), *Pasternak: A Collection of Critical Essays* (Englewood Cliffs, N.J., 1978)

EYKHENBAUM, B., *Anna Akhmatova: opyt analiza* (Petrograd, 1923)

GIFFORD, HENRY, *Pasternak: A Critical Study* (Cambridge, 1977)

GLADKOV, ALEKSANDR, *Vstrechi s Pasternakom* (Paris, 1973); also tr. into English and ed., with introduction and notes, by Max Hayward, as *Meetings with Pasternak: A Memoir by Alexander Gladkov* (London, 1977)

GUMILYOV, N., *Sobraniye sochineniy*, 4 vols., ed. G. P. Struve and B. A. Filipoff (Washington, D.C., 1962–68)

HAIGHT, AMANDA, *Anna Akhmatova: A Poetic Pilgrimage* (New York, 1976)

HUGHES, OLGA R., *The Poetic World of Boris Pasternak* (Princeton, N.J., 1974)

IVINSKAYA, OLGA, *V plenu vremeni: gody s Borisom Pasternakom* (Paris, 1978); also tr. into English, with introduction and notes, by Max Hayward as *A Captive of Time* (London, 1978)

KARLINSKY, SIMON, *Marina Cvetaeva: Her Life and Art* (Berkeley, Calif., 1966)

N.   MANDELSTAM, NADEZHDA

N., 1   ——*Vospominaniya* (New York, 1970); also tr. into English by Max Hayward as *Hope Against Hope: A Memoir* (New York, 1970)

N., 2   ——*Vtoraya kniga* (Paris, 1972); also tr. into English by Max Hayward as *Hope Abandoned: A Memoir* (London, 1974)

M.   MANDELSTAM, OSIP

M.s   ——*Sobraniye sochineniy*, 3 vols., ed. G. P. Struve and B. A. Filipoff: vol. 1, 2nd ed. (Washington, D.C., 1967); vol. 2, 2nd ed. (New York, 1971); vol. 3 (New York, 1969)

M.bp   ——*Stikhotvoreniya*, ed. N. I. Khardzhiyev (Biblioteka poeta, bolshaya seriya, Leningrad, 1973)

    ——"Mandelstam's 'Ode' to Stalin," ed. Anon., *Slavic Review* (Columbus, Ohio) No. 4, December 1975

MARKOV, VLADIMIR and MERRILL SPARKS (EDS.), *Modern Russian Poetry: An Anthology with Verse Translations* (London, 1966)

MARKOV, VLADIMIR, *Russian Futurism: A History* (London, 1969)

MAYAKOVSKY, VLADIMIR, *Polnoye sobraniye sochineniy*, 13 vols. (Moscow, 1955–61)

NABOKOV, VLADIMIR (ED.), *Eugene Onegin: A Novel in Verse by Aleksandr Pushkin*, tr. with commentary by Vladimir Nabokov (London, 1964)

P. PASTERNAK, BORIS
———*Doktor Zhivago* (Milan 1957)

P.s, 1 ———*Stikhi i poemy, 1912–1932*, ed. G. P. Struve and B. A. Filipoff (Ann Arbor, Mich., 1961)

P.s, 2 ———*Proza, 1915–1958. Povesti, rasskazy, abtobiograficheskiye proizvedeniya*, ed. G. P. Struve and B. A. Filipoff (Ann Arbor, Mich., 1961)

P.s, 3 ———*Stikhi, 1936–1959. Stikhi dlya detey. Stikhi 1912–1957, ne sobrannyye v knigi avtora. Statyi i vystupleniya*, ed. G. P. Struve and B. A. Filipoff (Ann Arbor, Mich., 1961)

P.bp ———*Stikhotvoreniya i poemy*, ed. L. A. Ozerov, with introduction by A. D. Sinyavsky (Biblioteka poeta, bolshaya seriya, Leningrad, 1965)

PUSHKIN, A. S., *Polnoye sobraniye sochineniy v desyati tomakh* (Moscow, 1956–58)

SAKHAROV, ANDREI D., *Progress, Coexistence and Intellectual Freedom* (New York, 1968)

TARANOVSKY, KIRIL, *Essays on Mandel'štam* (Cambridge, Mass., 1976)

TROTSKY, L., *Literatura i revolyutsiya* (Moscow, 1923)

TSVETAYEVA, ANASTASIYA, *Vospominaniya* (Moscow, 1971)

T. TSVETAYEVA, MARINA
———*Stikhi k Bloku* (Berlin, 1922)
———*Tsar-devitsa: poema-skazka* (Moscow, 1922)
———*Vyorsty: stikhi* (Moscow, 1922)
———*Remeslo: kniga stikhov* (Moscow–Berlin, 1923)
———*Posle Rossii* (Paris, 1928)

T.bp ———*Izbrannyye proizvedeniya*, ed. A. Efron and A. Saakayants (Biblioteka poeta, bolshaya seriya, Moscow-Leningrad, 1965)
———*Pisma k A. Teskovoy* (Prague, 1969)
———*Lebediny stan; Perekop*, 2nd ed., ed. G. P. Struve (Paris, 1971)
———*Nesobrannyye proizvedeniya*, ed. Günther Wytrzens (Munich, 1971)
———*Neizdannyye pisma* (Paris, 1972)
———*Neizdannoye: stikhi, teatr, proza* (Paris, 1976)
———*Izbrannaya proza v dvukh tomakh*, ed. A. Sumerkin (New York, 1979)
———*Psikheya* (Paris, 1979)

ZHIRMUNSKY, V. M., *Tvorchestvo Anny Akhmatovoy* (Leningrad, 1973)

INDEX

Acmeism, Acmeists, 7, 8, 16, 27, 29–34, 40
Adalis, Adelina, 114
Afanasyev, Aleksandr, 90, 91
agriculture, collectivization of, 157–8, 179–80, 197, 207, 214
Akhmatova, Anna Andreyevna (*see also* poets, four), 7, 18–27, 28, 33–4, 36, 43–4, 56–62, 89–90, 91–3, 106–9, 122, 185–6, 201–3, 210, 221–7, 236, 237–9, 244–7; birth, 5, 6; parents, upbringing, 6, 12–13, 14–15, 21; and Acmeism, 8, 16, 29, 34; recitals by, 9, 237–8; and politics, the State, 11, 111, 143, 179, 221–5, 237–9; and Western Europe, 13–14; marriage, *see* Gumilyov, Nikolay; Punin, Nikolay; Shileyko, Vladimir; obscurity, difficulty, in her poetry, 16, 24, 34, 43, 244; appearance, 19–20; and the Mandelstams, 20, 76–7, 84, 114, 143–4, 179, 182, 183, 184, 185–6, 190, 192, 202–3, 219, 244; love affairs, 23, 59–60, 61; "half nun, half whore," 24–5; and Blok, 26–7; and Stray Dog, 27; restraint cultivated by, 35–6, 40; and First World War, 45, 56–8; and Pasternak, 50–1, 136, 139, 141, 142–3, 173, 203, 224, 226–7, 238, 244, 245; and Tsvetayeva, 62–4, 108, 229, 232–3, 244; and emigration, 77–8, 108–9; and Civil War, 84–5; Trotsky on, 114–15; and Mayakovsky, 161–2; and Second World War, 226, 237; death, 236, 247; *see also under* Leningrad; *By the Sea Shore*, 21; "Cleopatra," 225; "Dante," 202–3; *Evening*, 19, 21; "Four of Us (Komarovo Fragments)," 246–7; *From Six Books*, 224–5, 226, 233; *Glory to Peace*, 238–9; *In 1940*, 226; "In the Evening," 23–4; "Little Geography, A," 210; "Lot's Wife," 108, 233; "May Snow," 57; "My Last Toast," 201–2; *Poem Without Hero*, 243, 244;

"Prayer," 57–8; *Requiem*, 25, 202, 223–4; *Rosary*, 19, 21; *Russian Trianon, The*, 143; *Selections*, 237; "Song of the Last Meeting," 22; "To the Many," 109; *Way of All Earth*, 225, 226; *White Flock*, 58
Aleksandrovich, Grand Duke Sergey, 137
Alexander I, Tsar, 9
Alexander II, Tsar, 136
Alexander III, Tsar, 5–6
Alliluyeva, Nadezhda, 170–1
Andronikova, Princess Salomeya, 27–8, 69
Annensky, Innokenty, 8, 13, 17
Anrep, Boris, 59–60, 77
Antokolsky, Pavel, 86
Apollon, 29
Ararat, Mount, 163
Arbenina, Olga, 97
Armenia, *see under* Mandelstam, Osip
Aseyev, Nikolay, 46
Association of Russian Proletarian Writers (RAPP), 158, 194

Babel, Isaak, 197
Bakhrakh, Aleksandr, 124
Balmont, Konstantin, 8, 11, 123
Baratynsky, Yevgeny, 7, 17
Bashkirtseff, Marie, 37
Batyushkov, Konstantin, 31, 178
Bely, Andrey, 1, 106, 123, 178, 179, 200
Beria, Lavrenti, 222
Berlin, Sir Isaiah, 244
Bernhardt, Sarah, 37
Black Earth, 192
Blok, Aleksandr, 8, 8–9, 11, 17, 19–20, 26–7, 64, 101, 107, 244
Blyumkin, Yakov, 93–4
Bobrov, Sergey, 46

Bolsheviks, Bolshevism, 72, 75, 81, 82; *see also* Lenin; Russia, Revolutions of 1917
Borodin, Sergey, 184–5
Brest-Litovsk, Treaty of, 72
Brown, Clarence, 11, 31
Bryusov, Valery, 8, 10, 35, 116, 117
Bukharin, Nikolay, 145, 183, 186, 195, 196,208
Bulgakov, Mikhail, 225
Burlyuk, Davyd, 47

calendar, Old and New Style, 81–2, 82, 235, 252
Casanova, Giacomo, 35, 87
Caucasus, 55–6, 166–8, 173; *see also* Armenia *under* Mandelstam, Osip; Georgia
Centrifuge, 46, 47, 48
Chaplin, Charles, 5
Cheka, 93–4, 106
Chekhov, Anton, 7
Chelyuskin (ship), 199
Cherdyn, 188, 189–90
Chistopol, 234, 237
Chukovskaya, Lidiya, 222, 223, 245
Chukovsky, Korney, 211, 222
Civil War, *see under* Russia
Cohen, Professor Hermann, 41
collectivization, *see* agriculture
Coster, Charles de, 145
Crimea, 179–80
Cubo-Futurism, 46
Czapski, Joseph, 244

Dante, 177, 202–3, 215
death, as theme in poetry: Mandelstam, xi, 217–18; Akhmatova, 21, 43, 225; Tsvetayeva, 38, 39–40, 43, 65, 89, 127
Decembrist coup, 9
Denikin, General Anton, 95
Derzhavin, Gavriil, 67, 178
Dostoyevsky, Fyodor, 136
Dzerzhinsky, Feliks, 94

Efron, Ariadna (daughter of Tsvetayeva), 35, 38–9, 64, 81, 88–9, 198, 228, 231–2, 234–5
Efron, Georgy (son of Tsvetayeva), 124, 198, 231, 232, 234
Efron, Irina (daughter of Tsvetayeva), 85
Efron, Pyotr (brother of Sergey Efron), 39
Efron, Sergey (husband of Tsvetayeva), 35–6, 81, 91, 119, 123–4, 147, 153–4, 198, 228–9, 231–2
Ego-Futurism, 46

Ehrenburg, Ilya, 28, 123, 210
Eliot, T. S., 5, 16
England, English culture, 14; *see also* Shakespeare
Europe, European culture, 13–14, 29, 70–1, 218, 226; *see also* Greek themes
Eykhenbaum, Boris, 24–5

False Dmitry, 69, 83
Fedin, Konstantin, 212
Feodosiya, 81, 96
First World War, 45, 56–8, 62, 70, 72
folk tales, 90–2, 131
Futurism, Futurists, 7, 8, 29, 43, 46–8

Georgia, 96, 166; translation of poetry from, 132, 209, 210
Gershuni, Grigory, 28
Gide, André, 209
Gifford, Henry, 47
Gippius, Zinaida, 8, 11, 15
Gorenko family, 21
Gornfeld, A. G., 145
Goslitizdat, 233
Great Purge, Great Terror, 171, 208, 221; *see also* Stalinism
Greek themes in poetry: Mandelstam, 33, 70, 72–3, 94–5, 97–8, 110–11, 216; Tsvetayeva, 87, 91, 127–8, 130–1, 150–2
Griboyedov, Aleksandr, 87
Gronsky, Nikolay, 199
Gumilyov, Lyov (son of Akhmatova), 19, 64, 201, 202, 221, 222, 238–9, 241
Gumilyov, Nikolay Stepanovich (husband of Akhmatova), 8, 10, 16, 18–19, 20, 23, 27, 29, 31, 34, 35, 58–9, 91, 106, 144; *Path of the Conquistadors*, 18
Gumilyova, Anna, (mother-in-law of Akhmatova), 19

Hamlet, see under Shakespeare
"Hamlet," *see under* Pasternak, Boris
Hayward, Max, 239
Hitler, Adolf, 5, 231
Ho Chi Minh, 114
Holliday, Sonechka, 86, 87, 230
Hulme, T. E., 31

Imagism, 29
International Congress of Writers for the Defence of Culture, 197

Ivanov, Georgy, 11, 68, 200–1
Ivanov, Vyacheslav, 8, 11, 13
Ivinskaya, Olga, 173, 234, 241, 242

Jakobson, Roman, 11
Jews, Jewishness, 14–15, 125, 164

Kamenev, Lyov, 75, 208
Katayev, Valentin, 165
Kerensky, Aleksandr, 72, 75, 81
Khazina, Nadezhda Yakovlevna, see
    Mandelstam, Nadezhda
Khlebnikov, Velimir, 8, 11, 46, 47
Khodasevich, Vladislav, 11
Khrushchev, Nikita, 236, 241, 243
Kiev, 95
Kirsanov, Semyon, 182, 186
Klyuyev, Nikolay, 8, 10
Kobylinsky, Lyov, 39
Koktebel (now Planyorskoe), 35, 179
Kollontay, Aleksandra, 25
Kruchonykh, Aleksey, 47
Kuzmin, Mikhail, 8, 229

Lay of Igor's Raid, The, 82–3, 168
Légende de Thyl Ulenspiegel et de Lamme
    Goedzak, La, 145
Lenin, Vladimir Ilyich, 75, 75–6, 132, 134
Leningrad, St. Petersburg, Petrograd, 12–13;
    formerly St. Petersburg, 13; Akhmatova
    and, 13, 20–1, 27, 57, 61, 84–5, 143, 210,
    225–6; Mandelstam and, 13, 27, 73–4, 97,
    174–5, 214; formerly Petrograd, 13; Stray
    Dog (night club), 27; seat of government
    transferred to Moscow, 72; named in
    honour of Lenin, 132; massacre in (1905),
    135
Lermontov, Mikhail, 6–7, 10, 17, 55
Literaturnaya gazeta, 178
Lokhvitskaya, Mirra, 46
love, as theme in poetry: Akhmatova, 21–3,
    58–62; Mandelstam, 69, 184; Pasternak, 52,
    141; Tsvetayeva, 37–8, 89, 91, 120, 126, 127,
    131; see also sexual themes
Lozinsky, Mikhail, 28
Lurye, Yevgeniya, see Pasternak, Yevgeniya

Malenkov, Georgy, 238
Malraux, André, 197
Mandelstam, Nadezhda Yakovlevna (*née*
    Khazina; wife of Osip Mandelstam), 94,

110–11, 144, 165, 179, 183, 186, 188, 189–91,
    193, 210, 211, 212, 217, 219–20; on Soviet
    oppression, xiii, 171; on Civil War in
    Kiev, 95–6; and Tsvetayeva, 121–2, 124;
    and Akhmatova, 122, 143–4, 219;
    comments on Osip Mandelstam, 145, 174,
    180; and Zinaida Pasternak, 173; and Boris
    Pasternak, 181–2, 187–8, 206; struck by
    Sergey Borodin, 184–5
Mandelstam, Osip Emilyevich (*see also* poets,
    four), 27–34, 43–4, 66–71, 72–7, 93–8,
    109–14, 144–6, 162–6, 174–85, 186–8, 189–94,
    210–20; and "Nightingale Fever," xi, 73;
    birth, 5, 6; parents, upbringing, 6, 12–13,
    15; and Acmeism, 8, 16, 27, 29–32, 34;
    recitals by, 9, 178–9; death, 10, 220; and
    politics, the State, 11, 28, 75–6, 93–4, 94–5,
    111–13, 162, 165–6, 174–7, 178–80, 182–3, 185,
    186–8, 189–94 *passim*, 210–13, 214, 218–20;
    and Western Europe, 13–14; Jewish
    descent, 14–15; obscurity, difficulty, in his
    poetry, 16, 33–4, 43; and Akhmatova, 20,
    76–7, 84, 114, 143–4, 179, 182, 183, 184,
    185–6, 190, 192, 202–3, 219, 244; appearance,
    27–8; and progress, 28; first published
    verses, 29; and Symbolism, 31–2; and
    buildings, cathedrals, 32–3; and
    Tsvetayeva, 35, 62, 66–9, 114, 121–2, 200–1;
    restraint cultivated by, 35–6, 40; and First
    World War, 45, 72; and government
    employment, 93; marriage, see
    Mandelstam, Nadezhda; and Pasternak,
    114, 180–2, 182–3, 186–8, 203; and
    Mayakovsky, 162; and Armenia, 163–6,
    166–7, 180; slaps Aleksey Tolstoy, 184–5;
    see also under Leningrad; "Age, The,"
    111–12; "Ariosto," 177, 177–8; *Buzz of Time*,
    13, 28, 165; "Clock-Grasshopper's Song,"
    73; *Conversation About Dante*, 177; "Do
    Not Tempt Alien Dialects, but Try to
    Forget Them," 177; *Feodosiya*, 96; "First
    of January 1924," 112–13; "Flat Is Quiet as
    Paper, The," 181, 196; *Fourth Prose*, 145–6;
    "Freedom's Half-Light," 75–6; "Golden
    Honey Streams from Bottle," 72–3;
    "Horseshoe Finder," 16, 113–14; "I Drink
    to Military Asters," 176; "I Love the
    Breath of Frost," 213; "It Is Night," 181;
    Journey to Armenia, 163–6, 180;
    "Menagerie, The," 70–1; "Mistress of
    Guilty Glances," 184; Moscow
    Notebooks, 162, 175–7, 191; "Not Believing
    the Miracle of Resurrection," 68–9; Ode
    to Stalin, 212–13; "On Pieria's Stony
    Spurs," 94–5; "Phaeton Driver," 166, 180;

Mandelstam *(continued)*
  "Poem on Stalin," 182–3, 186; "Rome,"
    215–16; "Stanzas," 193; "Stary Krym," 180;
    Stone, 29, 31, 32, 33; "Straw, The," 69–70;
    "Straw-Strewn Sledge," 69; "This
    Province in Dark Water Season," 214;
    "To Cassandra," 77; "To the German
    Language," 177; "Today We Can Take a
    Transfer," 176–7; *Unknown Soldier,*
    217–18; Voronezh Notebooks, 162, 191, 192,
    193–4, 211–12, 213–19; "What Can I Do
    with Myself This January?," 214; "Wolf,"
    176, 186; "You Aren't Dead Yet," 213
Markov, Vladimir, 46, 47
Mayakovsky, Vladimir, 158–62; and
    Futurism, 8, 46; death, 10, 132–3, 158–9,
    162; European culture, slight knowledge
    of, 14; recitals by, 14, 159, 205; Pasternak
    and, 47–8, 159–60; and politics, Soviet
    society, 82, 109, 118, 158–9, 196–7;
    Akhmatova contrasted with, 109; praised
    by Tsvetayeva, 118, 147, 160–1; and
    Georgian poetry translations, 132;
    Akhmatova's lyric on, 161–2; "To Sergey
    Yesenin," 161; Mandelstam and, 162;
    Vladimir Ilyich Lenin, 133
Mejn, Marija (maternal grandmother of
    Marina Tsvetayeva), 64, 88
Mirbach, Count, 94
Mniszek, Marina, 69
Moscow, 12–13; Pasternak and, 13, 78–9, 135;
    Tsvetayeva and, 13, 65–6, 83, 86; seat of
    government transferred to, 13, 72; Presnya
    revolt, 78–9, 135; Art Theatre, 86;
    Mandelstam and, 175, 178; Museum of
    Fine Arts, 200
Mussolini, Benito, 215

Nabokov, Vladimir, 13
Napoleon, 37
nature, as theme in poetry: Mandelstam, 216;
    Pasternak, 48–50, 79
Nedobrovo, Nikolay, 59
Neygauz, Zinaida Nikolayevna, *see*
    Pasternak, Zinaida
Nicholas I, Tsar, 9–10, 170
Nicholas II, Tsar, 6
"Nightingale Fever," xi, 73
Nilender, Vladimir, 35
NKVD, 207, 208, 220
Novy Mir, 163

OGPU, 106
Oxford University, 246

Parny, Evariste, 26
Pasternak, Boris Leonidovich (*see also* poets,
    four), 7, 28, 41–4, 45–56, 98–102, 132–42;
    166–73, 236, 239–44; and politics, the State,
    xii, 11, 133, 168–9, 173, 180, 195–6, 197,
    205–6, 207, 208–10, 239–41, 241–4 (*see also*
    Russia, Revolutions *and* Stalin); birth, 5;
    parents, education, 6, 12–13, 15, 34, 41–2;
    and Futurism, 8, 43, 46–8; recitals by, 9,
    205, 239–41; visits to West, 13–14, 106; and
    Shakespeare, 14, 99, 129, 138 ("Hamlet"),
    210, 226, 240, 241; Jewish descent, 14–15,
    15; obscurity, difficulty, in his poetry, 16,
    43, 172, 244; religious motifs, 25; and
    Tsvetayeva, 36, 41, 46, 50, 55, 79, 98,
    129–31, 138–9, 141–2, 147, 152, 197, 201, 233–4,
    234; first verse collection, 42; and First
    World War, 45; and Second World War,
    45, 237; and Akhmatova, 50–1, 136, 139, 141,
    142–3, 173, 203, 224, 226–7, 238, 244, 245;
    imagery, similes, 53–4; and Revolutions,
    Civil War, 78–80, 98, 133–40; and
    Pushkin, 99–101, 170, 229; and
    Mandelstam, 114, 180–2, 182–3, 186–8, 203,
    220; and Stalin, 132, 168, 169–71, 187–8, 204,
    209–10, 238, 240–1; marriage, *see*
    Pasternak, Yevgeniya; Pasternak, Zinaida;
    and Mayakovsky, 159–60; and Caucasus,
    166–8, 173; and First Writers' Congress,
    195–6; and Writers' Union, 196, 203, 209;
    residences, 205–6; death, 236, 244; and
    Nobel Prize, 242; "About These Verses,"
    55; *Aerial Paths,* 140, 246; *Afterglow,* 237;
    Autobiographical Sketch, 141; "Autumn,"
    245; *Breach, The,* 101–2; "Century and
    More, A," 169–70; *Childhood of Lyuvers,*
    The, 140; *Doctor Zhivago,* xii, 45, 80, 85,
    98, 133, 137–8, 140, 197, 207, 237, 241, 241–4;
    Earth's Spaciousness, 237; "First View of
    the Urals," 49; "Hamlet," 138, 241; "I
    Realized That Everything Is Alive," 204;
    In Early Trains, 237; "Intoxication," 245;
    "January 1919," 101; "July Storm," 50;
    "Kremlin in Blizzard, End of 1918," 101;
    Lieutenant Shmidt, 133, 137–9, 195; *Lofty*
    Malady, 133, 133–5, 140; "Looking Glass,"
    48–9; "Marburg," 51; "Meeting, A," 98–9;
    My Sister Life, 46, 48, 52, 54–5, 79, 98,
    129; "Nobel Prize, The," 242; *Over*
    Barriers, 45–6, 79; "Permanently
    Momentary Storm," 50; "Poetry," 102;
    "Poet's Death," 159–60; *"Raspad,"* 79;
    Safe-Conduct, 140–1; *Second Birth,* 166–9,
    172–3; "Shakespeare," 99; *Spektorsky,* 133,
    139–40; "Spring Rain," 79; "Stuffy
    Night," 49; *Tale, A,* 140; *Themes and*

Pasternak *(continued)*
Variations, 98–102, 133; "To a Friend,"
169; *Travel Notes*, 227; *Twin in Clouds*,
42, 47, 49; "Waves," 167–8; "Weeping
Garden," 50; *When the Skies Clear*, 242;
"Winter Night," 51; *Year Nineteen
Hundred and Five, The*, 133, 135–7, 195
Pasternak, Leonid (father of Boris
Pasternak), 6, 34
Pasternak, Rosa (mother of Boris Pasternak),
34
Pasternak, Yevgeniya (*née* Lurye; first wife
of Boris Pasternak), 133, 168
Pasternak, Yevgeny (son of Boris
Pasternak), 133
Pasternak, Zinaida Nikolayevna (*née*
Neygauz; second wife of Boris
Pasternak), 168, 172–3, 209, 227, 233
Paustovsky, Konstantin, 242–3
Peredelkino, 205
Perets, Isaac Leib, 232
Perovskaya, Sofya, 136
Peter the Great, 83, 191, 192
Petrograd, *see* Leningrad
"Petropolis" (i.e. Leningrad), 73–4
Petrovykh, Mariya Sergeyevna, 183–4
Pied Piper legend, *see* Tsvetayeva,
Rat-Catcher
Pilnyak, Boris, 158, 225
Planyorskoe, *see* Koktebel
"Poetesses' Evening," 116–18
poetry, xiii, 52, 102, 197
poetry, Russian, 6–10; "Golden Age" and
"Silver Age," 6–8; recitals, 9, 14, 85,
116–18, 129, 147, 159, 178–9, 205, 237–8,
239–41; obscurity, difficulty, in, 16, 24, 34,
43, 118, 172, 244; themes in, *see* death;
Greek themes; love; nature; sexual
themes; *see also* Acmeism; Futurism;
Symbolism; writers, and the State; *and
individual poets*
poets, four (Akhmatova, Mandelstam,
Pasternak, Tsvetayeva, *qqv.*), compared,
considered as a group, xi–xiii, 5–6, 7, 8,
11–12, 12–17, 43–4, 45, 84–5, 109, 236, 246
politics, *see* Stalinism; writers, and the State;
Russia; *and under individual writers*
Potyomkin, battleship, 135
Pound, Ezra, 5, 16, 29
Pravda, 180
Presnya revolt, 78–9, 135
prose fiction, Russian, 7
Pshavela, Vazha, 232
Punin, Nikolay Nikolayevich, 143, 201–2,
221–2
Punina, Anna, 143, 201, 221

Punina, Irina, 143, 201
Pushkin (place), *see* Tsarskoye Selo
Pushkin, Aleksandr, 6, 9–10, 17, 26, 73,
99–100, 199–200, 229–30; *Eugene Onegin*,
229–30; "Prophet, The," 100; "Stanzas,"
170
Pyatakov, Grigory, 208

Rachel, Elisa, 20
RAPP (Association of Russian Proletarian
Writers), 158, 194
Razin, Stenka, 86
Reichstadt, Duke of (Napoleon II), 37
Reiss, Ignace, 228
Revolutions, Russian, *see under* Russia
Rilke, Rainer Maria, 141, 152
Rostand, Edmond, 37
Russia: Civil War, 80, 81–2, 84–6, 94, 95–6,
98, 105, 116–17, 119, 153–4; emigration/exile
from, 77–8, 105–6, 108–9, 122–3, 147, 198–9;
poetry, *see* poetry, Russian; prose fiction,
7; Revolution of 1905, 78–9, 135, 137;
Revolutions of 1917, 5, 72, 75–6, 78, 79–80,
80–1, 119–20; Tsarist oppression, 12;
writers, *see* writers, and the State; *also*
poetry, Russian; *see also* Stalin; Stalinism
Russkiye zapiski, 230
Ryleyev, Kondraty, 9

St. Petersburg, *see* Leningrad
Sappho, 25
Savinkov, Boris, 28
Schwab, Gustav, 150–1
Second World War, 226, 234, 236–7
Sevastopol mutiny, 137
Severyanin, Igor, 46
sexual themes in poetry: Pasternak, 245;
Tsvetayeva, 88, 89, 90–1, 120, 130, 151–2; *see
also* love
Shaginyan, Marietta, 165
Shakespeare, William, xiii, 14, 99, 210, 226,
240; *Hamlet*, 128–9, 138, 226, 241
Shileyko, Vladimir, 91–2, 143
Shmidt, Lieutenant Pyotr Petrovich, 137
show trials, 208, 221
Shtempel, Natasha, 211
Shteyger, Anatoly, 227–8
Sinyavsky, Andrey, 79
Sirius, 18, 20
Skriabin, Aleksandr, 41
Slepnyovo, 58
Socialist Realism, 194, 205
Sologub, Fyodor, 8
Soviet Union, *see* Russia

Sreznevskaya, Valeriya, 223

Stalin, Joseph, 12, 87, 157, 162, 207, 236, 236–7;
Akhmatova and, 224, 238; Mandelstam
and, 166, 182–3, 187–8, 212–13, 218–19;
Pasternak and, 132, 168, 169–71, 187–8, 204,
209–10, 238; his wife, 170–1; and writers,
the arts, 132–3, 158, 196–7, 207, 239

Stalinism, the Stalin epoch, 12, 157–8, 171,
207–8, 221, 222, 236, 241; *see also* writers,
and the State

State, the, *see* Stalinism; writers, and the
State; *also* Russia

Stray Dog (night club), 27

Surikov, Vasily, 225

Surkov, Aleksey, 239, 239–40, 243

Symbolism, Symbolists, 7, 8, 29, 31–2

Tagantsev affair, 106

Tenishev's (school), 13

Third Studio, 86

Tiflis, 96

Tikhonov, Nikolay, 175

Tolstoy, Aleksey, 106, 184–5

Tolstoy, Lyov, 6

Trans-Sense, 47

Trans-Siberian Railway, 6

Trotsky, Lyov, 93, 114–15

Tsarskoye Selo (since renamed Pushkin), 13

Tsvetayev, Professor Ivan (father of Marina
Tsvetayeva), 34, 35, 87, 200

Tsvetayeva (paternal grandmother of Marina
Tsvetayeva), 88

Tsvetayeva, Anastasiya (sister of Marina
Tsvetayeva), 235

Tsvetayeva, Marina Ivanovna (*see also* poets,
four), 6, 25, 34–41, 43–4, 62–8, 85–9, 116–31,
147–54, 197–201, 227–35; exile from Russia,
xii, 35, 106, 122–3, 147–8, 197–9, 227, 228–9,
230, 231; birth, 5; not affiliated to any
group, 8; recitals by, 9, 116–18, 147; and
Pushkin, 9, 199–200, 229–30; death, 10, 232,
234–5; parents, upbringing, 12–13, 14–15,
34–5; and Western Europe, 13–14;
marriage, children, 15, 35–6; *see also*
Efron; obscurity, difficulty, in her
poetry, 16, 43, 118; first published work,
35; return to Russia, 35–6, 201, 231–3;
praised, 35, 36; and Mandelstam, 35, 62,
66–9, 114, 121–2, 200–1; love affairs, 36, 124;
and Pasternak, 36, 41, 46, 49, 50, 55, 79,
98, 129–31, 138–9, 140, 141–2, 147, 152, 197,
201, 233–4, 234; prolific, 36; personal
themes, 36–7, 38–9, 62–3, 88–9;
assessments, development and

achievement, 36–7, 40–1, 43, 62–3, 118, 124,
126, 200; chief characteristics, 39; and
First World War, 45, 62; and
Akhmatova, 62–4, 108, 229, 232–3, 244; and
Blok, 64; and Revolutions, Civil War,
80–3, 85–6, 116–18, 119–20, 153–4; and
theater, 86–7, 150–2; in government
employment, 87–8; and Czechoslovakia,
123–4, 197, 230–1; and Paris, 147, 198–9, 201;
and Mayakovsky, 160–1; politics,
indifferent to, 198; prose works, 200–1,
229–30; and Second World War, 234;
Adventure, 87; *After Russia*, 123, 126–9,
130, 131, 141, 151; *Alleyways*, 118; *Ariadne*,
87, 123, 127, 150–1; *Attempt at Constructing
a Room*, 152; "Attempt at Jealousy, An,"
127; "Bush, The," 199; *Captive Spirit*, 200;
Cloudburst of Light, 46, 129; *Craft*, 118,
123; *Death of Casanova*, 87; "Elderberry,"
199; *Enchanter, The*, 39; *Evening Album*,
34–5; *Evening Elsewhere, An*, 229; *Fortune*,
87; *From Two Books*, 36, 40; "Garden,
The," 199; *History of a Dedication*, 200–1;
"Homeland," 199; *In Praise of Aphrodite*,
120; *Insomnia*, 64–5; "Longing for
Homeland," 198; *Magic Lantern*, 36;
March, 231; *Mileposts*, 63, 66, 87, 123;
Moscow Verses, 65–6, 66; *My Jobs*, 87; *My
Pushkin*, 229–30; *New Year Offering*, 152;
"Ode to Pedestrians," 199; *On Red Steed*,
120–1, 131; *Parting*, 123; *Perekop*, 85, 153–4;
Phaedra, 87, 127, 150–1, 151–2; *Phoenix*, 87;
Poem of the Air, 152; *Poem of the End*, 123,
124, 125–6; *Poem of the Hill*, 123, 124–5;
Poets, 126; "Prayer," 38; *Psyche*, 123; *Pupil,
The*, 118; *Rat-Catcher*, 123, 148–50; *Red
Bullock*, 154; "Roland's Horn," 90;
September, 230–1; *Snowstorm*, 87; *Staircase
Poem*, 152–3; *Stone Angel*, 87; *Swain, The*,
123, 131; *Swan Encampment*, 82, 87, 116;
Tale of Sonechka, 86, 230; "To Germany,"
62; *To Mayakovsky*, 160–1; "To You—in
a Hundred Years," 89; "Trees, The,"
199; *Tsar-Maiden*, 90–1, 105, 123; *Verses to
Czechia*, 230–1; *Verses to My Son*, 198–9;
Verses to an Orphan, 227–8, 230; *Youthful
Verses*, 36, 38–40

Tsvetayeva, Mariya (mother of Marina
Tsvetayeva), 34

Tukhachevsky, Marshal Mikhail, 209

Tyutchev, Fyodor, 7, 17, 73, 178

Uritsky, Moisey, 94

USSR, *see* Russia

Vaksel, Olga, 144
Villon, François, 31, 218
Volkonsky, Professor Sergey, 118
Voloshin, Maksimilian, 35, 199
Voloshin, Yelena Ottobaldovna, 35
Volya Rossii, 197
Voronezh, 190–2, 210–11, 213
Vysotskaya, Ida, 42, 51

Weidlé, Vladimir, 47, 136
White Sea Canal, 219
White Volunteer Army, White forces, *see*
   Civil War *under* Russia
women, the woman question, 14–15, 25, 116,
   168, 169
Wrangel, General Pyotr, 96, 153–4
writers, and the State, xii, xiii, 9–10, 111, 158,
   194; *see also under* Akhmatova;
   Mandelstam; Mayakovsky; Pasternak;
   Tsvetayeva; *also* poetry
Writers' Congress, First, 194–7
Writers' Union of the USSR, 194, 196, 205,
   209, 219, 235, 246

Yagoda, Genrikh, 183, 186
Yelabuga, 234
Yenukidze, Avel, 186
Yesenin, Sergey, 8, 10, 14, 132–3, 158, 161
Yezhov, Nikolay Ivanovich, 162, 208, 222

Zadonsk, 214
Zamyatin, Yevgeny, 158
Zavadsky, Yury, 86, 87
Zhdanov, Andrey, 24, 238
Zinovyev, Grigory, 75, 208
Zoshchenko, Mikhail, 238
Zvezda, 163

A Note on the Type

The text of this book was set by computer-driven cathode ray tube in Janson, a recutting made direct from type cast from matrices long thought to have been made by the Dutchman Anton Janson, who was a practicing type founder in Leipzig during the years 1668–87. However, it has been conclusively demonstrated that these types are actually the work of Nicholas Kis (1650–1702), a Hungarian, who most probably learned his trade from the master Dutch type founder Dick Voskens. The type is an example of the influential and sturdy Dutch types that prevailed in England up to the time William Caslon developed his own incomparable designs from them.

Composed, printed, and bound by
The Haddon Craftsmen, Inc., Scranton, Pennsylvania.

Typography and binding design by Maria Epes.